BUT BY THE
CHANCE

RICHARD C. LYONS

LYLEA

LYLEA™ CREATIVE RESOURCES

Published in the United States by Lylea Creative Resources

First Edition

ISBN: 978-0-615-53205-9

Published in the United States of America

Book design and illustration by Kevin McHugh

LYLEA is the trademark of the Saryan Corporation

This book has demanded a working lifestyle as closeted as an ascetic's, with long hours of solitude and the despairing weight of wondering whether the objective would ever rightly be achieved. During this time, my wife Erika brought light into the darkness, companionship into the solitude, and hope that scattered my doubts.

Therefore, to her this work is lovingly dedicated.

The work is also dedicated to the memory of
Second Lieutenant Edmund Lyons Leach,
28th Marines, 5th Division.
Died March 3, 1945 at Nishi Ridge, Iwo Jima,
following the battle for Mount Suribachi.

FOREWORD

Several persons who have read this book have asked me: "How did you come to write such a work?" The first answer is that I have been beset throughout much of my life by the burdensome blessing of an intractable muse, which has acted on my mind like Io's gadfly, never allowing me the peace that might accompany being quietly stationary, at home. Thus, at the muse's will, to an elusive poetic promise I have always roamed.

I was equally beset by the need to comprehend and then address the problem this work presents: of what occurs at the end of human history's ages, of the cataclysms that inevitably obtain during those violent and tragic periods. Of the effects wrought upon humanity in these times of crucible. Of what is fought for by the conquerors and the defenders, of the virtues that bind them or the weaknesses that doom them. Finally, the idea of the collection of opposites into camps based on differences in material lineaments, variations of geography, differing institutions or classifying names, rather than on the universal motives or spiritual truths held in common by all mankind.

So, driven by the muse and given the objective of the subject, this work has impelled me to pursue a sojourn through every part of human history, through the world's various philosophies, through the ancient and modern sciences, through every form of literary style of expression and argument, to the culmination of this work. I once put it succinctly by saying I began this work in the anatomy of a mouse; through labor, I hope I have brought to a birth an eagle. Now, let's see if it can fly!

A NOTE ON STYLE

I chose for an organizing style the tetralogy, a system of four related play compositions, which allows for the dramatic evolution of an idea. It was used in ancient Athens during the Dionysian Festival. I have made one exception: in place of one Satyr play, I have maintained the tragic form.

I also chose to write in heroic couplet as symbolic of what the work is attempting to achieve, the reconciliation of two physically opposed lines, through the relative harmony of melodic rhyme.

TABLE OF CONTENTS

"In the crucible of this uncertain hour."

BUT BY THE CHANCE
OF WAR

PART ONE
"MATHURA"

CONTENTS
PART ONE
"MATHURA"

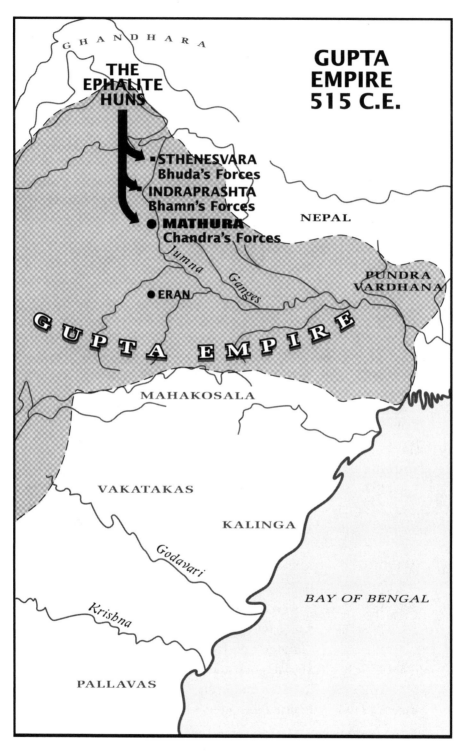

CHARACTERS
PART ONE
"MATHURA"

ROYAL GUPTAS:

King Bhamn Gupta	Emperor of India
Prince Chandra Gupta	Son and Heir of Bhamn Gupta
Prince Samudra Gupta	Son of Bhamn Gupta
Princess Sita	Wife of Prince Chandra

BHRAMIN:

Madhu	Bhramin of Mathura, Hindu Priest

GENERALS OF INDIA:

Ashara
Darshan
Amedkar
Tukarem
Asrani

COMMANDERS OF BHAMN'S FORCES:

Shekar
Jagjel
Silesh
Ashwin

ADJUTANT:

Mahedhara	Prince Chandra's Second

EPHTHALITE HUNS:

Tomara	The Ephthalite Khan
Mihirakula	The Son of Tomara
Uldin	A Warlord of the Huns

OTHERS:

Asunaya	Wife of Ashara
The Mayor of Mathura	
Ashok	Jailor
Sudhile	Merchant / Trader
Gowind, Atmaram, Ajay	Sentinels
Mother and family of Ajay	

ACT ONE
SCENE ONE

ON THE OUTSKIRTS OF MATHURA

Place: In the vales and fields to the south of Mathura, the principal Temple City in the western provinces of the Gupta Empire

Present: Prince Chandra Gupta and Ashara, a general of the Eastern Indian Armies; later Sita and Asunaya, their respective wives.

Scene: *The drama begins with the joining of the two great armies of India in the year 515 C.E., just to the south of the provincial capital of Mathura and to the west of the Jumna River. The armies represent the recruitment of soldiery throughout the subcontinent to meet the menace of Hun invaders, led by the warlord Khan Tomara, whose forces now populate Ghandhara, a northwestern province of the Gupta Empire, and threaten the invasion of the Indo-Gangetic plains. Leading the forces from the south is the commander, Chandra Gupta, the son and heir of the reigning emperor, Bhamn Gupta. Leading the armies from the east is Gen. Ashara, among his army are his wife, Asunaya, and Chandra's wife, Sita, who is with child.*

Chandra:	Dear friend! You are ever good as your word:
	You bring an ample corps, prepared to serve!
	Since our first days at the academy
	Your friendship has always brought me remedy!
	How was your passage across yon river?
Ashara:	We crossed on waters barely aquiver.
Chandra:	And our brides, they made the passage aright?
Ashara:	All's well, they are at the rear of our line;
	Seeing your host, Sita is moving forth
	To greet her husband, love, and noble lord!

7

Chandra: I am overjoyed you passed through the press
    Between Spring and Monsoon's[1] yearly event:
    When warmth opens the locks of winter's vault,
    And mountains melt beneath the Sun's assault
    Loosening the crystal, moon-kissing snows
    That flood these streams from Himalayan abodes…

    And when Koel[2] flocks fly before the clouds
    Which bear Ocean's pregnant rains from the south.
    Whence nature's made bountiful in the deluge
    Which pours upon us through the blessing monsoons.

Ashara: I've seen their flocks meander through the sky
    Foretelling the season that's cruelly kind:
    When whirlwinds form in heaven to invade
    Earth to its roots-renewing as they slay:
    Cleansing the globe of its senility,
    Flooding hollows with bright vitality,
    Clearing fading fields for fertile vigor,
    Seeding the lands through the Monsoon's rigors!
    Then will come a stirring of calm rivers!

Chandra: I believe that the rains come with sunset,
    By then, within good Mathura we'll rest;
    For a night secure from Monsoon's first shoots;
    Then, with tomorrow's dawn, forth we will move,
    From temples and gardens of Mathura,
    That one-time cradle and city of Krishna,[3]
    To join royal arms 'fore Indraprashta![4]

Ashara: We've received no current news since two days past
    With what may unfold of the Hun's advance.

Chandra: Nor we. I know we have them in a net
    Leaving no escape - save their promised death!

---

1 Monsoon: A seasonal reversing of winds, accompanied by heavy precipitation, effective in India June through August.
2 Koel: A bird species, which migrates with the monsoon, native to India.
3 Krishna: Mathura, according to legend, is the birthplace of Krishna, a central figure in Hinduism.
4 Indraprashta: See map.

Why show barbaric foes further lenience
When they do our patience further offence?
Were we not patient before their invasion
Through northwest corridors of our kingdom?
Did we not give the Huns lands and massy gold
To abide in peace and to leave us alone?
Did we not afford them arts of civilization,
Which they now use against our nation!

Ashara: Our generosity is thought weakness…

Chandra: Yes, their attacks are fueled by our kindness!
             We thought to wear them down in Ghandhara.[5]

Ashara: Now we make war before Indraprashta!

             You know the child's tale of the babe leopard:
             Once mature, he listens to no shepherd!
             They follow only when they've need of food;
             When full of red meat, they become obtuse:
             Though you pet and feed the starveling infant,
             You cannot rule the adult's feral spirit!

             They say the Hun's soul bears the scar of the cold
             Of Caucasus[6] from whence their race is known
             And that their babes are born from wombs of stone!
             They furrow with iron their newborn's cheeks
             Before giving them a mother's warming teats!
             Before their babes take infant strides in life,
             They're lashed to a horse's back and made to ride!
             They're taught to eat their meat bloody and raw...
             Can hearts formed so cold be then made to thaw?
             Born and bred frozen as mountainous steppes:
             They have in their chests the ice of Caucasus!

---

5 Ghandhara: See map.
6 Caucasus: A rugged mountain range extending from Russia on the north to Iran and Turkey on the south, whose highest peak is Mount Elbrus at 5,642 meters.

Chandra: Bhamn, Darshan and I now share your opinion,
All the Hun ever wanted is dominion!
They're a madness of wind and lightning,
Perverse herds beyond the scope of taming!
Their liberty is full of menacing:
We must fight these hyenas as lions
Colliding prides embraced in defiance!

Ashara: They do move like a vigorous cancer:
From sickened provinces to those yet pure,
Where they roam they bring malignant danger!

Chandra: Cousin Bhuda comes in arms from the north[7]
While King Bhamn holds 'fore Indraprashta's fort,
We with our corps will ascend from the south -
The Hun are in a hellish net, don't doubt!
They're in the vice, with the numbers we bring
We will destroy their barbaric armies!

Ashara: Within my column we've twenty thousand.

Chandra: I've the like sum, troops well trained and hardened!
But I've tales to tell of a city damned -
Have you heard what we met at Eran?[8]

We arrived to that city's immense ports
With our requests of men, money and stores,
As writ in the terms of the covenants
We hold with cities of our provinces:
That for fruits of common justice and peace,
Sacrifice of men we expect from each!
This is the central hold of our union,
Since 'twas consigned as a gift of Heaven!
'We need men and means with immediacy
To conquer the Huns - our common enemy,'
Said I. Then a man came forth on the wall

---

7 Bhuda's forces: See map.
8 Eran: See map.

10

To say: 'We are not by princes enthralled
We are capable of standing on our own,
We need no protection from distant thrones!
We manage the scope of our government
 And dissolve the laws of your covenant!'

'Should we abide prayers of foreign men
Who demand we send youths on paths of death?'
'You crack,' said I, 'the prop of that justice,
That's held since the empire was an infant!

I've brought two essential deities to plead:
Those of Reason and Necessity
Who demand men for our common army!'

'We've gods of our own we follow' said he,
Those of Peace, of Ease, and of Luxury...
Besides', said he, 'I've at home a pet bird,
Who finds no enemies within his wing's search,
Why then disturb the soft peace of our perch?'

'Huns,' said I, 'are enemies of the world,
Whose range nearly threatens all that is yours,
Even your haunts of luxury: your taverns!
Think before denying our great union:
Your parting may breed riots of ruin -
Breeding division and scatter'd fission
Cleaving Empire through every dimension!
You may as well seek to sever a heart,
That cannot self exist, when cut apart;
While severing access to sacred blood
Which feeds the organs of all that we love!
You may as well tear the blessed connection
'Twixt yourself and your nearest relation:
And be self-devoured in the conflagration!
You can't divide what is fundamental,
Without sequel, both horrible and fatal!'

'Strike me now,' said I, 'and swift for my life,
Than to let me witness with bleeding eyes,
The choking necrosis by slow degrees,
Of sinew and limbs from our empery!'

'I would be glad, 'said he, 'to battle you here!'
'But the hour of my lunch and nap draws near
Should you want the resources of this town,
You must spend precious days tearing her down!'

'For you,' said I, 'I am to a battle due,
Should we lose; the Huns will come lunch with you!
Good appetite, cur, while you've time to dine,
Should we lose, joy of your future is mine!'

Ashara: Good gods, have they no sense that perils near!

Chandra: The groin and belly by themselves have no ear!

I tired of insults from rebel tongues,
And without time, this coward city to crush;
So withstood, we moved off.

Ashara: Damnable slouch,
While we bleed for him, he'll snore on his couch!

Chandra: We're better hunting without sleepy hounds!
At all events, they lost us an entire day,
While we battled with words on that dusty plain!

Ashara: Here's a rider, by dress a messenger.

Chandra: Who's ridden hard by his temperature.

Messenger: Prince! At the place appointed! Here is a missive,
From Prince Samudra, from his encampment!

Chandra: Good, we'll now know how matters are arranged -

Man, how long have you been riding?

Messenger: Two days.

Chandra reads his brother Samudra's letter to Ashara

Chandra: "Chandra, health, I hope this post finds you close,
               And free of any hindrance in your approach.
               We have noted a rising energy,
               In the Huns and their lightning cavalry!
               They descend on us in mighty waves,
               Their third attack was just repulsed today;
               We have fought them well but their numbers grow,
               Nor do we yet know what reserves they hold:
               So much for gold spent from our treasuries -
               The Hun paid our gold to mercenaries!

               The buildup of Hun horse is our concern.
               While of our horse there is naught to learn:
               Sudhile, the trader, says our horse are gathered,
               Are training now and will be delivered,
               To our three allotted encampment sites,
               Horses ready for mounts, but he needs time.

               Meanwhile, in intervals, as planned, we train:
               Moving spear to cavalry and back again,
               Adapting forces between disciplines
               For when this late supply of horse comes in!

               We feel a growing sense of nervousness:
               Timing in war bears the strongest currents;
               If we don't soon reap these vital shipments,
               The Hun may surprise our best resistance.

               At all events, we are buoyant and pleased
               That you come to reinforce the armies.
               We hear that Bhuda is at Sthenesvara -
               And you will soon be passing Mathura.
               Don't loiter for garden tours with Sita!
               Use all haste to make for Indraprashta:
               That we may rule empires happy with tears,
               Singing joys of peace for a thousand years!

               By the way, we look forward to that birth

13

Sita will endure to renew the world!
I hope the Prince has Sita's eyes and face,
Should he look like us - what a damned disgrace!
Yours in love, as in our blood, Samudra"

They have been fully engaged for a week!
God! Hold up our hopes and their strengths!

And here comes my princess, my dear Sita!

Sita: How I've searched horizons of misty morn
To find the vivid frame of my Love's form,
Abandoning the gaze with drowning eyes,
For I found not my house of paradise!

Chandra: But at long last, we meet and even now,
My heart bursts to see you in beauty crowned!
You are my lodestar, wherever I roam,
My soul orbits your own - that is my home!

Sita: Yet necessity called, the world we've paved,
While love's denied, for the better of the State!

Chandra: If Love could adversaries overcome,
Eternal chrysolite[9] would kingdoms become!

Tell, love, how's your health and of our unborn?

Sita: We thrive. Ashara keeps us safe and warm.
Here are some flowers, plucked before the storm.

Sita hands Chandra a bundle of flowers...

Chandra: *To Sita's womb*
Tender vessel in a vessel gentle,
You must soon be swathed in the world's mantle,
Where adverse winds and chaotic thunders
Play at edges of Earth's divine wonders.

---

9 Chrysolite: A mineral believed to possess adamantine properties.

14

It seems you come cradled in a tempest
As Monsoon's rains will soon be upon us.

In a whisper...

I'll defeat our enemies' dread designs
That you, a greater Empire may colonize!

Thunder is heard rumbling.

Ashara: We must go achieve the city's cover
            Time to move, Prince, with our ready lovers!

Chandra: This thunder sounds from pleased deities,
            Applauding us from the sky's magazines!

Ashara: No, Prince! God keeps his mind on timeless designs
            Scarce gazing on mortals, with careless eyes.

End of Act One Scene One

MATHURA

ACT ONE
SCENE TWO

MATHURAN SENTINELS

Place: The southern watchtowers of Mathura

Present: Gowind and Ajay with Atmaram arriving

Scene: *The southern walls of Mathura overlook the rolling approaches to the capital city. It is late afternoon and the horizon has begun to fill with the clouds of looming monsoon rains.*

Ajay: How fragrant and how soft are these breezes.

Gowind: Seasons are their fairest as they leave us.

Ajay: No, old man, this wind brings no end of Spring,
              But portends further days of blossoming!

Gowind: You're young, unknowing of the attendant signs,
              That the advent of the Monsoon draws nigh:
              Her onset of winds from the south start soft,
              But as powers converge they become rough!
              You should know the marks of seasons by now,
              Though the sun still shines, she's closing in clouds;
              Seasons after seasons have their sights and sounds,
              Naught stays the march of their eternal rounds.

Enter Atmaram

              Old friend, it's time for the guard to rotate?

Atmaram: Aye, I'm uneasy, things are in a strange state
              When sprawling Mathura goes all quiet!

17

Gowind:	Is the town not watchful and temperate?
Atmaram:	It's more than that: signal citadel fires, Which the defense of our fortress requires, Have gone dark from Indraprashta's bastions!
Gowind:	Maybe the Monsoon has already reached them, Drowning their fires, debilitating their flare?
Atmaram:	Even through rains, signals are usually clear.
Ajay:	Gaze south! Heraldic banners fill the air – With colors waving, through forests of spears!
Atmaram:	Chandra's armies from the territories Of southern India are approaching!
Gowind:	Men, we may yet be mercifully saved: The prince arrives on the appointed day! Signal the town with the blasting of horn - Clarion the city! A new hope is born, A savior Son emerges, before the storm!

End of Act One Scene Two

ACT ONE
SCENE THREE

ENTRY TO MATHURA

Place: Advancing through the southern approach to Mathura

Present: Prince Chandra and Princess Sita, Gen. Ashara and wife Asunaya, Aide de Camp Mahedhara, and attendant troops.
Later: The Mayor of Mathura and assorted citizenry

Scene: *The armies of Chandra Gupta have achieved the southern rise overlooking the city of Mathura, renowned throughout the ancient world for its school and manufacture of colossal sculpture and for being the birthplace of Krishna. The Jumna River curves behind and defines the city's eastern margins. The sunset casts its last beams on the prominent forewalls of Krishna's birthplace. To the south of the armies, the sky is threatening. As the scene proceeds, the army is moving to the great portal doors of the city.*

Chandra: Cast an awful introductory eye
On yonder city, eclipsing the sky:
Witness what hands of men, who lowly trod,
Have artfully wrought to mimic the gods!

Asunaya: Sita! View spangled light of roseate hues
Trembling on walls as the sun is subdued:
Deep colors suffused - luminous as pearl -
Encircle ramparts of yon novel world;
Fewer stars people the infinite spheres
Than are sky-inhabiting steeples here;
Woven with colossal images and forms:
The huge frames of gods lustrously adorned!
What mortal can so beautifully range
So animated or effulgent a stage,
Than this scene that bids the soul weep and burst
With joy, as midst a spiritual birth!

19

May we have a moment to linger here?
This view forcefully moves emotion I bear!

Chandra: No, Naya! We must move steadfastly on:
Striving with the wake of the setting sun.
Disaster engenders at feet of sloth
As with the warts, boils, or pustules that rot!

But wake the inner sanctum of your ear
And Mathura's storied history hear:
Two centuries past, this "Samudra's Path,"
Wended north and west through wild savage tracts:
'Twas a post abandoned: to law unknown
Since Sakas[10] held a regional throne.
This place was prostrate 'neath a savage age,
Void of reason, and of all civil grace:
Both man and beast were a single kind:
Ruled in pursuits by lust and appetite.
Justice and the tenants of the Heavens
Were fallen in gross ruins, defenseless:
Temples were stables of jackals and thieves;
The courts were caves of unheard griefs.
Whence came on the place in a manner fierce,
Warlike Samudra to subdue frontiers![11]
A warrior whose orbiting sword and shield
Bid contraries: perish or bend or yield;
So small tyrants and shadow-borne brigands
Took to armed field, or fled in cowardice!
Where this lion thunderously tread
No haunt, hill or mead was unconquered -
The West was scourged by fire and purified
As an evil generation fled or died.

Thence, as voices of nature's denizens
Tone in scales 'neath the cries of the lions -
Harmony, long dead, arose in forests,

---

10 Sakas: Scythian tribe that formed a regional kingdom in the northwest area of the subcontinent of India.
11 Samudra frontiers: The western frontiers of the Gupta Empire in 238 C.E.

Cities were built on their disused relics;
Cultivation grew in once-abandoned soils;
Earth's good fruits became universal spoils.
Neighboring spheres are not more firmly held
By the Sun's sweet radiance - soft compelled,
As Samudra's light did warm all to awe,
The virtues inherent in majestic law!
Allied regions sang praises in a wedded choir:
Like constellated tapers in a canopy of fire!

Through this first portal of light: Mathura,
Through this ancient, blessed birthplace of Krishna,
Grew a beautiful and a lasting aura...

This ingress was nourished by gilt legends
Till glossed to a mineral resplendence:
Outpouring the vigor of a lodestone
Luring the learned to this central home!
Wondrous structures grew among the admix
Of a teeming and talented populace,
Building various schools of novel thought,
And temples where faithful prayers were wrought!
Ménages of artists and divers crafts,
All framed a flourishing city and lands:
A safe harbor for persons of soft hands
The sensible or sentient of man!
Where, freely, they may the world enfigure
With the bounds and lines of sacred number.
Or in peaceful breath send their orisons
To the numberless stars of the Heavens,
Or devise with their fleeting hands and eyes
The fixed brow of a god's eternal guise!

This safe harbor has also proved a seed,
Whose petal and filament blossoming,
Has sent spawnings from these soft encasings:
Shipping souls on the Jumna and Ganges,
Spreading their artistry, faith, and teaching,

As threads of a new, living tapestry,
Interweaving this region with beauty!

Thus, from seacoasts to the Himalayan arc,
And from the Ganges west to the Kandahar,
Mathura is the crystalline lodestar -
Of our mind and soul, she is the hearth,
She is the heart of India's three worlds!
Standing as she does at the intersect
Between the ancient east and regions west,
She is, with Sthenesvara, the gilt key
To the ranged wealth of the Inter-Ganges:
She is where our Indian destinies meet!

Sita: Chandra! Please pause with your storytelling!
Look fore, to the walls we are approaching:
The whole populace has thronged en wild masse
In every door, window and portcullis,
As bees about a flower's bright calyx
To cast beaming eyes on a beloved prince!
Petals are pouring from without the turrets
Like waves of colored rain in soft tempests,
And the low-hung, huge ramparts are eclipsed
By purple clouds of a welcoming incense!
Note, musicians play a composition
To match the pitch of this jubilation.
I feel blessed to be such a witness
To joyous frenzy of happy madness!

Ashara: These are now a crew light in heart and mind
With a feeling they've deathly fate defied.
If you were dweller of this solitary town,
And heard issue of the wolf's packs deep howl -
Beheld the grisly, menacing brood advance
With open jaws stalking about your flanks,
Fear would enthrall you and keep you cabin'd -
Until a hunter killed the haunting savage!

Then the city would erupt in hope's joy
For the late parent of fear was destroyed
And no matter what the object of fright,
Joy's counterpoise would bear an equal weight.

Pardon, Lord, or do my eyes play me false
Or is there adequate height to those walls?
I'm seeing false if they are of regular scale;
These imposing statuaries loom so hale!

Sita: The scope of Siva's graceful proportion
Is framed a heaven-aspiring mountain
Shadowing the lesser crown of Vishnu[12]
Ought they not be equal in attitude....

Chandra: Perspective creates the difference.
They are equals in compared prominence
Standing intermediate you would see
Among magnitudes, their equivalency.
If the sculptures are proper in measure
Vishnu by line and scope should be higher,
Lest all forms be beneath Siva's shadows,
There unknown, and obscured in the dark's throes.

Ashara: Chandra, are these walls military scale
Or is this city, in defenses, frail?

Chandra: The city was finished last century:
Victory bred peace, peace sanctuary,
Sanctuaries ease; ease a lethargy!
Concern was for naught but true artistry:
Not for hoarding siege nor warlike engines,
Nor magazines, nor elaborate defenses,
As the frontier had moved far to the west
And with Gandahar sealed in alliance -
These great circuit walls became ornaments.

---

12 Siva/Vishnu: Two members of the Hindu trinity, in which Siva represents the destructive principle and Vishnu represents the preservation principle.

Ashara: If masons have mimicked war's battlements,
              As the artists mimic the gods' lineaments,
              Then, given we've defense but in appearance:
              We need gods, with their power's inherence!

Chandra: Mathura has been blessed with long peace!

Ashara: Thus, she's burdened to meet necessities!

Chandra: But allow this city its joyful sighs,
              A moment of light, midst thundering skies!
              After our entrance, assess defenses.
              Address weaponry and our dimensions.
              But before this assembly bare no frown
              It's the light of hope we bear to this town!

Asunaya: Regard in peace, Ashara, that they
              The fruit-laden figure of Ganesha[13] convey,
              In casual strands of lotuses[14] dressed
              With plenitudes of sweets embellished!
              Before the portal we must make prayer
              That all our future ventures work out fair!

Chandra's adjutant arrives to the city's gates and so relates:

Mahedhara: Gatesman! Here is our prince and noble lord
              Trooped with thousands of the stoutest sort:
              I introduce the Prince of Magadha,[15]
              With compliments, our Lord Chandra Gupta,
              Descendant in name the empire's founder,
              First born of Bhamn, India's undoubted heir!

              Congressed with great nobles of India:
              From Cedi, Kasi, Asmaka, and Vatsa

---

13 Ganesha: A deity of the Hindu pantheon who takes the form of an elephant and is associated with success, good beginnings and the removal of obstacles.

14 Lotus: An aquatic perennial which normally grows on the surface of marsh waters; considered symbolic of virtue and divine beauty, it is revered in connection with the divinities Vishnu and Lakshmi.

15 Magadha: Seat of the Gupta family power, the original Gupta kingdom.

Who descend on this capital of Mathura,
To relieve beleaguered Sthenesvara.
The prince bids: open the city to him
Allowing our strengths proper admission.
Tell the foremost of this great capital
Chandra Gupta would swift convene with all
Having to do with its good governance.
He seeks an immediate audience,
That orders be received throughout his troops
With grant of food and storm-defying roofs!

The Mayor of Mathura steps before the gathering to address the herald.

Mayor: Welcome!   Allow the gates to be opened!
                Throughout the city, allow through these men!
                Kindred you are, that banish our despair
                We invest in you the sum of all our care!

Chandra has now ridden to the fore to address those convened on city walls.

Chandra: Peaceful calm is what we've come to afford,
                Trooped with iron shields, staves, and sharpened swords!

                Mathura! We request your great largess,
                We petition to be your sometime guests.
                And thank you for this, your beloved greeting,
                Which blesses the Heavens with its fealty!

                What parental ear, formed with filial care,
                Can the plaintive tears of a prone child bear?
                Does not the frightful and dolorous tone
                Bore irresistible avenues to the soul!
                Thence the soul is roused and animated
                And corporeal members are elevated
                To a sense! To perform impassioned tasks
                Regardless effort, pain or offered thanks!
                Or what grave wound or disease can invade -
                Through apertures of a vulnerable frame,

Fore the body's generous nutrients
Are recruited through profoundest passages
To war for health of every member
In a wild, heated, feverous manner?

We have heard the province's bellowed cries,
Since war's horrid note rent India's skies,[16]
And felt deeply this grieving injury:
Blazing pain through our common arteries!
And to this wounded cry we now answer -
With the foremost arms we may deliver!
To counter the Hun's miscreated tribes -
The dogs of Siva! These Empiricides!

Lift your eyes to the horizons to observe,
Our fabric and magazines of thunder:
India's soldiers, her archers and casters,
Her engine builders and weapons makers,
Her dense arbors, metals and minerals,
And the select of her warlike animals!
We strode India's animate gardens
Filling our arms with these warlike harvests,
Assembling India's bounty for you,
Responsive the cry, healing to the wound!

Weak and unwilling souls we cast aside;
Like lions leaving weakling runts behind
To assure the greater strength of the pride -
Preserving the character of our line!
Here, great numbers we bring in sacrifice
To defend our sacred Indian life!

We, however, then ask of you, a dear part:
Sacrifice to us something of your heart!
We must request of you a great kindness:
We wish time for future reminiscence,
A time to enjoy the warmth of the hearth,

---

16 War's beginning: The Hun/Gupta War began with the invasion of the northern province of Ghandara.

Time to converse in familiar mirth,
Time to calmly hear the temple's chime,
Time to repose in the half-moon's light,
For fields of war where we must inhabit,
Are not of peace, but her darkest opposite!

Our thanks to you again for this kindness
Thanks to you, Mayor, and to all subjects.
Sing, Mathura! In a manner exultant
For our soon return to you - triumphant!

The thousands gathered of the city and the armies let swell a clamorous cheer.

Ashara: I would this were of victory itself
           Not the saturnalia of her pelf!

Mayor: I am here, my good sir, for your serving.
           Note before, an edifice for bathing!
           You may in armory or citadel
           Commission your troops and attendants dwell
           While you, your family, and retinue,
           With other provincial nobles too,
           Should stay in your ready royal palace!
           You may make of that your strong nucleus,
           From there exert your authority's radiants.

Chandra: Previous to our making any entrance,
           Ganesha needs prayerful obeisance:

                   Through the arc of this fortress,
                   Bless the steps of our progress;
                   Through the fire of your forces
                   Bless the chart of our courses;
                   Through the channels of your heart
                   Bless the potence of our arms:
                   Be aident with great power
                   In this, our now needful hour!

27

MATHURA

*A gathering of devotees of Krishna sing joyfully and dance before
Chandra and his retinue inside the city gates.*

        Let them sing joyfully, as is their way,
        Nor God, nor we will allow a savage race,
        To invade joys of this - Krishna's birthplace!

End of Act One Scene Three

ACT ONE
SCENE FOUR

MADHU AND MISSIVES

Place: The principal administrative chamber of the Royal Palace of Mathura

Present: Chandra Gupta meets with the Bhramin Priest, Madhu.
Later, they are joined by Gen. Ashara.

Scene: *The chamber is a very large square with upright pillars ranged in geometric colonades. The aperture of the door through which Madhu enters is arched with a titular head over the archway. Before the walls of the chamber, evenly spaced and at half the height of the ceilings, are beautifully wrought sculptures of mythical and divine figures of Indian cosmology. Chandra is seated but rises at the sight of Madhu.*

Chandra: Who would guess Madhu's face is made of flint?
            But the fires of bright joy are sparked by it!
            Of all my father's dear friends, the dearest,
            Of favorites nearest me, the nearest!
            Madhu, embrace me with all your love's might
            Demand time stop now, that we may share life!

Madhu: Wishes cannot interdict a star's path,
            Or halt light's unalterable advance.
            Time is the deity without an ear -
            Regardless the petitioner or prayer!

Chandra: Have you seen father? Tell me how he does.
            How holds Bhamn, The Steadfast, whom we all love?

Madhu: He emits a lighter glint in his eye
            The nearer he hears you and Sita nigh.
            But endless business has wracked his life:
            With continued drain of unending strife,

29

Even adamant stones, of granite form,
Are by the slow assaults of ocean worn!
It were as though his mother's rueful throes
Were prelude, at birth, to this tragic ode:
Timed by cracking drums and suffering groans
Quaking prone footholds of his sacred throne!

And you! In your youth did you know peace?
Or hear your lover rhythmically breathe?
Or were vestures of the university
Exchanged for hard molds of an armory?

Chandra: Calm Madhu! We are all bestowed our lots
You know, we are not the liberal gods.

Madhu: I feel, Chandra, the need to apologize
We are come to this crisis by my advice.

Chandra: You looked kindly in the Hun's direction
And assumed you viewed our own reflection:
Your hopes clothed them in your aspiration!
It is to the credit of your spiritual stature
You assume the best of our human nature!

We offered the justice of our laws of state -
You, the spiritual mercy of your prelates;
We had hoped to foster their nobility -
We pay the cost of its callous discarding!
The Hun deceived us with shallow, false words
All the time preparing to act the scourge!
We, on our part, fell into their trap
As hope for peace lulled us to relax.
We had hoped that our hopes would be proved right
We had hoped mere hope would avoid this fight:
We lived in a mirage of delusive hopes
Until this reality arrested us by the throat!
We on our part, were willfully blind
While we dallied and strayed and played for time!

While the Hun's appetites played upon our vice!
We must be wary of faith we place in hope,
For it bears a weighty darkness - in its shadow.

Madhu: And that shadow has fallen on my dear friend,
            Bhamn suffers so under this dread burden.
            Normally, one must suffer and is blessed,
            By varied chance: good and ill interblent,
            Ocean ever bears ebb and flow of tides:
            Bhamn bears solely the tide of war in his life!
            And, as Cassia[17] bows under the weight
            Of blossoming fecundity grown great,
            Bhamn bows beneath a wilderness of sorrows:
            For our losses birth a burden which harrows
            Upon his mind, taxed with apprehensions
            Vast as the Empire's living dimensions!
            All these lashing blows that his soul has bourne
            Have carved their currents in his graven form:
            Once strong, broad, square shoulders are now rounded,
            Eyes, once afire, bare the brows of the hounded...
            It is I! I am to blame that Bhamn must suffer this!

Chandra: Enough, all right! Your words become weapons -
            Their fall upon my ears makes me dark and pensive;
            You did as you thought fit to forge a justice!
            It's the Hun, not ourselves, who did not accept it:
            Justice among friends must come from both ends!

Madhu: Thank you and your valorous family
            For blessed peace that had lasted centuries!
            If life is a wheel wherein we must exist,
            The Gupta have lived - on its burning rims!

Chandra: Whilst all of you, that we cherish and love,
            Flourish unassailed in the wheel's smooth hub.
            For this gift, I thank you, dearest Bhramin,
            For keeping India's beloved pure portrait.

---

17 Cassia: A tree native to India, noted for growing so lushly that its branches droop to the ground.

Of priests praying and debating mysteries,
Of vast heaven from frail sanctuaries,
Whilst forces light and dark battle between
Where oppositions are dutifully ranged -
From sky-high mountains, to shadowy plains!

If love lives in pure chambers of our heart
We can perform our duty, however hard;
Of marble shall we be, Earth's hardest shell
Within which your kindred's jeweled souls dwell.
Are we not of that mold Kyshatrian:[18]
An order to battle born and dominion!
My forces are here with great suppliance,
And with Bhuda's and King Bahmn's convergence
We'll leave no more of bloody war to chance!
Thereafter, we'll regreet this still quietness,
Which the prayerful and studied relish.
And come together Madhu, without regrets!
I have now scant time, my friend, but prefer
You rejoin Sita and me for dinner.
I must view Ashara's inventory -
Indexing this city's ability.

Madhu: Chandra, I wish you peace.

Chandra: And soon there will be!

Exit Madhu, who greets Ashara as they pass.

Ashara: Chandra, I come from every quarter
            Knowing all that we need to consider.
            Forces man every vital tower;
            Eleven armed gates are in our power;
            Camps inhabit about the city wall;
            Our troops are now resting for the nightfall;
            And over the police in civil trust
            Authority has been delivered to us.

18 Kyshatrian: Hindu caste of warrior knights.

Chandra:	How stand our armories and magazines?

Ashara:	Deafening chambers, full of echoing! Necessity visited and bore hard On Mathura's token amounts of arms; She is but a sinewless skeleton!

Chandra:	Speak on, how are her outer dimensions?

Ashara:	Everywhere fragile as an eggshell. You've said: she's a beautiful temple.

Chandra:	Our hearts, seated in frames corporeal, Have throning ribs - vaults armorial; But this heart of India is laid bare: Unsafe for any but a lover's care! We must deem this a vulnerable nest And thrust north our arms, our bristling crest, Surge winged to victory where we trust, For we can't survive here, even if we must!

Ashara:	There is yet something else beneath this town, Which I found as I did my exhaustive round: They have reopened a pit, a deep dungeon, One that had been used in days of the ancients. It is filled with antique and rusted instruments, And its lord is a fearful man named Ashok Who has some unfortunates chained in stocks.

Chandra:	Doubtless they were well judged before punished - The chaos of this time breeds miscreants! Anyway, we've a place to store the dung, A good place to put any surviving Hun!

Enter a messenger bearing dispatches.

Messenger:	The latest of the King's correspondence, Is herein annaled, for bearing to his Prince.

Chandra: Deliver the missive and thank you,

Chandra reads his father Bhamn's letter to Ashara.

"Chandra,
I wish you the best health, dear son!
If you have surpassed hard expectation
And have followed our stratagems' courses,
You are now within reach of our forces,
Which is well, for we have much to contend,
As the scope of our danger has grown again!

News arrived in the dark midst of last night,
Doubling the coming peril of our plight -
Bhuda, coming south, encountered repulse,
Blasting assigned plans to conjoin with us!
We know he lost some strength of his army,
And dare not engage immediately,
Since that correspondence we have no word
But hope that Bhuda's force may still come to serve!
Till then, our gathered arms and men must suffice
To face the utmost battle of our lives!

Eight times now our armies have been engaged
In half the count of death-infested days.
The Hun and ourselves have equally bled
And dealt mortal blows but escaped undead!

Unlike us - the Hun is a Hydra[19] in injuries:
From wounds, he breeds further armies!
And from such purgings the Hun is learning,
Even at the edge of death's sharp urging,
That in all contests it is ever best
To mass one's main forces in lines of depth.
He also assembles a seeming few
In manner to obscure his multitudes!

My mind misguides, forgive my digression:
Tomara's a whirlpool of attention.
This fiend to whom we are now bound by fate,
As opposed poles wedded in lasting hate -
No force can we summon, nor tether find -
To keep this ambitious panther confined!
He is all want, desire and fierce power

---

19 Hydra: Mythical dragon of nine heads who grew two new heads with the loss of every one.

That, with right means, may seize a fatal hour!
Turn quicksilver whilst I have his dread throat
Lest some sudden thrust, overwhelms our moat!
My gaze can no more foresee what may emerge
From these hell-born miscreations of the world!

Is it novel, I am failing in my faith.
I feel the gods desert our reverent race!
Leaving us carrion to these hyenas,
These able feeders in blood-soaked arenas!

Chandra: What message is this! It doubles our perils!
We must move now, before the Sun so heralds!

Ashara: We cannot move now after our forced march!
It would be quarter-speed through storm and dark;
The men must rest at least until the morn,
We will make up time - even through the storm!

Chandra: Our cousin Bhuda's is a quarter of our force!

Sita must not know of this change in course
Or she will be filled with fear and remorse!

Ashara: We are to dine, listening to persons anyway
A palace full of legates and magistrates
Who will foist on our hope their full praise!

Chandra: Our sense of hope we must through this news sustain!
Though it doubles our labors and our pains.
We must fulfill obligations, seem at ease,
Or this town behind us…will fall to rioting!
I cannot think of anything more we can do,
Than we must be calm through night's interlude!
Hold, Father!   Hold through the time that intervenes,
Then will our forces join in a victory!

End of Act One

35

ACT TWO
SCENE ONE

THE CHANGELINGS

Place: The great Banquet Hall of the Royal Palace

Present: Ashara, Chandra, and royal servants. Entering: Sita, Asunaya, and the royal physician. Later entering: The Mayor and Magistrates of Mathura, legates of the provinces, Mathura citizens and stage players

Scene: *The great hall serves as both a dining chamber and a theater; the seating areas are arranged in a large square with the entertaining area occupying the center. Many servants are arranging the dinner and the central stage. Tripods of various heights are being assembled to lend the proper lighting to the event. The scent of lamb and curry is filtering from the off kitchen. Arrhythmic rumbles of thunder attend, from the storm beginning outside.*

Ashara: Ladies, physic, welcome to the hall for dinner
            We hope you rested well in your bedchamber.

Chandra: Physic, how fares my love, and our unborn?
            Publish your results, are they within form?

Physic: The baby's fine and in right position,
            Sita's beautiful and in healthful condition!

Chandra moves to Sita, kneels before her, and puts his hands and ear to her womb.

Chandra: Nourished and sustained on a slim tendon
            A tender thread and a supple organ!
            Nature's great miracle of mechanism
            That feeds and protects her organism,
            In a soft, supple, radiant world
            Where she lies gently, delicately curled!

37

Sita: Naya just asked where and when we conceived
This prince or princess who's within, dancing!
Remember where we all met in Tosali
For the inspection of the gathered navy,
When the wintry moon cast silvering beams
Across the undulating roof of the seas?
Chandra and I took to ship that evening,
Casting crew and soldiers over the lee;
With them went all the cares we had
Of wars, revolts and a world gone mad;
So nothing was left but our love alone
And the will to love 'neath the swelling dome.
Harboured for a time in a sacred bower,
Lovers enchanted by a romantic aura,
Revelry we knew, as is known to few,
And I begged the moment never conclude!
But war cries crashed in upon our ears:
The rousing of troops to their careers!
What a contrast to soft notes of subtle waves
Are clashings of swords, shields, and staves!
Though it was just a moment in our time
In the frame of a child, the moment took life!
In the time of that brief and magic interlude
Darts of love rushed and flooded my womb,
Conjuring the frame of a new creation,
Forged of love and insuperable elation!
Our hearts will forever be cast and twined
In the reflected spirit of our newborn's eyes,
Which shall harbor light of our emotional crest,
In the pupil's deep gaze and the iris's depths!

Ashara: Here are Madhu and provincial legates,
With Mathuran citizens and magistrates.

Mayor: Dear Prince! Welcome to the place of our feast
Tell me, how is your army and our city?

Chandra: The troops are resting well round the citadel

We have found the city here quite passable.

Sita: Mayor, can you secure Chandra and me tours
Through the city's vast temples and arbors?

Chandra: Sita!   We'll be marching by the Orient light
That demands we fly immediate to fight!
Take Asunaya and venture a walking turn!

Sita is fighting her tears.

I'll see the city with leisure, upon our return.

Mayor: Here now's a troupe we sponsored for the arts:
Who will sing and dance into your very hearts!

Chandra: Does the subject touch on war?

Leader: No, I'll be sworn!

Chandra: Be the subject anything else, then play on!
To All   It lies within our sovereign power
To eclipse our cares in a restful hour:
Wombed in the harmony of soft minstrels,
Whose measured tones touch our restless souls,
And bid them progress to dulcet repose;
As cares, round our senses, sensibly close.

The leader of the dance troupe comes forward.

Leader: Our humble offering this evening
Incorporates the dance of the 'Changelings,'
A blend of the Tandava and Taysa,[20]
In an ancient spiritual drama
Put forth as humble prayer to Siva.
We will see the Earth, Water, Air and Fire
Through Volcano, Ocean and Storm aspire,

---

20 Tandava and Taysa: Two styles of the Sivan repertoire of ceremonial dances.

To work the will of neverending Change,
Which in all times and places Earth sustains.
We are even now composed and ready
So, if all of you would find your seating!

THE CHANGELINGS
-VOLCAN-

Players: Energies of Earth, Air, Fire and Water

When first primal energy burst
Into formed orbs of a universe,
Seminal fire became our hearth
Nestled in burning gulfs of Earth:
The first born of that maiden spark,
First offspring of life's sacred heart,
We thrive in the world's mineral wombs,
Treasured ores, a-flow in fulgent pools!

Thus Earth and Fire give oblation
Nestled in cauldrons of creation

Mingling, we forge mighty children
Beneath our iron veined pavilion.
With a world-circling flow
We heat the arc of the moving globe
With our malleable living fire;
We allow Earth motion unmired
Quiescent we go through realms unknown
Till revolution rends our home!

Thus Earth and Fire give oblation
Riving in cauldrons of creation

With gathering power, tensing force
We burst through the Earth's corridors -
Cataclysm cracks the granite ribs
And roots of dem-eternal Mountains!
Our pent fires make dreadful strides
To cleave the mortis of stone confines -
Thence through brazen veins we break
And blast beyond the rock bound way!

In ash and fire and floods of stone
We issue from Earth's inmost throne,
We hurl golden orbed meteors
To the verge of Sky's outmost borne -
Earth weds in a chaotic sphere
With all subtle elements of Air
And from the wound we issue a flood -
Rivers of Earth's most sacred blood,
Streams forth through fiery arteries -
Renewing the world's fertility!
We glow in the emerald ember
Which becomes the globe's new vesture:
New life holds on our open pores,
Intermingling with glistering ores.
Glory to Siva in this great hour -
When Volcan births and sheds his power!

Earth, Air and Fire give oblation
Through the Volcanoes of creation!

Noise erupts of many elements of soldiers, horses and carriages from the city gates.

Sita: What earth-rending noise shakes my womb's sphere?
               And cracks harmonies with shrieks of nervous fear!

Ashara moves swiftly to the window.

Ashara: The royal carriage is at the northern gate
               Voices attend, accented with furious haste!

Chandra: Ashara, Sita, Madhu, come with me,
               Immediate to learn what news there is to meet!

Sita: Lord of heaven - let it once be of peace!

End of Act Two Scene One

MATHURA

ACT TWO
SCENE TWO

BHAMN GUPTA

Place: A Royal Bedchamber of the Palace

Present: Bhamn, Shekar, physicians and servants. Entering: Chandra, Madhu, Sita, Ashara and Mahedhara

Scene: *The bedchamber is lit only by wall and hand torches in the area immediately surrounding the bed where King Bhamn Gupta lies. He is surrounded by physicians, their attendants, and his adjutant Shekar. The entering group, led by Chandra, are all hurried, restless, and incredulous. There are agitated conversations occurring in the corridor from Bhamn's corp of followers.*

Chandra: I pray: gods of mercy, eclipse my sight!
                    Horror is forming 'neath this cope of light!

Bhamn: Thus you find your Father's not made of stone:
                    Vulnerable born, couched in a brief throne,
                    Mutable as summer's glorious flower,
                    That is mangled by some meager power!
                    Gaze how swift has changed a once-youthful frame
                    All my beauties are scarred, and my strengths maimed!
                    I swear, my son, I was born by that orb[21]
                    Convulsed by the vivid motions of war:
                    Tossed through life by chance and force,
                    Who inflict their wills on a soldier's corse!

                    The crown we wear, of a sacred fire's blaze,
                    It's alloyed gold, fused with infernal pain,
                    Whose ponderous weight and confining brace
                    Are prisoning cogs of a king's doomed fate!
                    The golden gloss of a monarch's fortunes

---

21 The planet Mars.

But mask afflictions, with gilded costumes!
I need not worry for my aging form
Look where chanced - the mortal javelin tore!
Look where the crimson tributary gleams
Pour from my fragile heart, in gory streams!
How many fallen? How many are fled?
How many perished that my banners had led?

Speak, Madhu! Are we the loathed of heaven:
The crushed flies and subject pawns of demons?
Or mere spawn to a creating divine,
That hoists us on high but to slay our pride?
Every moment our enemy breeds...
Beasts who feed on the supple hearts of Kings!

Madhu: Oh dear Heaven! This horror I never dreamed!

Physic: His brain is infected by great fever
Leave us that I may tend to the matter:
Medicines will blunt his pains and rages;
Give me time to bring him back his senses.

Bhamn: Where's Samudra? He's engulfed in dangers!

Shekar: He rode south with guardian rangers.

Bhamn: You must alert me when he does arrive,
Though 'twere the quietest watch of night!

Chandra: Father, hold still for a tranquil while.
We are here, the other side of the aisle;
If we hear the arrival of my brother
I'll alert you, even from your slumber.

Mahed! Send to the north a full storm brigade
To bring home safe what survivors they may!

Mahedhara exits. Chandra, Ashara, Sita, Shekar, and Madhu move to another corner of the chamber while the physician attends to Bhamn's wounds.

Chandra: There have been the several stable holds
             Life hath lent me as all-enduring posts,
             Unshaken foundations to host my hopes,
             Countering my fears, allaying my woes,
             As stable as the skies' constellations -
             Stars and galaxies nestled in heavens!
             Bhamn is the beloved and stablest light
             That ever pierced the veil of clouded night!
             I feel his sphered light fading in the sky:
             I feel sorrow delusive hope can't defy -
             'Whelming my soul and mind with rueful flood
             The dark newborn of the death of my love!

Sita: Death hold, hold! Oh Krishna! In heaven bow
             Take hold of dear Bhamn's threatened life now!
             He hath been nothing but loving to thee,
             Forebear he comes before death's ministry
             Or interdict the free range of love's pain
             And seize from my heart its sentient strain!

Madhu: Do not blame Heaven nor fall in sorrows
             Though sight of Bhamn's wounds the soul harrows!
             He suffers fulfillment of devotion,
             Like an avatar of our blessed nation!
             The destiny of his birth ordained this
             Sacrifice of life, for love most cherished.
             Bhamn in all things has been my dearest friend
             And our great Empire's ablest guardian!
             Not dolorous sadness but solemn praise
             Should attend on this: the end of Bhamn's age!

Ashara: Chandra, we must know of this the full cause:
             To swiftly react, to prevent further loss!

Chandra: The cause? The cause of all that we have lost?
We trusted too much and now pay the cost!
Madhu! Go to your friend, then let us know,
If Bhamn's sense revives, in wake of this stroke!

Sita, tend on our tormented father
Be his brightest hope, in that dark bower,
Commander! Come forward here and relate
How chanced a battle that destroyed the State!

Shekar: I will do my best in the utterance,
Though to make known events this disastrous
Demands plaintive tongues of Hell's dominion
Groaning from the deepest knot of perdition!

You know that we had bourne hard skirmishes
On series of recent days, in surges,
Until yesterday, when we invested
Our forces before Prashta's[22] entrenchments.

The night previous we had heard the word:
Bhuda's force engaged in battle northward,
In the region surrounding Sthenesvar[23] -
And no joining could be made of our arms.
Bhamn hoped that, with no further engagements,
On the morrow, you'd reach our encampments.

Chandra: We should have done!

Ashara: The Hun knew our motions!

Shekar: The dawn was suppressed in a humid mist,
We could not view their forward encampments:
Light and vision were both ambivalent,
Then began hard rains from the firmament,
And the mists to lift on our horizons,

---

22 Indrashtha – see map
23 Sthenesvara – see map

Unveiling a wide front of massive squadrons,
Of horsemen and archers, a gross number,
Arrayed in strength for a swift encounter!

As you know, we had been in anticipation
Of ten thousand horses from merchantmen
Engaged from Bactria some months before -
When our long-term plan of war was formed
For conversion of your and our infantry
To bring up numbers of our cavalry.
We received missives of soon arrival
But our strained hopes were always baffled!

I say this for on horizons we saw massed
Harnessed horse divisions, filling the compass!
With woven troops and auxiliaries
In formations we'd never before seen!
We readied fiercely to form our phalanx,
Hurriedly, fearful of instant attacks!
In our corps, orders were given to form,
Though the heart of our force was weak and worn
From the incessant fighting of days before!

In intervening fields gangs of dogs roved
By sense of battle instinctively moved:
Keening and barking echoed through the sphere
Kindling our senses of urgency and fear.

Bhamn signaled the attached musical corps:
'Go forward and begin the martial score
Which preludes the orchestrated advance -
Of universal motion - horse, foot and lance!'
The Huns began their ear-piercing howling.
We strove forward toward the enemy…
Then their long inexorable march began
Slingers, darters, lancers of the first van -
Flung spears and stones, fire and arrows were hurled
Until their massed numbers obscured the world!

Elements joined the gathering chaos:
Horse's hooves, beaten shields, charging elephants -
The plain trembled with the resounding mass,
Soldiers sang hymns of death and tragic chants!
Over all was screamed the repeated order:
'Hold line for the King, hold to your banners!'
As you both know, the strength of the phalanx
Is union through her indivisible ranks...

On the left of our forward formations
Where we expected great infestations,
Bhamn was visible with his retinue,
His sacred guard, "The Undefeated Troop!"
On his squadron the Hun cavalry flew -
First in order, then in manner confused,
While some Hun infantry held on our right
Working slowly to break our phalanxed might!
Bhamn's post bore innumerable chargers
And the hard impacts of horse-borne archers:

He held our cavalry in rear reserve
Until this time, to counter the Hun surge,
The Huns adapted their horse to lances
Which repulsed our cavalry's advances!

Hun resistance faded along the central span;
Samudra's center then drifted from Bhamn:
Rather than lend assistance to the King,
Samudra was blind to necessity!
Pushing forward along his entire line,
He moved from us - by not moving in time!

Thence o'erseeing our corse like a vulture,
Tomara soon sensed our grave error.
He allowed time to measure impatience,
Then loosed massed horse on gaps in our salients,
Falling on soldiers singly and in mass:
Tearing through the hollows with vengeful wrath,

They made a perfect pattern of motion:
Hitting us at the apex of momentum!

Ashara:
Tomara has learned the most fatal point:
All things may divide at their weakest joint.

Shekar:
Our troops were torrid in their rage and fear,
Pushing when seeming victory appeared!

Chandra:
Samudra's confidence consumed caution -
His rage was deaf to reasonable motion!

Shekar:
Bhamn saw the line move forth and swerve outward,
And ordered men to fill the interlude -
Maneuvers taxing to his defensive ring,
Which snapped back on us like a broken string!
Then closed around the Monarch his members
As great walls form round vaults of rare treasures,
All energized in valorous splendour
Fighting to defend the King's threatened honor!

Darshan and Asrani moved to the fore,
And raised all the defense they could implore,
But the dread Hun… had more for us in store!

Tomara, no less, viewed our dire distress
And converged his horse into a vortex,
Then ranging himself opposite our navel
He propelled on us with great upheaval!
Cleaving the finest of our soldiery -
With massed horse careering in density!
The king himself fell beneath a long spear -
Unerringly flung through the crowded air:
Then universal hope groaned in fell despair!
Spirited strength exhaled in doubtful wail,
As our great legions exhausted and paled,
Our stern military rank caved and broke
Like wrenching a wheel's axis from the spoke!

We felt the dread, breathing in that environ,
Grappling the hell-born, to save our Sovereign!
Though all beheld the grave, sorrowful sight:
Our fallen, near-extinguished throne of light,
The fading crown and dying fire of hope,
Symboled the gravity of our losses' scope!
We braved battle hand to hand, eye to eye,
Who had fought for Empire, now struck for life!

Swords continued to clash, battle to swell,
Turning Bhamn's pavilion to churning Hell!
Until the heart of the royal cordon
Became a locus of desolation,
Till all the gilt regalia of the Empire
Was strewn over the blood-soaked quagmire!

We broke forth with a surviving cohort
And rode for Mathura, our last recourse!
The wretched left behind were ridden down
Transfixed by spear and horse to bloody ground!
The men, the camp, all our gathered legion
Were lost, scattered in annihilation!

Chandra: You said Asrani and Darshan were front line!
            Do you know whether either has survived?

Shekar: I remember the last I saw of them
            Fighting bravely among the bravest of men!

Ashara: If we lose Darshan, our strength in Ghandhara,
            We will have no chance to save Mathura!

Chandra: Whether he and Asrani are dead or alive,
            With dawn for Indraprashta we ride!
            To give this Hun his death! Or fighting die!

Shekar: Don't waste time preparing to venture there.
            He's slaughtering all before him - he comes here!

He comes, and all between us does he slay,
He comes, and Death rides post in his train!

Chandra: Then to battle we subject all demands
            All our hearts defy him, and all our hands!

Physic: Your father now awaits you, Lord... a word:
            For a word is all his life may yet afford.

Chandra: What hope remains when all of heaven falls?
            What do but bear it! And in virtue bear all!

*Chandra moves into the chamber where Bhamn is attended by
Madhu, a physician and Sita*

Bhamn: My failing spirit starts to beg transport
            To the shrouded gardens of Bhrama's court,
            The battle's lance severed me to the nerves.
            We must speak now! While yet each organ serves...

            How could I have trust in barbarians?
            How could we have been so damned generous?
            All the gifts we gave - they use against us!
            How could we have owned so weak a will
            That we lived to ignore the gathering evil!

            Siva, to the Huns this bloody job assigned
            To fell empires and to destroy mankind!
            Or nature, in her wombs of creation,
            Molded monsters beyond imagination,
            Raising the Hun to interdict man's ascent,
            And cast us back to the jungle's rude deck!
            Caging men again in scopes of nature
            Where hope is known solely to survivors!

            Have we not heard the thunder of Rome's fall
            As barbarians cracked her millennial wall?[24]

---

24 Millennial Wall: The walls around the Imperial City of Rome stood for a thousand years.

Or seen palaces fall of the Sassanids
Cracking their ancient thrones and diadems,[25]
Or known the Han's once-vast morphia
Walled and shuddered in corners of Asia?[26]
In this convulsed world, what has not been changed?
Her monuments razed, her continents maimed!

Once our brave troops were vast and numberless!
Now we may account without an abacus...
Once we were courageous, we were dauntless,
Now we are subdued, fear-worn and cautious!
Once we drove our foes before us like sheep
Now we've been driven to this long retreat!
Once a land bursting with generation,
We're barren! At an abyss of destruction!

The world's environed in a circling fire
While glories of humanity feed the pyre!
The architecture of the world is ablaze...
With flames now kindling at Mathura's fane!
Are we not the globe's last erect column?
Trembling against universal ruin!
Are we the last pillar and podium
Which upholds the laws of civilization?

Nature or Siva were the alchemists
Who stirred this all-transforming catalyst -
Who armed Huns to pull the world asunder,
And shatter the face of Lakshmi[27] for plunder!

But they'll not litter their horses and dogs
To feed and piss in temples of our gods!
Nor house their camp of mongrel prostitutes
In halls enshrined with our holy statutes!

---

25 Royal Pars: Refers to the royal family line of the Sassinid Empire of Persia.
26 Han Asia: The Han dynasty was fragmented into the Wei and Jin dynasties in 265 C.E.
27 Lakshmi: Hindu deity associated with prosperity, wisdom, courage, fertility and good luck. Also equated with Mother Earth.

Though Huns brought with them cold, frozen winter
Which at our height of spring begs we wither,
Our roots fold too deep in the soil of history,
Producing harvests of strengths o'er centuries,
To be cropped by tribes of no lasting dower,
These passing tempests, these wonders of an hour!

Chandra! Meet this season of intemperance
With defense of Heaven-forged ordnance!
Have faith, luminous in the profound dark:
To guide the path of our kingdom's heart!
With virtues that are mettle of our crown
Kingship and empire are thus so endowed –

In youth or age, virtues are just the same
Time and change our mortal forms maim
But the virtues, and their patterns sustain!
Virtue is a fort of its own construct;
'Tis the frames of life that change and corrupt!
May not mind and principle be erect
Though the corpus about be imperfect?
May not body be wounded or diseased
But the mind and soul lay beyond time's siege?
Composed of an immaculate membrane
No brute force can penetrate or profane?
Only the virtues survive the agents of change
Striding faults of fortune... underanged,
Whole and entire is the virtuous mind,
Mind that's unchanged by circumstance of time,
Though the circling props of heaven fall in...
Or though the once-fixed poles of earth contend!
Our virtues shield what must remain the same:
The true magnitude of our crown and name!

Most sacred are those oaths by us given
To justice, service and our covenant:
It is the fulcral and central promise,
That's living between we and our subjects!

With its protections, we are not alone,
But myriad hosts compose round our throne!

Chandra: I learned this entirely, Father, from you
                  While in my simple infant robes of youth.

Bhamn: Learn it well! For now it's put to proofs
                  Lest Mathura be set ablaze to her roofs!

                  Fear, sorrow and worry frame your features
                  These are not emotions of conquerors!
                  You need constancy and adamant valor
                  In the crucible of this uncertain hour!

Chandra: My sorrows and worries are all for you….

Bhamn: Don't wed living thoughts to my coming doom!
                  Time is always bearing and burying….
                  Transform despair, for hope in the living!
                  And, dear son, be whole in the coming trial!

                  Give me to drink, anything, that near vial!
                  That is the last thirst in this life I'll know,
                  Besides thirsting not to leave you alone!

                  Have we heard nothing of our Samudra?

Shekar: He has yet to achieve the gates of Mathura.

Chandra: I have sent forth, Father, a full brigade
                  To redeem such soldiers as may be saved.

                  We've yet the men, arms and hearts set to thrive!

Bhamn: On altars of our love, a sacrifice…

Chandra: Whose eyes now fill with the salt of despair?
                  Betraying your lifelong love and care.

Bhamn:	Embrace me, I feel my spirit lightening
	And my trembling limbs tingle with flushing.
	Take from me this now-ancient carpet,[28]
	The crown, this jewel and golden ornament,
	The eternal emblems of true kingship.
	Promise you will be Vishnu's model son,
	In trials you bear and battles to be won!

Chandra: I'll be all that, for being your firstborn,
               I'll be that, though I inherit the storm!

Bhamn: I have felt more for you than you can know
              I leave you all my love and all my hope!
              When I first grasped your small infant hand
              I little dreamt this horrid fall of man!
              Good Lord! I never should have trusted them!
              Or if so, with a ready sword in hand!

              Remember! Victors oft triumph but to fall -
              And the fallen rise, and rise to conquer all!

Bhamn expires.

Chandra: Oh God!   No!   No!

Physic: The light of his soul has fled the iris;
              He is now an incorporeal spirit.

Madhu: What more will yesterday bear the morrow?
              How could my good intent birth this sorrow?

Chandra: He flies, but his flight we cannot follow!
              Like a fissure in the Sun's gravity,
              Which revolving orbs cling to in harmony
              Of a symphony tuned through eternity:
              So divides this: the royal heart of a king!

---

28 This now ancient carpet, crown, jewel, ornament: The official emblems of the Gupta emperors.

Ashara: So may soon divide our hold on empire,
Orbits of known affections, ally's desires,
Might bend or bolt to neighboring powers,
Assuming potency in these fell hours!
'Tis certain loyalties will be shaken:
Futures weighed and faiths forsaken.

Sita: What came of our brilliant spring morning
When all was fragrant in the Sun's dawning?
Where this night is a covering awning
To shelter us from the torrent's storming!
Have I travelled the world's perimeter
To imperil my unborn as I lose a father?
Do I witness the end of our empire?

Chandra: Sita, be calm, and recess for a time
Find Naya, I'll come to you by and by...
Embrace me now and fly!

Exit Sita, weeping

Ashara: Tears are well, but acts at present better -
The warlike soul of Bhamn to remember.

Chandra: The husk of Bhamn's body is for the fire -
Living, he would share our martial desire!
While I live, his will within me shall burn -
And his spirit rule me, even from his urn!

Ashara: I will notify guards at every gate
To convene the generals still astray
In the palace, to assess some living means
Of patching strengths, from cerements of defeat!

End of Act Two Scene Two

ACT TWO
SCENE THREE

STAGGERING BACK TO MATHURA

Place: On the northern walls and over the main portal of the city

Present: Ajay and Atmaram

Scene: *Viewed from its walls, Mathura awakens to chaotic motion. Retreating and broken troops return to her walls. Within and without, there is a growth of chaos, a heightening of sound and gathering of despair.*

Ajay:	How the city has transformed in a round - All that was ordered has been crushed to ground!
Atmaram:	The royal litter arrived with our King - His life is despaired of: he is dying! Wildfire was ignited by his messenger, Who brought news of the battle's disaster! He told a person of his acquaintance That fell news as he passed through this entrance… The acquaintance told two, who made four aware Of the perilous fortune that we bear! Eight then to equal numbers bore the weight; Thence sixteen echoed the knell of our fate. The number knowledgeable multiplies While every telling our fate magnifies! Word moved in an expanding cataract From this gate through the alleys it passed - Flying to eastward, toward the river, Resounding here - in shuddering thunder! Of hearts broken through portals of the ears, Of new widows and orphans, steeped in tears! See the hollows of their sorrow-seized eyes! Hear the abandoned souls issue broken cries… Whose depthless sound cleaves the bounds of the skies!

Ajay: Look west for Echo's answering horror:
      Ragged remnants of the conflict's survivors
      Return sans regal ensigns of the princes
      Or the orient banners of the provinces;
      Soldiers return, torn to ravelled messes!

Atmaram: They descend on us in disordered waves
      Like death-bruised spirits looking for their graves!
      They show a horribly deformed guise:
      Crushed by violence of a shattered enterprise!

      As swift as sound through the tenantless air
      Or lightning's dread fire through the atmosphere,
      Fortune has turned on this metropolis
      And Chaos governs in a wild demesne!

Ajay: I must seek my parents!

Atmaram: See about it!

Ajay flies from the platform.

      If monarchs by the barbarians are slain,
      Into what abyss will we be cast this day!

End of Act Two Scene Three

ACT TWO
SCENE FOUR

GATHERING OF THE MILITARY COUNCIL

Place: The Administrative Chambers of the Royal Palace

Present: Chandra, Ashara, Samudra, Darshan, Madhu, Tukarem, Amedkar, Asrani, Shekar

Scene: *The vanquished and surviving generals of the battle for Indraprashta assemble, joining Chandra, Ashara, and Shekar. The room is tense, and the vapor of sweat and fear and uncertainty are palpable.*

Shekar: Herewith, Lord, are the generals returned
               With Samudra and Darshan, so I've learned.

Chandra: Samudra, Brother! Bear this loving embrace.
               I am elated you survived those fates
               That fractured our father's radiant light
               And have left us here, alone to the fight.

               Darshan! This chaos of battle you survived,
               I am overjoyed to see you alive!
               We will need your wisdom the more,
               Being now doubly challenged by this war!

               My friends, I bear with you this horrid loss
               That we a father, you a King hath cost!
               It's an event we deem irreparable,
               Whose gnawing wounds run deep and palpable!
               I am stunned with amaze at these reverses -
               That must be answered with stern purposes.
               The measure of this measureless sorrow
               Must gauge resolve and strength of our marrow!
               It's certain we've suffered loss of sinew -

But forty thousand troops herewith renew
Our strengths which now do battle for the crown,
Our houses, altars and ancient renown:
All the flesh that still animates our frame.
And that still composes our common name;
Time affords opportunity and room
To overturn this dark fortune of doom!

Once more we must rouse ourselves to duty,
Redoubling desire for our victory,
Once more, tried in courage and constancy,
We must answer with sacrifice and fealty!
To bring us victory, and the Hun's defeat,
We must leave no act of virtue unachieved!
I ask once more you battle the profane
And fulfill faith given the Gupta name!

Tukarem: Is not thanks now owed to the Gupta name?
Now Chandra brings tardy armies too late!
And what courage this true Gupta has shown,
Providing armies, now mine are of bone!
Doubtless you are of that kind of physic
That enquires of the dead whether they're sick,
Who provides healing salves to fleshless limbs!

Ashara: What manner of speech is this?

Chandra: Allow it!

Tukarem: Allow me to proceed with an index
Defining our great Gupta's excellence
As it's a catalog - worthy of contempt!

When the Hun's first incursions bruised the ribs
Of our array of northern fortresses,
I pled to our Guptan king and his son here:
'A babe tiger has issued from its lair
And we should kill it now with some slight snare,

While the teeth are small and ineffectual,
Its motions few, and strengths contemptible.'
'No!' said our great sovereign! Our conqueror!
'Why upset this little infant's temper,
Allow him satisfy a just hunger;
He may well prove to be a friend hereafter.'

Well, the infant fed as much as it could:
This tiger grew to an ambling childhood!
I then said to our invincible King:
'This toddler is vigorous in growing,
With paws maturing and fangs sharpening;
We must not feed this tiger any longer -
Let's hunt him now before he grows stronger!'
I said: 'Sovereign, you've heard the old law:
We should never feed beasts who have sharp claws.'
'I have my eye on him when at my ease;
Thus disturb no further our well earned peace,'
Said Bhamn, our lord, our King, precious prince -
While these beasts fanged and clawed my province!

When this tiger felt pangs of adolescence
Fervent wants took form in rage and license!
The King was then aghast with his questions:
'Hasn't the Hun understood our kindness?
Such thanks are returned our benevolence!'
'Your boundless generosity and support,'
Said I, 'create war, while thinking it sport!'

Then King Bhamn raised needed troops and armies,
But formed a dilatory policy,
Of seeking merely this tiger contained
Allowing him to become fledged with age!
The slight blows and defeats we gave to them
Served as the slide and rule of education
In military strengths and weaknesses -
Which, with vigor, they now use against us!
They use the same methods in their attack

We once used vainly - to hold the beasts back!

Now my cities are studies of desolation,
Moldering pyres and ruins populate them!
The earth itself is saturate with floods
Of cracked skulls and bones and innocent blood!
Such has become of what once was my home:
The Huns ravage it and call it their own!
Now they have grown so great, and are of such kind,
No force of ours can govern or hope to bind!

And Chandra bids I fight once again -
Who have no province or a surviving friend!
No friends, no lands, but I should fight for a name,
One that rings hollow of its former fame!
What is sacred in the sound I pronounce,
That failings and mortality announce?
"Gupta," I know this august family:
They give lessons in how to bleed blindly!
"Gupta," I know this great august master:
They have lorded over our disaster!

To Madhu

And do not think I forget you - damned priest!
You! With your blind missionary zeal
Who ignore all that part of the world that's real!

Madhu: I believed the best in humanity!
If there is fault - leave the blame fall on me!
Blame me! For I sought Bhamn thus to sway
And did not know - we would unleash a plague!
Did I know these Huns would grossly ignore
The law in which God's glory is stored?
Or that they would be more enamored with trinkets
Than of the dearest gifts of the Bhramins?
They gave us their word!

Tukarem: And how good was it?
By abandoning Ghandhara to the dogs

You thought the Hun would embrace laws of God!
I don't care how they sang empty prayers!
For your love of God - their people have no care!
When it's love or brotherhood we would extend
It must be a bond that is firm at both ends,
Before you open our doors - to a pestilence!

Amedkar: Easy, friend!   We are all at severed ends;
But must sanely discuss what to do next.
For myself, I find that things are blended
What occurs, what we do, what is destined.
We found enemies unasked on our frontiers,
And tried to hold a dread panther by its ears,
But failed by all those aggregate chances,
Woven in the destiny Siva dances!

The Hun is armed with more than sword and lance;
More, with advantages of fortune and chance!
I'm certain the Gupta star is fallen,
There is naught left to defend but the ruin!
The family tree is a hollowed arbor,
Naught of the fall remains but the clamor!

The Hun populates all of Ghandhara,
And now push south beyond Indraprashta,
It's simple then - they'll conquer Mathura!
This side Jumna, we are at their mercies
Lest we enlist gods as auxiliaries!
Fly we must: to save at home what remains:
Of families, friends, possessions, estates;
We must take on the habits of the tortoise
And carry our houses about upon us,
Outrunning the appetites of these fiends,
Saving what may be carried and redeemed!

What of covenants of a kingdom's bond?
'Twas of breath and a necessary nod,
Empty as a sound in tenantless air,

Now scattered by shattering cries of despair!

Asrani: I've tired viewing moving catastrophe,
I would dive in fire, if 'twere unchanging!

Tossed in this gulf of sickening motion,
I prefer the currentless deeps of ocean:
Where nothing living disturbs buoyed sleep,
Oysters make no sound, even as they creep,
There are golden worlds habited elsewhere,
Where the hardest hurt is a lover's glare!
But a lover's tempers are changeful things
And following the currents can be draining!
Leave me alone in cold, remote abodes
Where there's no lovers, nor enemies, nor thrones!

Madhu: Oh my dear Lord!

Darshan: Asrani's reason is blown.
Affected by gruesome things we have seen:
Of the human physiques' mutability!
Then to witness the felling of one's king,
To view, in a sea of blood, a world overturning!

Asrani: Enchain me that my mind may move no more,
Chain me now! Fix me to the unmoving floor!

Madhu: Come within my soft offered clasp and hold,
Love of God's the sole eternity we know!

Tukarem: There he goes! It's Madhu's reason that's blown!

Darshan: Asrani! I was years ago in a vast library,
In Taxila,[29] where I chanced to read something,
Writ long ago by a Greek, Heraclitus,[30]

---

29 Taxila: The city of Taxila was home to a famous ancient library.
30 Heraclitus: Greek philosopher of Ephesus 535-475 B.C.E., renowned for his theory of the universal mutability of the elements.

Who taught that all living things are in flux:
Transformation affects all creations
Even to the dark floors of deepest oceans,
Among living things smaller than oysters,
Ever at war, even in their cloisters!
Asrani, Heraclitus had wept too,
That there's nothing of Earth that doesn't move!
War is expression of ultimate motion:
Bred like loosed winds in the throes of monsoon -
Spun in the vortex of a prone vacuum!
Where war is horrid father of all things,
Where oppositions reach extremities.
War is considered of all things the father,
Who balances, as everything alters!
Determining the new victors and orders:
Foisting new balance, among survivors!

To what do we cling, to what do we hold?

Democritus,[31] another sage of old,
Saw, beneath all the elements, a sole
Atomic core round which elements form...
Impervious to the force of all storms!
Such is courage: an indivisible altar,
A main strength - no counterforce can conquer.
Such is faith, the basis of a kingdom,
Round which is formed our Indian union.
Such the sacred oath that we have all made,
To this king's crown and to the Gupta name!

In this universe, this flexuous state,
Weak elements are consumed by the great.
There is not in existence a law more sure
Than Nature's: 'Rule is of the Mightier.'
And naught is more certain to make us weak
Than if the faith of this kingdom here breaks!

---

31 Democritus: Greek philosopher of Abdera 460-370 B.C.E., renowned for his theory of the primary incorruptible structure of the atom.

If the courage of our persons proves lame
Or we forsake our oath - to our king's name!

From the contested Pillars of Hercules,[32]
Across worlds, barbarians are sweeping,
Through our weakness or their capital merit,
The Hun have grown our mighty opposite.
Divide before this prodigious power,
Then we and all we know will be devoured!
Or we'll be cast adrift, a vagrant pismire,
To wander the hollows of our fallen empire!

Amedkar: Enough of this war that we cannot win
Before this tempest, let's scatter with the wind!

Madhu: It was prophesied man has four ages,
And war attends the ends of these stages:
When laments are sadly sung for the living,
And the dead accounted felicitously.
In this cauldron, this great extremity,
God calls you the more, not less to duty!
In this you, not your enemy, controls
Faith to the oath which you gave with your souls!
Failing that oath, you're your own enemy
And in eternity - already dying!

Tukarem: I will recognize no man as my King!
Not Chandra, this heir to imbecility!
Nor will I listen to his unworldly priest!
We are dying, for he inspired this peace!

Chandra: Tukarem! Of your insults I am tiring!

Samudra: There is one here of the same Gupta line,
Who believes survival is not a crime!
For my part, with the death of my father,

---

32 Pillars of Hercules: The sea gate between the Atlantic Ocean and the Mediterranean Sea, spanning the Rock of Gibraltar and Monte Hacho, at the farthest edge of the then-known world.

The kingdom and all its forms have altered!
I weary of being at all points pursued:
By Hun savages through our native wood!
For peace we must adapt to changing time,
And plead for terms, in order to survive!
Terms I've sent to the Huns by embassy:
For surrender of contested cities,
And creation of a peace, beyond the Ganges!

Tukarem: Now here's an heir who bears an equal weight
And steers us, with like name, to differing fate!

Chandra: You know full well who is your rightful prince -
What king embodies his father's faithful wish!

Amedkar: Sure, that's open to interpretation,
Your brother and you, so close related?

Chandra: You would make of me some new Damocles[33]
Who gained and lost a kingdom on a string?
Where's the hanging sword and disabling wine
To waft me to the loss of my resolved mind?
Surrender Mathura? Our fairest jewel!
To the arrogant enemies of the world?
To my death, this place will be defended,
Though rebels of Earth and Hell contest it!

Ashara: Our pains blaze over the springs of wisdom!
Let's all return to cool wells of reason.
The Hun, though distant and yet far afield.
Have a force in this chamber we all feel!
Bewildering woes make the wisest err,
Take this time to think, beyond our common fear!
We have oft overcome these tireless foes,
These are not gods - immune to mortal strokes!

---

33 Damocles: The legendary courtier who envied the King of Sicily; when invited to enjoy the ruler's life of privilege, Damocles was humbled by the suspension of a sword over his neck, held by a slender thread, and symbolic of the precarious nature of kingship.

If we compose our force in a strong union,
It's possible to regain our lost dominion.
Union is a weapon of our armories' helm
That only we can divest of ourselves!
Should each verge to retreating paths and ways -
All paths will have their ends in the same place:
Under swords of this all slaughtering race!
This merciless crew would sense bloody wounds
Following all, redoubling their pursuits,
They are a force in full career of motion;
That will never pause, lest we oppose them!

Should we bend a knee and beg for a peace?
A dream of tranquility beyond Ganges?
What fealty to an oath shall a Hun show,
If we debate here an oath given to our own?
Would they keep oaths to end their savagery?
When we keep not ours to defend our King?
No mumbled oath will stop their ravages,
But defer battle, to our disadvantages!
We may choose where to make the battleground
But not avoid battle, nor from it bound!
Our choice is not whether to fight or fly,
But where to fight, gain victory or die!

Lastly, first failings are always moral,
Whose linked and gathered effects are mortal!
If now, our better selves we first conquer,
And we break our oaths of martial honor,
We'll prove we are cripples in our nature,
Hamstrung lions, self-borne 'fore our slayer!

Asrani: I feel that the floor is now quaking, moving:
            The walls trembling, this palace is cleaving!

Tukarem: I care nothing for breath-borne mortal oaths
            Or joining hands with doom devoted heroes,
            I have a Gupta king named Samudra,
            With him I intend to fly from Mathura!

Amedkar:	I too renounce any covenant or bond - You too are a man, Chandra, not a god! Names and syllables can be interchanged Depending on what's emphasized or strained. I too follow the lineal Gupta If you will lead where we wish, Samudra?
Tukarem:	Yes, let's see writ a plausible treaty, To live and to plead for the Hun's mercy... For peace beyond the defendable Ganges. What say you to this, good friend, Asrani?
Chandra:	You plead for the peace 'gainst which you were ranting!
Asrani:	Cannot you all feel it, everything shifting? Yes, I would be gone - But cease be moving!
Chandra:	What a body is formed before our eyes: The weak of heart and the broken of mind! This is how my father's death is answered: Our Empire's strength – suddenly surrendered? Love and duty have been three times denied - I owe to our fallen King once more to try! Will you not observe the King's covenants And present arms for the Empire's service? Think before you deny to me again Constancy belonging to long-known friends!
Tukarem:	You want victory that we cannot gain I am for peace, even with the profane! And for flying from this contested plain!
Amedkar:	Again, I tell you I'm with Samudra, If he flies from the battle for Mathura!
Chandra:	And you, who owes us the most, Samudra?

Samudra:	Peace is necessary, that is the offer!
	Though it bankrupts wealthy Mathura's coffer!
Chandra:	I wish the Hun had slain more by a few,
	Than have left me this rebellious crew!
	You are Mathura's guardian porters,
	Caving in doors that protect her altars?
	The fall of your virtues, the grating sound,
	Fissures sacred ports of the inmost bound:
	The soul of ourselves at its most profound!
	Samudra! Speak to me aside awhile,
	Come here, to the quiet of this near aisle.

Chandra moves Samudra aside.

How can you here take my heartfelt embrace,
And counsel the swift end of our whole race?
Poisons have crept into your princely blood,
Weakening your mind to abandon our love!
Is even the bond of our love threatened?
Does this war leave such sacred holds broken!

Samudra: Of all the world's wonders, what's the foremost?
That though all around him their lives have lost,
There is one thinks, he'll not pay the same cost!

Chandra, you weren't on battlefields to see -
Tomara's fearful strength will make you bleed!
Save us! Let's go home to save what we can;
This place is reserved to the cursed and damned!
If you throw a stop where the Hun would trod,
You may as well wield feathers - to bar a god!

Chandra: Our dear Father tried to create his own peace
While the Hun were few, relatively weak!
You think they'll accept peace at present strength?
They will pursue our end with all that force,
To which our early errors gave so much support!

Samudra: If you don't use those closed ears to listen,
             Tomara will use them to feed his python!
             He is nature's sablest son of Earth
             Who comes to shake us from our preening perch!
             To smite the edifice of our creations -
             And nothing beneath heaven can sway him!

Chandra: We are the Kingdom's and Heaven's first servants -
             And 'tis you, our first strength, that deserts us!
             This grotesque war has wrought a mutation
             Severing paramount bonds of brethren!

Chandra leaves Samudra and pulls Ashara and Shekar aside to confer.

             Ashara! Guard these persons for a time
             I must pause, or become of Asrani's mind!
             Our troops are also in need of orders:
             Assume to new corps, the returning soldiers!

             Shekar! Ready flotillas, skiffs and boats -
             We've a city on a river to set afloat!
             Those incapable of bearing sword or spear
             Must by swiftest means get away from here!
             I will inform our wives not to unpack
             But move their things from the wagons to rafts.
             We have to hope the storm is not buttressed -
             Or the Jumna too, turns rebel in this tempest!
             Return here, after you start the process!

To himself I'm a rightful King and a great King's son...
             Fled by many, heard by few, obeyed by none!

Shekar turns to go but is met by a guardsmen with whom he talks.

Shekar: Lord! Would you believe? The trader Sudhile's arrived!

71

Tukarem: Chandra! Here's another of your swift kind -
               Who brings horses now their riders have died!

Chandra: By my reading, one cause wrought this calamity,
               And it came among us through one activity -
               And that cause does deserve a full hearing.
               Let this Sudhile enter our royal company!

Sudhile the horse dealer enters.

Sudhile: Pardon, Lords, I have ten thousand horses,
               That I've brought here by perilous courses,
               To bolster the ranks of your cavalry,
               Where would you like to take delivery?

Chandra: Shekar! This man followed all our movement,
               Withholding our horse until this moment?

Shekar: Yes, we informed him of our intention,
               How else meet many armies in motion?

Chandra: Indeed, how and where to meet us in the field…
               Of information, the least we could yield!

To Sudhile   Thanks, for this grant of aid, and your timing,
               Before the due time, you have made me a king!

Sudhile: I need to know with regard to the herd,
               Which side the river they need be delivered?

Chandra: That very question has been in debate -
               You must be the first to know, can you wait?

Sudhile: I should really be on my working way;
               He wastes a life away, who wastes a day.

Chandra: You can't wait moments? For you we waited months.
               You'll have our plans and good reward of us!

Darshan!   Let this our guest not part your eye -
Nor from this guarded chamber let him pry!

Exiting Chandra, Ashara and Shekar

To himself   Every room I move in is a prison
                  And every person met, bears a poison!

End of Act Two Scene Four

MATHURA

ACT TWO
SCENE FIVE

CHANDRA AND SITA

Place: In the Palace, a Royal Bedchamber

Present: Chandra and Sita

Scene: *Chandra solemnly enters into the palace's royal chamber.*
Various oil lamps blaze along the stone walls. Intermittent to the
lamps are vast tapestries depicting several courtship scenes of Hindu
mythology and Indian history. Sita is alone at the window with
brows knit in fear, anxiety, and sorrow. On seeing Chandra, Sita
makes attempts at cheer but cannot lift the weight of her worries;
Chandra answers with a desolate look. Sita turns her gaze out to
the storm.

Sita: What's now become of those thriving flowers
I picked for you in this Morn's sweetest hours?
What's become of the fragrance of this day,
That time, night, and storm have borne away?

When we wed I thought our life was composed
In a pellucid shell, a crystal dome,
Wherein we might live with our love alone,
Closed from shocks that emanate from thrones!
This world's fragile, and mine's a frail dream:
The arced glass of our dome is shattering!

What will come of our child yet to be born?
Who engulfs my senses, my body's form:
Careering in a current of peaceful joy,
Joy this one night's passing, now bends to destroy!
I've rode through a thousand miles of upheaval,
To see our father die and a villain revel?
If Tomara topples kingdoms and kills kings,
Tell me, husband, Chandra, what hopes have we?

Chandra:	I too thought we lived in a crystal sphere
	Until Huns sundered forts of our frontier;
	I thought Mathura our unpierceable heart
	Though it may soon burst into burning shards!
	I thought Bhamn's life indestructible,
	Now he's lost! And our brother's turned rebel!

Sita turns fiercely

| Sita: | Rebel! Who would turn rebel? Against you! |
| | Who in such a trial could be so removed? |

Chandra:	Can you believe the night and this tempest:
	Fierce gales surging in the gathered darkness
	Mirrors our fate with a perfect likeness?
	A dying of light steals over Earth's womb,
	In shadows, time labors, birthing our doom!
	Fate arms with sword and arrow the Hun tribes
	While to our friends she lends close striking knives!

| Sita: | Can you make sense! |

Chandra:	Of *friends*, who survived the fray,
	A moiety among them turns renegade:
	A chorus sings "Surrender Mathura,"
	Of these the high voice is our Samudra!
	I've lost my hope, a father and a brother
	In the crippling span of an accursed hour!
	The time of love, Sita, which we have known
	Is a time this one night has blasted and blown!

| Sita: | Why would these generals break the Covenant |
| | That binds to you the service of provinces? |

Chandra:	They believe we are too weak, the Hun too strong;
	That we neglected Ghandhara too long,
	That we misused her until she was lost!

Sita: You thought land traded for peace worth the cost!

Chandra: It doesn't matter what's done! What I would propose!
            Half the assembly has come out opposed
            This loss has split us apart like the Earth's poles!

Sita: Tell me the truth! Are we to lose Mathura?

Chandra: There's more here than you know, of cousin Bhuda,
            His advance was repulsed near Sthenesvara.

Sita: Ye gods! Then their council is quite right!
            From this prone position - we must take flight!

Chandra: Then I should be last and worst to betray
            The word of our Kingdom and a father's faith!
            I cannot break the word that ordered this age,
            No matter what the savage hardship I face -
            For survival of our faith, beyond my grave!
            There must be a sole core beneath all tresses
            That holds strength, ungiven to severance,
            I must save Mathura, according to covenants!

Sita: Such was your oath and promise given to me!
            That our love would not suffer - dividing!

Chandra: If I allow the devil here to trod
            Onto foundries dedicated to God,
            The whole of western India will fall in;
            What will come of our faith, hope or life then?
            I cannot betray the source of those strengths
            Which upholds our justice and our beliefs!
            I must keep my oath, my father's true word,
            For it's our word that has ordered this world…
            Better to fight, though a chorus bid me fly!
            Better to die, yet keep the faith alive!

Sita: Kingdoms are living things, things of a day

And like anything living, must pass away!
Leave these dusty constructs of earth and stone
Think of the life of our child - our life alone!
If we are the true source of all that you love
Carry us, love, to the interior of the Kingdom!

Chandra: Mathura is more than mere earth and stone,
It was raised by the faith that footholds my throne!
This kingdom's faith is in justice: its fruitful spring -
If we betray our word, that is life giving,
From whose source all loves are tributary.
The whole empire will die...eventually!

Sita: Is this empire so near to unraveling!

Chandra: As long as we are of a posture that's weak,
The Huns advance with mechanical certainty!

Sita: Given the Huns' history, there's no arguing!
Your power is halved, while that of our foe
Is double the strength you forethought known,
And you would stay here - to persevere alone?

Chandra: I have Ashara and Darshan to count on
And I may yet douse these sparks of rebellion.
If survivors of battle prove a good sum,
And we maintain strict military union,
We may yet see a great victory won!

In meantime, you and I must not play the fool!
The Earth teaches how to save rare jewels:
Hiding them in the coverts of the world!
Are not gems hid in caverns of adamant
To hide the allure of their inbred glint?
The greatest treasures I shall ever know
Lie in our unborn and your sacred soul!
While time and our strength allow us means,
We must put these treasures past war's reach!
While the storm surges and Earth's aquiver,
We must send you, love, beyond yon river!

	I will find for you the very ablest craft, For over that full river you must soon raft.
Sita:	A thousand miles to view an empire severed. So many to see a kingdom dismembered, All this way to feel my family shattered! The sole constant is this force that changes – States of persons and things that we hold sacred!
Chandra:	True! Thus I move as does a constellation, Predictable in my light and motion: A King who bears the great wheel of the crown With duty, strength and loving faith unbowed! Fighting as a member of a royal brood Whose virtue is nor altered nor subdued! As long as I fulfill my father's will As long as your love is alive for me still My heart and spirit will arise the victor, Our soul's crystal dome will go...unconquered!
Sita:	You must give Samudra a chance to be recalled! He cannot be easy as he betrays us all! Remind him, if the Huns should venture here, I, his sister, will take up the bloody spear!
Chandra:	I know, my bride, that you are without fear! I hope to recall them all from betrayal, So I must leave you in this interval. I go to pray to the gods in the temple... To aid us to overcome this obstacle! Then I'll return to the rebellious council, And hope I may reclaim our generals. Then I'll return to you, Love, at the soonest, To let you know first, how these things progress!
Sita:	You must return to me, Chandra, at the soonest As every moment's vital and cherished.

End of Act Two

ACT THREE
SCENE ONE

REFLECTIONS IN MATHURAN TEMPLES

Place: The Temples of Mathura

Present: Prince Chandra

Scene: *Chandra is within the main Pantheon Temple of Mathura. There are numerous statuaries of various divinities, but dominant and gathered at the back stupa of the oblong edifice are colossal statues of, at center, Bhrama; to his left, Siva; to his right, Vishnu, and next to Vishnu, Krishna. Chandra walks the length of the temple and kneels before the triumvirate, looking first toward Vishnu, then round the sacrarium, then again to the members of the triumvirate.*

Chandra: Vishnu, cannot you give me 'neath your vault,
                Where colossal forms adorn the hall,
                Moments for prayer, free from these assaults?

                Images of gods! Elaborate frames!
                Expressions that spawn millions of names:
                Aspects of God, of a source all the same!

                Through fear of you, Lord, the sun shines, winds blow
                From you, Lord, life comes and fates are bestowed.
                How unlike you is our prone doubtful world:
                Bristling havoc, while you go undisturbed!
                How unlike you is our prone, doubtful state:
                Riving in change, while you form molds of fate!
                How unlike you is our prone, doubtful heart:
                Prisoned shadow, while you're light to the dark!
                How prone to doubt are we in relation:
                In tumult, while you abide above creation.
                We are of you, but suffer constant winds,
                Nothing of us begins, but to an end shifts.

Nor are we free, even if the twice born,
From your sun or the specter of your storm!

'Tis evident your wisdom commissioned
Earth to purify through opposition:
Where swiftly wings the ornate dragonfly,
Freely from the bird's insatiate eyes?
Where strides the deer, even amid his herd,
Free from peril of the haunting leopard?
Where stands the fruit tree, thriving and alive,
Free from struggle with the ambitious vine?
Where in the river swims the turtle's child
Free from crushing jaws of the crocodile?
What fish swims into the profoundest seas
Free from leviathan's wanton foragings?
The inhabitants of earth, sky and sea
Vie predator beings, testing their strength.
Even you, Vishnu, have an alter, Siva!
Counterpoints beneath the poise of Bhrama.
What Vishnu preserves, Siva would destroy
Where weakness lives, Siva's strength is employed!

Earthly beings must have adversaries
Keeping all pure, to punish mistreading;
Much as poles have their base in contrarity
To keep the Earth upright and evolving!
Siva! Maybe it's right, raising homicides
To correct our lives and scourge our weak hides!
Thus the law of contraries is observed.

Why then, Vishnu, are a king's laws unserved?
Where is aid from faiths of similitude,
That should be drawn mettle to our magnitude?
Our great strength is in the covenant made
Which escapes us now, in this trial of faith!
Where's the firm, loyal and impregnable
To stand 'gainst foes with me – immoveable?
Where am I to find affectionate friends

If friends I expect, serve an enemy's ends?
Where shall I find a loyal force of arms?
If friend's swords bow to adversary charms?
Where's in the realm the magnetic circuit
To defend justice and the King's Covenant?

This chaos shifts all from true ordinance,
As if the Earth's shelves loosed her continents!
The mettle of friends dissolves unalloyed -
Yet, there is a greater bond here destroyed!
Are not immune to laws of polarity
Blood-borne bonds of a sacred family?
Brothers bound from the womb and nursery,
And common affection from their infancy:
United genus, of a single train,
Descendant fires derived of common flame!
What is family, if not fire of the soul,
Lighting our heart's love, making it whole?
It is reflected in the filial hearth,
That warms souls it may destroy, if it burst!
My brother blasts embers of filial fire,
Scattering them in an all-destroying pyre!

If we allegiance expect of our friends,
What fealty from brethren should attend?
If not reverence, then not estrangement;
If not loyalty, then not rebellion!
How to survive in a world overturned,
When enemies are joined and brothers spurned?
How might I a tottering empire save,
How succeed, if love, by which we relate,
By war's chance is consumed in fires of hate?

We are shaken even to our soul's core
By this world-cleaving Hun, this meteor,
Who baffles the poles now loosed in the storm!

Siva! Compliments, you seem to flourish

Even in souls that owe us love to nourish!
Souls whose love of us hath been fully purged,
Leaving wanting even the virtues of a herd,
Which should cling, in the face of a predator!
So far we've fallen from heavenly grace
Our love's beneath that of a jungle race!

If family and friends leave us with dawn,
We'll venture forward as an injured fawn:
Crawling forth a prey to packs of wild dogs,
Who will claw from us our rich, ornate hide,
Fanging our strength till our weakness has died!

Krishna! Your own will die by this Hun brute:
Can you stand aside motionless and mute?
Are you oblivious as your stone statue,
Which, by its immensity, is unmoved?

Lords, view the beauty of this sanctuary
Which we built as our love's testimony!
In the sculpture of these statuaries
Our souls seek to achieve your harmony,
But through these vast works you will doubtless find
Slight imperfections of various kind,
Where sand doesn't perfectly hold with lime.
Though we labor to perfect the sculpture,
Blemish in our efforts proves we're mortal!
I'm mortal and cannot keep my minions
In the sculpt of our King's covenant!
But if your voice could descend from Heaven
To stir our virtues with your resonance,
It is the breath and measure of your word
Whose cadence binds all in the universe!
Cannot you lend my hopes but a whisper?

My monarch's voice is of mortal timbre
That can't call mine own to love remembered:

Imperfect as these statues which we raise
That are just sand without the lime of faith!
Lord, your word binds orbs of heaven at night,
Can't you relume the faith we need to unite?
If we rebel against our better selves
By our weaknesses we'll be overwhelmed!
Lend your voice till evil is exhausted
Aid us, that justice may be exalted!
If we will lose your love's guide from our heart,
Justice will be lost and we, bound for the dark!
The four fold world[34] will join a single fate
Of learning empires are mortal... too late!
We'll witness as did people of Ephesus,
Though we meet foes stronger than Herostratus,[35]
That in the night, with a miscreant flame,
One may raze to dust... glories of an age!

Here am I, perfect only in agony
And hear no god, only my frail echoing!
'Tis truly said by Madhu and those that pray:
God! You understand most and have least to say!

In the silence, I'll make you yet this pledge:
To defend your altars to my last breath!
Aid me to fortify mortal weakness,
Help me to my right thoughts and right actions,
To right motives, free of weaker passions.
I am prepared to make the sacrifice
Of my imperfect self - for your greater life!
In defense of your sacred hearth, Mathura,
Which holds in her precincts your sacred aura.
In defense of this your monumental figure
Which inspires us, that your love we remember!
And though they prove we are not of your kind
But are fickle, feeble sand, without lime!

---

34 Four fold world: Refers to the four principal empires of the later Ancient World: the Roman, the Han, the Sassanid, and the Guptan.
35 Herostratus: Set fire to the Temple of Artemis at Ephesus, one of the seven wonders of the ancient world, on July 21, 356 B.C.E., destroying in a night what was said to have taken an age and all the wealth of Asia to build.

Have you nothing to say from your vast throne?
Nothing more, colossal images of stone?
With hearts as cold, that leave us here alone!

End of Act Three Scene One

ACT THREE
SCENE TWO

A GATHERING OF REBELLION

Place: Administrative Chamber of the Palace

Present: Princes: Chandra and Samudra; the Priest, Madhu; Generals: Amedkar, Tukarem, Asrani, Ashara, Darshan and Soldiers: Shekar and numerous of Chandra's soldiers under arms

Scene: *The place is the same as that of the first council, but all present are more tired, more thirsty; the blood and mud of the battle have turned to dry, powdery paste and dust. The dispositions of those present have become dry and hardened as well.*

Tukarem: Damn, if you do not greatly try patience
                Allow us leave or you'll taste our rages!

Amedkar: I note the river is populating
                With varied skiffs, rafts and barges plowing
                Along the city's eastern boundary!

Chandra: Well, while King, precedence goes to the weak!
                Ah, right! You both should be foremost sailing!
                They're now boarding the old women and girls;
                Given your natures, you two should be first!

                I ask once more you observe covenants
                And return to duty's proper orbit;
                This is the final plea of my kingship!

Tukarem: Our several intents we have made known
                And no mortal power can bind the hold.

Samudra: Our enemies have beat us to this stream,
                Where surely they'll drown us, if we don't leave!

By our defeat that the Hun has won,
The life of our monarchy is overthrown!
Her laws, her authorities and decrees,
Her provinces, dimensions and energies,
Are with our comrades left afield, dying!
The monarchy's last breath is transpiring:
A monarchy's life must die with its armies!

Sorrow, I know, much more than anyone,
Proclaiming the death of another love!
Thus and so has this pestilent wind blown
That all life, as once it was known, is gone:
With a once-great king and a kingdom lost!

Chandra: Amazed I am such circumstance exists:
By operation of this hacking prince,
Mathura's ribs are laid bare to expose
Vulnerable tissue of her heart and soul!
Hearts you abandon to suffer alone,
Hearts now abandoned from above and below!
If by rebellion the crown is cracked,
Beware the issue of the cataract!
You know not the issue of what you do,
But it will do and do and do and do
When the hold of our order is confused!

Amedkar: Is there aught in Mathura to defend?
Odd outworks and poor constructions of men?
For dwellings and temples of granite and brick
For all this lifeless molded sand and flint,
Ought we to sacrifice our life and limb?
Nor heart nor soul resides in these old crags,
If we save them, shall they utter us thanks?

Madhu: Schools which teach the precepts of harmony,
Proportion and ethics of philosophy;
Temples raised in answer to Heaven's word
Whose sung cadences move the universe!

Structures of brick themselves have no spirits,
But these great halls breed glistering millions,
Whose trains are raised tapers to the heavens,
Like star fire, of which they are reflections!
These are the hearts and souls of Mathura
Breathing storehouses of God's sacred Aura!

Tukarem: Priest!   We'll see if all your lights and your songs
Last against the grim iron of swords very long,
When Tomara ignites a miscreant flame,
Razing this place to uninhabited plain!

Madhu: God's semblance does not need this defense,
But love in ourselves - that is God's essence;
The best and eternal aspect of man!

Tukarem: Keep gibbering, priest, while the Huns advance!

Chandra: Bhamn the king is dead, but defend Kingship!
Which centuries of justice established
Along patterns exalted in heaven:
Defend we must, sources and ends of justice
For sense to be made of our existence!

Darshan: Ashara and I are of constant mind;
We'll fight so to steady the jostling time!
To the justice of heaven make sacrifice,
As it is virtue of the cause makes all,
Honoring one's life, even in its fall!

Ashara: Yea, we'll be conquerors of greatest kind:
Those who subdue base instincts of the mind!
Who stand the course through stormiest seasons,
Biding the blast of war, by strength of reason!

Chandra: Greater praise there is not than reverence,
Greater love there is not than obedience!

Tukarem:	What use is it to reason or speculate,
	If we do not leave soon, we cannot leave late!
Chandra:	Asrani, is your temper better quelled?
Asrani:	Wherever I sit is a moving hell!
Chandra:	Madhu, take this man to some good remove
	With your best unguents let his head be soothed.

Exit Madhu and Asrani

Sudhile:	Prince? Uh, King! I know not your proper naming?
Chandra:	Without you, Prince; with you, with us, uh - King!
Sudhile:	With what I've heard…
Chandra:	and heard and heard and heard…
Sudhile:	Many horse you'll need that side the river
	For these generals to observe surrender?
	While you remain to brave a coming siege;
	As matters stand, do I properly read?
	If that is so, I should then get going -
	Most of your herd needs caparisoning.
Chandra:	A blithe creature of the time you seem,
	Knowing when to come, knowing when to leave.
Sudhile:	May I apply to the city treasury?
	There is the billing, a balance pending.
Chandra:	Yes, there's a balance.
Amedkar:	Have we time for this?

Chandra: Generals, please, a last breath of justice,
            Before your leave, let us go with a flourish!
            Shekar! You said this merchant was present
            In those talks when we formed our stratagem
            Congressing three bodies of our forces,
            And knew all the details of our courses?
            When and with what numbers we were to meet:
            Knowing thus the whole of our strategy?

Shekar: Yes, in fact, he could our future foretell:
            Where our arms would venture, where we would dwell.

Chandra: Had any else outside these closed numbers
            Thorough knowledge of all these maneuvers?

Shekar: No one, he was a spoke within a closed wheel;
            Such the great necessity of the deal!

Chandra: And of Hun cavalry was there increase,
            While of such needed horse we were starving?

Shekar: In the late battle, we noted a trebling!

Chandra: Sudhile! Why of a sudden such trembling?

Sudhile: I really should be going!

Chandra: What rare clothing!
            In fact your appearance is quite refined
            As though you had found a bejeweled mine,
            With these glossy objects on your finger?

Darshan: I discern the figure of mass murder!
            Fools! We've been betrayed like Roman Crassus[36]
            Led blindly by a smiling spy to death!

---

36 Crassus: Roman General of the first Triumvirate, betrayed by a spy of Hyrodes of the Parthians, whose conspiracy claimed
both Crassus and his son.

Chandra: What price delivers a King to his end?
What yield buries our kingdom in a trench?
Now you're trembling! You groveling thing!
Enamored by the lure of blood money!
Enormous must be the mounts of electrum[37]
Whose weight can sink a whole civilization!
To think the riches we mine from the Earth -
In base pockets, bury us with their curse:
Fixing our worth into living fossils
That will refill the mines on a scope colossal!
You worm! You pioneer of the muddy lurks
Feeding on corpses – blood-soaked scavenger!
We're treasure to such rummager miners,
When we're fallen dead and they our gravers!

Sudhile: I'll make amends, if we can be friends?
I know full well all that the Hun intends!

Chandra: What heart resides in this all-biting dog?
For treason to the Hun, I'll have you flogged!

Generals, Princes, I ask your judgment
On a spy whose lies are triumphant!
They've proved mighty enough to fell a king
While securing to himself our treasuries!

Samudra: How dare he breathe!

Tukarem: Let me do the hanging!

Amedkar: Take months to administer the torture!

Tukarem: May all such treasons find deathly halter!

Chandra: At last, I find you plaintiffs for justice?

Samudra: Killing the cause does not cure the effects

---

37 Electrum: An amber colored alloy of gold and silver used in ancient times.

Of what this galling spy has wrought on us!

Amedkar: Let's make justice, but do so as we go!

Tukarem: On the river, let's knife the poison toad!

Chandra: Justice hasn't achieved her ultimate ends,
But must to all and everywhere extend,
Through the Gupta's subject peoples and lands!
Allow an echo of India's gloried past
I'll have that, if the act may be my last!

Observing Sudhile weeping and trembling

I expect treachery from this whining fraud,
Born to be little better than a dog,
Raised as he was, taught to bite and to fawn:
Ever a slave... to his desires a pawn!
But his birth does not mitigate his crime;
Death has been pronounced as our court's design?

Amedkar: Yes, death!

Samudra: Make sentence!

Tukarem: We have all sworn it!

Chandra: How then to judge a general or prince
Blest in both education and origins?
Sudhile counsels courage to gain his gold,
You counsel fear and bid our world be sold!
He seduces strangers to serve his own ends,
You serve enemies, by the betrayal of friends!
Sudhile's acts have shaken and bruised the crown,
The same crown, your surrender cracks aground!
His treason imperils just Mathura,
While your broken faith would lose India!
What this miscreant spy hath but begun,

93

Your actions finish - and round the sum!
If he deserves hanging to end his life
The lot of you deserve skinning alive!

No mortal king living can so survive
With wolves before him and foxes behind,
When evils within and without combine,
Howling dissonant ends as they harmonize!
A future India, as yet undefined,
Shall curse your weakness, your wavering minds,
That made allies of enemies and spies,
Completing the ruin of our own kind!

You want calm, quiet and security?
Find it! In a dark prison cavity!
I'll house rebels in earth's mutest cavern
Where there's time to weave a coward's garland![38]
You say you won't defend these sacred walls?
Find a home beneath them, wherein to crawl!
Wait in the dark of a dungeon's confine
For light which lumes: we or the Hun survive!
As you send us alone to fight these beasts,
Here! I send you to Hell! Happy howling!

Samudra: You can't do this! By what authority?

Amedkar: We do not recognize you! You're not King!

Chandra: If you deem I'm not King! Iron vaults will be!
Enjoy your time below! To it on your knees!

Guards! Take them to haunts of the jailor,
Have them chained in his infernal parlor!
Mahed! Tell Ashok I don't care to hear
Aught more from rebel tongues, while I've ears!
Tell Ashok to keep them in his confine -
Until our death or victory is proved by time!

---

38 Garland: An ornament of honor normally given to a victor.

Sudhile:	King! Please! Is there a price for liberty?
Chandra:	And you would pay me from my treasury? All the general's will applies to you: You've earned agonies of a traitor's doom!
	Clear these miscreants from this fetid room!

Samudra, Tukarem, Amedkar and Sudhile are taken by Mahedhara and the guards from the room.

	The crown begins to crack from deep within: Fissures gape along faults of rebellion; Earth quakes as from her deep volcanic shafts: Eruption comes! Brimming with fires of wrath!
	Is it possible I and brother Samud's Hearts sounded first in the same supple womb? Shared simple laughter and joy of childhood Yet strive against each - to our common doom?
Darshan:	In war's chaos and the extremes which exist The fondest bonds may heat to divisiveness; Affections stretching to when we were born Break under pressure of a catalytic storm!
Chandra:	How do you bear our crown such reverence? Why are you so steadfast in our defense?
Darshan:	Take not that what I would say to you ill But crowns do crack and royal blood does spill: Crowns and family trees are mortal things, Mutable by nature, full of failings! Justice, reason, faith and their great precepts Are those that guide and yet survive the flesh, To which the Gupta have been great servants, Thus, you've my loyalty, even to my death!

They have not one name, nor frame, nor color
But I serve the aura of their flower.
Concepts are beyond effects of fortune,
But, in shift of time, determine motion.
They serve not the stomach, as does the spy,
Nor seek for the self, as our old allies,
But we are served in giving them service,
As they're upheld by unfailing courage,
We're upheld by their unchanging pattern.

Chandra: I should renounce the crown and follow you.

Darshan: Defending the crown which serves them, you do.

Shekar observes from the window

Shekar: Look! On the arc of Mathura's horizons,
Pitch fires are lighting, a thousand cressets,
Defining the darkness, forming a crescent:
Fires that long cindered and burned the wide Earth
Approach the walls of Mathura's sacred hearth!

Chandra: Timely as the tide are our conquerors:
They have their hands securely on the hours,
While by the moment, we grow more scattered:
We're frenzied motion, when all is at hazard!
Loyal ones! How to extend our grasp
And embrace the aid of our late fallen ranks?

Ashara: To say that necessity makes demands:
We are in need of all strengths from all hands!

Chandra: Into our troops the others organize!
While the Hun moves swift, we fall far behind!
Darshan! Ashara! Match the men to their armor!
Shakar! Return to save those on the river!

Darshan, Ashara and Shekar exit; Madhu re-enters

Madhu:	What do I hear - that Samudra's been jailed?
Chandra:	In the test trying all hearts, his has failed!
Madhu:	Your father loved him too!
Chandra:	Yes, as I do, I cannot be wise and merciful too! He has my love but cannot have my faith He, by his own will, turned a renegade!
Madhu:	For love of your father, can't you agree?
Chandra:	On loving Bhamn, yes! But not in the legacy. In how best to serve, we see differently. Don't worry; he's only being detained, No one will harm him, I am not profane!
Madhu:	He is your brother! I tell you this as your priest!
Chandra:	Enough! Enough of all you assorted beasts! By gods! Where's a corner wherein to find peace?!
Madhu:	I'm sorry, Prince. I feel all this weighs on me.
Chandra:	Must I now nurse your emotional bruisings?
Madhu:	Your father, your brother, even Mathura All lost on false hope - all India! Let me talk once more of peace, though late! Let me go! As I once did, as your legate, To Tomara, into the camps of the Hun, That I might save this place from perdition - Try to interdict the Hun's dark ambition!
Chandra:	You can stick truth in the center of their eye Or shout it in bowels of their ear, deep inside! But they will spit on you as they put you by! Madhu! What you would do is suicide…

Madhu: I must try!

Chandra: The Hun, ourselves, you! All blind!
            You've been misled by hope, we by our vice,
            And the Huns, as ever, by their appetites!
            And India dies, as our blindness collides!
            They'll give no ear to your beneficial will
            Only to clamors, pleasure or pain instill!

            I understand you. Try what talk may do!
            I must prepare for what battle will prove.
            Look! Take troops bearing the royal ensign -
            Take mine! It will help you through their front line.
            If it's true that fortune favors the brave,
            I hope your bravery will win us the day.
            But it's surer still, your virtue will be slain!

Madhu: I hope you're freed from this wheel's burning rim....

Chandra: Where is the hub, Madhu, that's free from sin?
            Take care, old friend!

Madhu: Ever yours, unto the end.

End of Act Three Scene Two

ACT THREE
SCENE THREE
CHANDRA AND SITA REVISITED

Place: The Bedchamber in the Royal Palace

Present: Sita, arriving: Chandra. Later arriving: Shekar

Scene: *Chandra enters the royal quarters with Shekar and the Monarch's guard. Sita is standing at the window, looking toward the Jumna River. The storm outside is audible. The winds and rains have intensified. Now and then, a flash of light and the low rumble of thunder sound the frontier of the gathering monsoon.*

Sita:	Chandra, my love, thank God, you are returned On the Jumna, the whole city has surged: Marauding citizenry in their fury; Scream deathly cries in the calamity!
Chandra:	The woven web of peaceful rule's broken - Terror thrives, flourishing through the ruin. They hear the approach of the homicide Who carves for us with a lunatic pride, Flaying the city's nerves, unleashing pain, Setting common holds of reason ablaze, Fraying the senses, unspinning the souls, Which were rooted before this death-wind had blown!
Sita:	Are your generals to duty returned? Have you the loyalty of their soldiers?
Chandra:	Samudra's rebels have the crown abandoned, For treason, I've condemned them to prison. Whether who stands of their wounded army Are loyal and will fight is a mystery - Answerable in war soon to try us all, Wherein trials of strength will judge who'll fall.

99

There was a time Bhamn's was a stable throne,
I am now his heir in misery alone!
Such the horrid, unalterable cost
Of broken faith, and a covenant lost.
Sound! Sound! Come you close, rupturing thunder -
Sound our sorrows, as we're cleft asunder!

The Kingdom and I have lost the gilt crown
Before I'd had the time to put it on!
The loose ties of the kingdom's empery
Fray like an unraveling tapestry!
The crown's columns, arches and cornices
Will soon lie in ruins of these edifices!
Colossal images of gods we've raised
Will crumble back to lime and sand again;
The limbs and brows of once sky-kissing gods
Will litter paths the barbarians trod;
Savage flames will melt the pavilion
Upholding our conception of Heaven!
When the city's leveled and strewn rubble,
There will grow pitiless realms of jungle.
These monuments, these glories of civilization,
Will become baubles for apes to gape on!

Oh my people! I hear your pain wailing:
Your single body, wounded past saving!
My beloved subjects you now must ride
Jumna's icy currents, unto foreign skies!
Whither can you run, where find a haven,
Where find defense, within this broken Heaven?

Sita: A haven? You've just put half of ours in prison!
           By your action we, in a manner, join them -
           We have divided again, before the opposition!
           You have left yourself with no alternatives
           But the prison of some retreating movements!

Chandra: Must I abandon more helpless thousands?

As I did in our northwest provinces!
It is for such failings within ourselves
That there are unleashed these forces of hell!
The crown didn't hold sufficient reason
To keep her kin from this fall of treason!
Nature armed these monsters to bring our doom
Our weaknesses gave them their motive and room!
It is the weak impulse within ourselves
Determines if Earth - be Heaven or Hell!

Tukarem was right! We made our own demise
While Ghandhara suffered, we turned our eyes!
We were the first our own covenant to break
Whence we were slow coming to a brother's aid
We of ourselves, unto our own, turned renegade!
When we allowed Ghandhara to suffer alone,
While too long coveting the couch of our throne!
While meandering in the comforts of our vices,
We allowed Ghandhara to be gashed to ruins!
Bhamn and I, and not our subjects, are to blame,
That we're condemned to die on this fiery plain!

Our wronged brethren wandered a province's waste,
Blinded and numbed by the torture of their pains!
They used their shields to dig their brother's graves,
And melted their swords to form the chains of slaves!
These visions I see give me keen sense of agony:
The suffering wrought... in this eclipse of majesty!
We failed our own basis of justice to uphold,
Now we're repaid with an India overthrown!

I should have been first, not the last, to meet death!
Not one more subject will die, but I will be next!

Sita: Damn it, Chandra! You must think of what to save!

Chandra: These acts have so bent the Empire's vast frame
            Her footholds break and her limbs are astray,

When so huge a frame slips and cracks,
The days of saving remedies are past!
The complex shell begins to disintegrate,
While it bleeds away the sinew of its faith!
When native loyalty of her children failed,
Where above nature, great India prevailed,
And when the web of her unapparent nerves,
That had the great ideal of justice served,
Become an agony of crucible, and a curse,
The mold of the living colossus must burst!
Then, no sculptor can create the patch overlay
To remold the core of her exploded frame!

We were the first! Do you see? Who broke our word!
Through the fissures fell - the order of our world!

Sita: Chandra! You must leave Mathura with us!

Chandra: No! My forces will make a final thust!
To retard the march of our conqueror,
I must keep him here! This side the river!
While our people escape as best they may:
I owe to their hope the lifespan of a day!
No more, before me, will die for my mistake!

Sita: I envy the more that your life you would fly,
Than exiled alive, I'm unable to die:
I prefer to remain, husband, to stay and fight!
They took my father and would take my husband -
They would murder our child! Set me upon them!

Chandra: So I do, Sita, and Love, so I must,
Though in manner that will bring continuance.

Enter Shekar

Shekar: Lord! The refugees are moving cross river
There's great tension, yet there remains order.

Chandra: Listen faithfully to what I say, Shekar!
Sita! I put the crown into your charge.

Go with Shekar and with our royal guard
To the waiting barge, join those that flee,
Organize them to order! Take their lead!
When you achieve that side of the Jumna
Attempt contact with our cousin Bhuda:
Send swift messengers for Sthenesvara!
Let Bhuda know what's become of Mathura!
If Bhuda lives, your forces may join with him.
Let him know, with my crown you're entrusted!
Take with you two thousand of our foremost men,
The best battle-hardened Kyshatrians!
Ride for strengths of our Ganges fortresses
To collect all their men and munitions,
And form new perimeters of defenses,
Protecting our eastern populations!
After I do them the gravest injury here,
If you can push the Hun to our north frontier,
You may be able to pin them in Kashmir!
Sita! You'll need bravery for your journey
Along which dangers and chaos will teem,
Our Gupta star, from on high, is now fallen,
Cracked like the core of a constellation:
Without guide and strength of our central orb,
Provincial law will fall, like a meteor!
Word of our fall has already transpired
And travelled swift as smoke of the fires,
Soon to consume Mathura's temple spires;
Cerementing skies in a funeral cloak
While beneath, organs of law stifle and choke!
Brigands and thieves will inhabit those roads
'Twixt here and Ganges' forts, where you must go!
Such will occur when love of a Kingdom
Severs at its core, blasted to ruin!

You, Love, will inspire India as you ride…
A new Semiramis![39] Our child at your side,
You'll soon reignite India's lost pride!

---

39 Semiramis: Legendary Assyrian queen said to have ruled as regent from 810-806 B.C.E.

Sita: Why can you not come, it is only right!

Chandra: Faith in the Gupta can only survive
If I remain here, as a sacrifice,
To that sense of justice which I left behind,
When gazing on Ghandhara, I turned my eyes!

Take all we love, and faithful to me - leave!
Death I must accept, even if you grieve!
Save what you can of our remaining power
To the safety of a surviving hour!
This is your rightful and lawful Queen - Shekar!

Shekar: Aye, Lord! I will follow her as I would a star!
I'll faithfully obey her every word,
And never be more loyal unto whom I serve!

Sita: Love! The joy of my life will soon die with you:
Swords will not fall on me but their shadow,
To eclipse light from my days forever…

Chandra: You are strong, Sita! And bound for the river!
Remember! In the rainbow's cincture
Lives the gold of all our foremost treasure
For there the essence of love is unspoiled -
By the dust of Earth! Its mutable soil!
There it is our best selves are preserved
In unassailable light, living forever!
That light I see! In the orb of your tear -
Glistening 'fore me is a light more dear…
Than all the crowns and kingdoms of the spheres!

Come, beloved! It is time for us to go:
I to my doomed troop; you to your painful road!

End of Act Three Scene Three

ACT THREE
SCENE FOUR

THROUGH A PRISON PORTAL

Place: The prison vaults far beneath the foundations of the city walls

Present: Tukarem, Amedkar, Samudra, Ashok (the jailor), Mahedhara and his guard and unseen but variously and dimly heard prisoners.

Scene: *Tukarem, Amedkar, Samudra, and a guard captained by Mahedhara are at the portal of the subterranean prison of Mathura. They have descended through an ancient labyrinthine chasm. With every descending step, the light from above has lessened, the passage has straitened, and the angle of the irregular stair has assumed a more precipitous pitch. A choking stench of decaying rot has thickened the nearer the approach to the door of the miasmic abyss. The darkness is palpable, the damp and humidity enclose the skin and the senses. One's sense of space is both closeting and infinite due to the narrow walls and immediate ceiling next to interjacent dark or invisible spaces. Shuffling movements of unseen prisoners and the indiscriminate scraping of chains and barely audible groans are the only sounds pervading the atmosphere. At the group's arrival, a brood of bats reorients their position, giving the dismal perception of a living, yawning ceiling made more strange by the eruption of high-pitched rodent squealing and the flushing sound of lizards moving in a wave along the uneven floor. Ashok, the jailor, meets the assemblage at the door.*

Mahedhara: I've unaccustomed guests for you, Ashok,
        Nobles and traitors to crawl in this muck -
        You are to keep these men for treason chained:
        Chandra wants no more to hear this rebel train!
        They are to be kept in your close confine
        Till our death or victory's proven by time!

        For Sudhile here, use agonizing device
        Which first inflicts pain and last takes his life!
        His treachery's the cause we are all here

Breathing the acrid, thick, motionless air!
For the rest, the price of their rebellion
Is to breathe the dead vapor of your dungeon.

Exit Mahedhara and Guard

Ashok: Oh, how the mighty herein are fallen -
Trading gilt scepters for chains of iron?
Once persons the bright world would exalt,
Prisoners are you now of my midnight vault!
I view the subject of profound proverb:
Touching the results of overturned worlds,
Which fell princes to provinces of worms!
It must say what havoc wrecks in a day
Whence from our duties, we are borne astray?
How when derelict, and though we act in few,
Our slightest wrongs can undue multitudes!
But that's work for philosophic thinkers
Not one who lives to confine prisoners!

For introduction, I am your captor,
Ashok my name, whose synonym is death!
None who fall in this den ever reascend.
To evil ones I am a scourge and curse,
Who keeps court here, in entrails of the earth!

Tukarem: We are prisoners, yes! To be close kept!
No one has mentioned a sentence of death!

Amedkar: The orders given cannot be construed
That we're here or elsewhere our lives to lose!

Ashok: While beneficent powers hold their sway
Persons such as myself are held constrained,
But you must be wary of the cascade
You created when such powers are deranged!
You yourselves eclipsed the beloved Crown,
Loosening the chaos that will make you howl!

Tukarem:	You have precisely heard the commandment - We're to be kept alive, not put to death!
Ashok:	I am dubious as to exact words: King Chandra wants that you should "never be heard." In this dark convex of all that's hideous We err, when words doubtful - to miscreance! You live in self-created tenements And will leave here as have other tenants: Your last home is fixed to this blood-soaked floor, Never to pass yon inexorable door! Your end I have determined and 'tis time: My accent is only known to those who die! Your death is nigh, and 'twill avail this night! I am by nothing at all further bound - Sure, not by fallen powers of fractured crowns!
Tukarem:	It's fit I should go. I watched my province die! This Earth no longer holds one familiar eye!
Samudra:	We're struck by the circle of our karma We would not raise, so we die 'neath Mathura: Here we are racked on shoals of our demise Wrecked by leveling storms of our own device!
Ashok:	First, the merchant, who came without his horse We'll first test the soft nerves of your mortal corse… A word must be kept! When words are broken, Do not you know that whole worlds may fall in?
To Sudhile	
	How dull your day, when you ought be riding, Such things you see, when you've not your pony!
Sudhile:	Jailor, I've means of making you wealthy; The Hun will reward you generously!
Ashok:	I was once a servant of stable justice But now I must serve the utter darkness...

More devoted to bringing the weak pain
Than seeking for the comforts of the vain!

Sudhile: I sold only to eat.

Ashok: Yes! Our country!
Now to drink, I'll give you a bloodletting…
First I must probe beneath your trembling breast
To search the shadows for unknown secrets:
How else know what really lay in your heart
Than by main force - to tear its pulp apart?

Sudhile: One atom of self sustains the universe
I, supreme, am beyond man's measure!

Ashok: I've known many an inhuman demon
Recite flawless the Bhagavad-Gita.
Do spare me false, empty iterations:
Faithless prayers never breach the heavens!

How make passage to the breast from the bowel?
These inches of transgression will make you howl!

Amedkar: Oh gods! That we have set this monster loose
Who'll open our noble veins like a sluice!

Samudra: How in this darkness I am enlightened
Here, where one sense dies, the others heighten!
Here, where I've not a sense that's ocular
My faults are luminous and spectacular!

I burst the genius of our common self,
All the cells of empire are overwhelmed,
The ring of heaven broken - brings our hell!
I couldn't bide to leave our inmost kernel,
The obdurate core of strength, unbroken
Round which foundation our life is woven!
My acts have made a fiery drowning wave,

Ripple with tidal force and gathered rage
Whose killing effects may not know a grave -
Strengthening on itself - then self-sustained:
Claiming all that lives with limitless range!

Please, Chandra! Forgive! I owed you love
Not rebellion. Do hear me from above?
My soul was convulsed with revolution
As I felt whips of unjust persecution,
I flew at power that faced me with a name
Though 'twere suicide of a moth to flame!
Self motivated, blind - a suicide
Whose cleaved life gravely sickens life beside
Wherein most of all - my love does reside!

Forgive, Chandra, in true mercy forgive
Though I die here, allow our love to live!
I hear the voice of Siva screaming within
"You're a villain of the most wanton sin!"
I burst the hold of our King's Covenant -
My King - forgive!

Ashok: We'll try the resistant ribs
To view what mortal evil bides within,
This to extract the evil from the good
You know, in this life - that's what you're to do!
Your slayer brings instrumentality
To wrench from you an ultimate agony
For being prisoner to your bestiality!

Many times I've tried this experiment
But it craves some superior physic
To make men better than mankind: perfect!
Yes, it is beasts that we are born and are
When once we take our eyes off heaven's stars!
Prone to all manner of faults, diseases,
While time and night avail it never ceases.
There now, I've made all my preparations.

I regret that I have not a sedative,
But dying you'll feel it most - that you live!

Sudhile: Forebear! Oh gods! That this be happening -
I'll pay anything, but don't torment me!

Ashok: Save your needed strength. Petitions are vain,
While you're lashed to my gory rack of pain!

End of Act Three

ACT FOUR
SCENE ONE

EMBASSY TO THE EPHTHALITE HUNS

Place: The Hun encampment north of Mathura

Present: The Khan Tomara, General Uldin, Tomara's son, Mihirakula, soldiers and Aides de Camp. Later, enters the Hindu priest, Madhu and Mahedhara

Scene: *Madhu is soon to arrive at the new encampment of the Huns to the immediate north of Mathura, which is in plain and prodigious view. It is the very end of the night, the verge of dawn. Rain is falling with a steady density; the winds are gusty from the south. The Hun soldiers form a vast arc intermingled with their horses. Torches and tripods blaze against the rains. At the center of the arc, seated before a fire drinking wine, are Tomara, the barbaric Khan, Lord of the Huns, his son, Mihirakula, and his warlord, Uldin, with several aides de camp present.*

Tomara: What sickly perfume assaults my senses?

Uldin: They burn lotus[40] from surrounding marshes…

Tomara: It's a horrid stench, this ornate fragrance!
             Fell some peepal trees,[41] add them to the fire,
             Lessen this atmosphere, too floral to respire!
             Slaughter some cows uselessly lingering
             And feed the troops! Their hunger is raging.

An aide de camp leaves while a messenger approaches.

Messenger: Prince Chandra, with forty thousand troops beside,
             To the precincts of Mathura has arrived.

---

40 Lotus: Supra. A symbol of beauty which pervades Indian culture
41 Peepal trees: A species of banyan that produces the sacred fig; also associated with Vishnu.

Tomara: Even chance the plans we create now abides!
A sun too late, he's precisely on time!

Uldin: What say? Will he comply with the surrender?
With such new forces, in loss he is bolstered.

Tomara: Chandra's army venture all this way
To surrender valor and sulk away?
Bhamn's bloody death makes Chandra fume,
Unleashing blinding passions to work his doom!
Fight they will, dangerously, to save their pride:
Furious as beasts, in their last throes of life!

Uldin: At least for now we have this docile time
To converse over meat and a glass of wine,
Before the beautiful prospect of city light!

Tomara: I devour this time: the rustling watch of night...

Mihirakula: With Mathura taken and victory sure,
To what new ventures will our armies turn?

Tomara: Mathura is the hard shell of a mussel:
Once shucked, inner India will prove supple!
We'll make peace with what remains of the Gupta
To secure victory over the breadth of India,
With positioning of chosen garrisons
To lord the distant Indian provinces,
Wrenching from the wealthy and the weak
Their worth in treasure - till their purses squeak!

Mihirakula: That all sounds in the prospect of probability;
To what use, then, would we put the new means?

Tomara: Next, we'll turn west on the realm of Egypt
Ravaging the river cities of lower Nilus,
Wheeling north to Alexandria and Memphis:[42]

---

42 Memphis: Modern-day Cairo, Egypt.

	To sack palaces in that limb of Byzantius, While denying what remains of that state The shipments of their necessary grains, Starving means by which that cripple is sustained!
Uldin:	Plans as that are a colossal ambition: To reduce Egypt and starve Byzantium, What purpose does all this activity serve?
Tomara:	In fullness of the discourse, you will learn! Our next attentions will turn on the Levant, Whose cities lie along the sea in a crescent: We'll reduce those cities and control those ports From which we'll launch piratical hordes - In a new built and ably manned fleet - To seize the weak underbelly of Greece!
Mihirakula:	We are not sailors who people the seas!
Tomara:	To every new enemy, boy, we adapt new means! Now listen! For this is where we fell imperium - For then we'll strike for the heart of Byzantium! Convening forces of army and navy To lay siege and attack on Constantine's city, Finishing what Attila[43] could not accomplish: To sack that capital on the Propontis![44]
Uldin:	I can say, since you were of years a child, Your ambitions have been insatiable and wild!

Tomara moves over to Mihirakula to embrace him.

Tomara:	Weakness in my enemies compels me to this - And what wider world will I leave to this prince! This is my heir, my able and fitting son, To whom I must leave hopes of expectation!

---

43 Attila: Known as Attila the Hun (406-453 C.E.), leader of the Hun Empire, conqueror of central Europe, who according to legend died following a nosebleed.

44 Propontis: Inland body of water known in modern times as The Sea of Marmara, straddled by Istanbul, it connects the Black Sea to the Aegean Sea, while separating Europe from Asia.

Uldin:	Having conquered the earth, to this vast scope,
	Might we then come to our rest and a home?
Tomara:	No! Then we strike an easy prize, fallen Rome!
Uldin:	Broken Rome! What the Goth[45] has not sundered,
	Our cousin Huns have looted and plundered -
	Even scraps left in that conquests aftermath
	Have long since been carried off by the Alan.[46]
Mihirakula:	We'll set about to plunder the plunderers!
Uldin:	You tire me, is there no end to our ventures?
Tomara:	Yes, when our powers have achieved the extent
	We've seized the last land bordering the sunset!
Uldin:	Excellent! When we have followed the sun
	And laid all barren to the ultimate horizon,
	All this done, then Tomara, what's to do?
Tomara:	To sit as now, drink this brew and talk to you!
	We will live at our ease, my dear friend,
	Spending days in drinking and conversation!
Uldin:	You propose to waste a thousand cities
	To raise and engage vast armies and navies,
	To battle onward to Earth's ultimate end
	For that which in peace, we have now at hand?
Tomara:	Don't you see! We possess power and means
	And live in a falling world: weak in its knees!
	There are no powers fit to interdict our motion:
	We can feed on the chaos of the commotion!
	The best of our enemies are a broken herd:

---

45 Goths: Visigoths, the Germanic tribe that sacked Rome in 410 C.E.
46 Alan: Referring to the Alani group of tribes originally from the northwest Caucasus region; some moved as far west as Gaul with invading Gothic tribes.

Sickened sheep without a guiding shepherd!
Without a single common principle -
They are a scattered mob, a frightened rabble,
Through whose lands we may ride invincible!
Some see these weak sheep and feel sympathy,
I prepare for a feast and march to victory!

Uldin: Nothing living survives the radius of your pride:
Full of ambition, insatiate and wild!

Messenger: Chandra sends from Mathura an embassy:
Madhu, chief priest, head of the sanctuary!

Mihirakula: Not much of an army that sends a priest to us?

Tomara: They are all-consumed, son, but for their tongues!

Enter the Embassy of Madhu and Mahedhara

Madhu: I am Bhramin over this part of India,
Prefect of yonder temples of Mathura,
I met you once, when we were both younger,
Now I view around, you are much stronger.

Tomara: I, Tomara, am Khan of this gathered army,
An army to slumbers of kings, unsettling!

Madhu: Impressive: these massive congregations,
Colors and banners of so many nations!
Tell me, how is it you still lead so many,
While you sacrifice hecatombs to Kali?[47]

Tomara: Those who come to us afoot, we give equines
To those with horse, we give chariots to ride;
On those whom we find with farms under tillage
We bestow the greater expanses of a village;
To those who govern village magistries

---

47 Kali: Hindu deity associated with time, change, and death.

> We give the land and slaves of ample cities;
> And to those soldiers who just want to be paid,
> We offer gold, not by count, but by weight!

Madhu:
> If the sole cause of the world becomes greed,
> The end of the world's soul is insanity!

The dawn begins breaking; the sun emerges in the eastern horizon, which is shrouded less densely in clouds.

> I suppose you are owed some compliments
> For so far piercing our strongest armaments
> That you have pushed our strengths to a precipice
> And view with vantage this abject edifice:
> In whose walls are a frightened citizenry
> Whose lives and welfare are at your mercy!
> So much so, that I must put to you the question,
> Having this advantage, what is your intention?

Tomara:
> India was valiant in times of yore;
> Now, to find a man, we must far explore!
> No! Here I find only a host of rabbits,
> Somewhat prolific, edible and harmless:
> Born the pet or prey to everything else
> That has teeth to grasp or gnash the pelt!
> Nature guides the lion, leopard and cheetah
> The wild dog, the jackal and the hyena
> To cull from the hapless ranks of the hare
> The sick, the slow and the lame round their lair,
> So I am here! And you are right, priest - to fear!

> We intend to reduce this prone capital,
> Harvesting yon monument's lustrous gold,
> Extracting the element from the dross stone,
> Refining and remolding it into simple form,
> To finance our way through a world at war!
> With gold's worth to purchase men and munitions
> We'll carve a conqueror's path through continents!
> Until growing, victory by victory,

116

Tomara points to the Sun

We subdue all that's lit by yon luminary!
Until, I may say with my name: "Conqueror"
I have fordone the feats of Alexander![48]

Madhu: Alexander crowned his great victories:
Constellating the globe with famed cities,
The same set aflame in your savage journeys!

And I'm accursed, for counseling lenity,
To the Gupta, who treated you generously,
You! Who are about to sack their greatest city!
It's owing to me we find ourselves at your mercy!
For upon a time I viewed you with pity!

Tomara: Then there is much to thank you for indeed!
You know, your face now returns to my memory.

Madhu: You appear guided and consumed by twin fires:
Those of personal pride and great desire.
If I show how to conquer worlds without war;
How amass treasures greater than earth's store;
How hold a demesne whose glory is eterne;
How do feats beyond even Alexander...
And demonstrate you may do so from your chair,
Would you then, Mathura and her peoples spare?

Tomara: Sure! Let's hear this all unlooked-for advice,
But if you waste my time, you'll pay with your hide!

Madhu: I will begin with the worth of Mathura,
With the work of her master artist Dinna,[49]
Whose soul molded the forms of yon beauty:
Glories you'd dismantle for your armory!

---

48 Alexander: Alexander the Great 356-323 B.C., conqueror of the Persian Empire and Near East Asia.
49 Dinna: Famous sculptor of the School of Mathura in ancient India.

Dinna's first labor was discovery in detail
Of the material that generally avails,
Through mining the veins of the world:
Her gems, her stones, her precious mineral:
Finding among shale the light of emerald;
Unearthing in quartz the luster of gold;
Lighting on marble, buried in wombs of stone.

Thence he used his artistic discernment,
With a cardinal eye of crystal judgment,
Culling the norm from the exceptional,
Sifting the base from the majestical!

Thence he gathered these proper elements
And bathed to pureness their inbred essences;
He hewed the rough jewels to a perfect form;
Remolded bricks of gold in his fiery forge,
And the rude marble he cut to colossal shape,
For the greater expanse of his designs to be made:
Designs latent in the genius of his mind,
Nurtured there by imagination and time!

As with harmony in an orchestration
He carved his vision with golden proportion,
With gouge, chisel and rasp he composed
Using geometry's mystic ratios.
Birthing forth correlation in complex shapes
Whose embodiments achieved divine grace!
Then with a soft delicacy he set to trace
Contours in the hands, the eyes, the face,
With softened features of a heavenly race!
Thence he detailed and inlaid their dress
Bejeweling symbols and gilding raiment,
Polishing the intervening stone to a finish
Until this great feat was accomplished:
Peopling this beautiful city that we know
With the blessed conceptions of his soul!
Then he built these symmetric vaults and domes

To give these exemplary gods their abodes!
This he did while he lived an existence
Which a mendicant would term penurious!
This he did 'til calluses of his hands cracked
Until these monumental labors bent his back!
Seldom he remembered whether he had rest
Seldom he cared if he had nourishment!
When beset by quandaries he could not solve:
His concentration delved in physical laws,
His dedication was of the sage degrees,
Equal to be the equal of Archimedes![50]
Such were his hardships and immense labor,
Such the focused faith of his hard nature:
The whole of his great life was a sacrifice:
To exercise his gifts in the noble devise
Of raising through art, his vision of the divine!
He birthed this not for thought of what he was owed,
But for beauty, this labor etched in his soul!

Lastly, you may search these temples and statues
From the colossal blocks, to the slightest grooves,
And nowhere will you find the form of his name -
For he dedicated his labors to his single faith!
His was a genius he deemed a mere tributary,
To be drained and lost in an anonymous sea,
Composed of those souls who serve Divinity!

Tomara: Oh! The frailty of all human design
When a conqueror rives a vortex in time!
'Tis sad: for so short a period doth stand
Even monumental works of mortal man -
That after our plunders must return to sand!

What you put forward is far too complex,
It needs a library and an index!
And yet, Priest! I've not heard the promised word,

---

50 Archimedes of Syracuse: Greek mathematician, engineer, inventor, and astronomer (287-212 B.C.E.); killed in the second
Punic War, reportedly while solving a mathematical problem.

How to conquer and know the tribute of worlds!
Have you forgot the hide I will be owed -
If you don't deliver soon along this road?

Madhu: 'Tis not a far road we need to travel
To unlock the mystery of the marvel!
For it is compassed in the round of your soul,
No greater than a mustard seed to behold,
But compassing in its frame the universe -
From the point of its womb to its utmost verge,
And is member to an infinitude of worlds!

First set to discover yourself in detail
Of the material there that generally avails:
Through mining the veins of your soul,
Perceiving what light or darkness enfolds,
Separating the dark of pride, desire, lust -
Shadows which sickly obtain in all of us
From light of mercy, temperance and love;
Using a moralistic sense of discernment
Abiding in the judgment of your conscience!
Hewing and forging these precious elements
To arrive to the virtue and pureness of Justice!

Use imagination to form great designs,
Orchestrating harmony in your acts of life!
Birthing forth correlation in societal shapes,
Whose embodiments achieve a divine grace,
Molded with a self-rule which is golden:
Relating to others - with love's proportion!
Jeweled with the soft light of the merciful,
Whose warmth aids, not assails, the pitiful;
Fashion smoothly your actions of justice,
With the evenness of a marble temperance!
Commit to this, not with thought of aught owed,
But for the beauty love will etch in your soul!
Make the beautiful works of Dinna your guide
Built with love, dedication and sacrifice!

Listen to the inner voice of love's dictates
Whence 'tis your hand shapes a people's fate!
This is the art needful in your hands, these the tools
Of those who are burdened with the weight of rule!

Your consuming goals of desire and pride:
Are delusive ends to which none ever arrives:
Futile ambitions which must be sacrificed!
For desire, let's use example of your troops:
For whom greater gain is life's sole pursuit!
He with a rupee desires for two or three,
He with three wants then four, six or forty!
He with forty seeks eighty or an hundred,
He with hundreds wants then for thousands!
They are ever greater slaves to ever greater wants
Which inhabit souls like Daemons with their taunts!
Tormenting the mind with ever greater assaults!
It matters not how much such desire is fed,
Greater feeding, leads to greater emptiness!
You may make a treasury of the globe,
But never may you own it as a whole;
Though you think you own it, it's but appearance:
With Death, all is "another's" inheritance!

Look to God, whose fruits are all creation!
Doth he take anything into his possession?
Or does he not give away everything
For others to divide in the giving or taking?
When once you define matters as yours or mine,
Are not half of all things, lost in the divide?
Who would possess all must want for nothing!
Who would conquer all things must conquer one thing -
Those desires of his soul which are limiting!
To know and hold the worlds of the universe
Wants for their slightest morsels must be purged!

As to the glory of your name, your pride,
How many Alexanders have strode this life?

Yet Earth's never in a name been circumscribed!
Again, God may be assigned millions of names...
But cannot by any one of them be contained!
He who could stamp creation with his fame
Has nowhere etched the definition of his name!
Knowing that by definition comes division,
And in defining, loses half its comprehension!

For your being to have tribute in eternity
You must recognize yourself as tributary,
To be drained and lost in an anonymous sea
Of those composed souls who serve Divinity!

Thus, if you wish without war to conquer worlds
You must defeat the base desires of your soul first!
If you wish treasures greater than earth's store,
Seek not to possess her slightest morsels anymore!
If you wish to hold a demesne and glory eterne,
Be a servant to God, that you will not be spurned
From His, the only empire of all, that endures!
If you wish feats and praise past Alexander,
Treat Mathura, a city at your mercy,
With merciful temperance and with lenity!
Of conquerors, you may surpass the foremost -
Turn yourself and your abject hordes to loving hosts!
You may earn heaven's love and all our own
You may end your hunger and make this your home!
All this you may do while sitting in your chair,
What say you then, shall Mathura be spared?

Tomara: That is rare! To have, I must abandon everything,
And to be remembered, I must become nothing!
And, oh! I must some ineffectual god serve:
While foregoing the worth of slaves and plunder?

Mihirakula: Here's our conqueror! What a sense of humor!

Uldin: Can't you put your gods in one catalogue,

And all their million wills into one law?
We Huns have but one law we all follow…
He leads who fills our stomach's deep hollow!

Tomara: My dear priest! It is with reality I must contend.
If I don't feed my armies with your prince's head,
It's my head in their stomachs will be next!
I am a man of this world! A man of this time!
You've wasted time, priest - so pay with your hide!
Stupid priest! To whisped things an abject slave!

Madhu: 'Tis you that desire binds in a thousand chains!
The skin of my mortal frame you can flay
But not crack the center of my lasting faith!
To the ends of Earth, peaceless you will roam,
Till a hill of worms is all that you own
When you might own heaven's eternal renown!
You are of the worms, unenlightened thugs,
Ever hungering to feed and conquer dust!

Tomara: This language, Priest, should come from a strong empire,
Not from the tongue of one, soon set afire!
Heaven favors me, priest! Repaying my toil
With your sacked temples and their barbaric spoil!

Madhu: More than jungle beasts, man is a horrid savage
When ungoverned in rage and slave to his passions!
Thank God! You can't command these skies and rivers!
Or disrupt the exile of Mathura's survivors!

Tomara: You will not be among them! Take him to his death!
Cut out his scurvy tongue, then cut off his head!

Aides de camp take Madhu, while Mahedhara sheds tears.

Madhu: God! What to do when your truth is spurned?
What can you do with those who never learn?
Mahed! Do not weep for me who gives his life

For a love that is superior...to this homicide!

Tomara: Guardsman! Let Chandra hear what I tell!
            If he dare venture 'fore Mathura's shell,
            Like an unhoused turtle, he'll venture Hell!
            Thereafter, it will be for Mathura's rabble
            To decide whether we range their temples
            With our blood-soaked spears raised or leveled!

End of Act Four Scene One

ACT FOUR
SCENE TWO

REVIEW OF BATTLE ORDER

Place: Atop the northern walls of the city

Present: Prince Chandra, Generals: Ashara and Darshan; Adjutant Commanders of Bhamn's late forces: Jagjel, Silesh and Ashwin; Aides to commanders and generals.

Scene: *Chandra ascends to a promontory wall overlooking the northern fields of Mathura. The rains have intensified; the winds are up in heavy gusts from the south; lightning and her reflexive thunders punctuate the skies with variable light and guttural percussive sounds, rolling and echoing through the horizons. On the Jumna, current and wind contend in chafed agitation. The skies remain shrouded in a dark grey vault, though the sun has risen. On the promontory walls are assembled generals, commanders, and aides. In the foreground are the Indian armies gathering in preliminary formations. In the distance are the massed multitudes of the Hun host, standing from the Jumna riverbanks in the east, arcing to the west, and southerly to the horizons.*

Chandra: Jagjel, Ashwin, and Silesh, you are well met:
                I pray your spirits are wrenched for revenge!

Silesh: This is the tenth of their waves of offense
                In nights and days of battle without rest!
                Their bivouacs blaze with like scope of light,
                Exhausting our eyes to the perimeters of sight!
                Our efforts are vain, their numbers still swell,
                Like blood-driven wolves, scenting a blood-filled well!

Ashwin: We've felled thousands, yet still they fill the orb,
                With forests of spears and glistering swords!
                To think, even as these curs round Mathura curl
                Their breed prowls the corners of a fallen world!

They move like the waves of a pestilent disease
Before which there can be nor victory nor retreat!

Silesh: The onset of this illness was slight indeed,
But spread swift with unchecked malignancy!
I agree with my General, Tukarem,
You Gupta were wrong in your stratagem!
Had you not acted in fear and weakness,
But with judgment and foresight of reason
This peril had been crushed in nubile season!
Conceding anything to tribes of this kind
Bates rather than satiates their appetite!
Like the drunkard at a room full of wine:
He'll eat the lees,[51] given the keys and time.

Chandra: You've heard then of Tukarem's rebel mood;
Don't waste words, what do you intend to do?

Silesh: I agreed his assessment of Bhamn and you,
But of his rebellion, I did not approve!
As Kyshatrians, we must serve India first!

Jagjel: The rebels in prison lessens nothing of our woe:
For labor we the more, the more the labor grows!
How powerful and magnetic is the coil
That breeds these multitudes 'fore a goal of spoil?

Chandra: Is it not better to fight this planetary plague,
Than be to such spoils an overmastered slave?
Is it not best to die in service of the highest cause,
Than to live by lesser and baser things enthralled?

Ashwin: Hence we here, against odds, with you remain
To wage battle for India - on yon infested plain!

Jagjel: Yet, look at the vast form of this demon:
Whose jaws gape to swallow us to oblivion!

---

51 Lees: Sediment or dregs that settle at the bottom of a bottle of wine.

Chandra:	Yet, in the swarming mass of these fiends from hell, There are none blest to battle beside Jagjel!
Jagjel:	Nor none who serve a rightful prince and King, Such is death's only redeeming destiny.
Ashwin:	I battle for ties that are familial, For the lives that we save by the hard exile Of survivors who now stream 'cross the river; By our efforts more souls may be delivered! If we dull the force of the Hun's horrid rage, Every effort might another life save…
Chandra:	Whether you serve a king or brethren filial, The life of India or a still greater principle, Or as Ashara serves his imperiled friend, We all battle here to serve the same end, We convene our strengths to shield what we love Against forces waging a war for their lust! We pray by our sacrifice, that God rides with us! How's the number and arrangement of our corps?
Ashara:	In need of munitions and men the more!
Silesh:	Some fled the battle, tired of persecution, Others bolted, who heard of the rebellion.
Ashara:	To form new corps we are still in motion, Patching needs created by the vacuum!
Ashwin:	There remains to say that which is the saddest: Some of our own serve in the Hun encampment!
Chandra:	Then the circumstance of dread Mathura, Is to be consumed by sons of India!

Ashwin: Who needs these wolves, when we breed our own dogs?
        Who needs fiends, when we abandon our own gods!

Ashara: They're sensible, moving to the rising power
        Of the Hun, shining in his triumphal hour!

Silesh: Faith in common men, as strong as frayed thread:
        Broken easily as the veil of a spider's web,
        Which, wavering in the wind, will swiftly attach
        To any object met, in the wind's first waft.

Darshan: Is not faith the strongest and weakest of bonds!
        It also holds us here in service, against all odds!
        And is the foremost strength favored of the gods.

Chandra: We are to blame! The Gupta are to blame, friends,
        That we have lost the love of these subjects,
        Who have lost faith in our covenant of justice!

        While meandering in the comforts of our vices
        We allowed Ghandhara to be chewed to ruins!
        Bhamn and I, and not our subjects, are to blame
        That we're condemned to die on this fiery plain!
        Sacrifice nothing for our bent regal frame,
        Sacrifice not for the broken Gupta name -
        What is in a name, if its meaning is betrayed!
        Sacrifice for the ideal that we mortally failed!
        For the justice, whose essence we ourselves assailed!
        You see, she lives yet, justice is unbroken
        She thrones safe, an underpinning of Heaven!
        Wanting in the souls of men, ushering servants,
        Who hold fast to the bonds of her covenant!
        Men who thereby serve best God and themselves
        And keep themselves aloft from the ports of Hell!
        Justice is based in truth, and it's truth to tell:
        The Gupta with the Hun wrought us here to dwell!

        I cannot lift from their roots the mountains!

Nor change currents of a river's fountains!
Nor can I pull from the skies the ranging clouds...
Nor catapult myself to synods of the gods!
Nor grapple with tolls and measures of Time,
Nor can I the fall of events redefine!
The Gupta crown is gold and of a perfect circle,
But sits on brows of flesh that are all too mortal!
The abject and iron fate we fall hard upon
If we could overturn it - wants a God!

Silesh: Chandra! Do kings hold a unique monopoly
On the common failings of humanity?
Then are they not also scions of her strengths?
You have spoken the truth eloquently,
Truth is the foundation of justice's equity,
And 'tis evident for India your soul bleeds;
Lead us forth with your great remaining strengths,
Battle with us now as you would have us bid,
Lead us forth in sacrifice for Justice!

Ashwin: Conceive a new title, let it be "Battle Lord" -
And convene for justice our ready swords.

Jagjel: Accept pleas the reign of necessity,
With all, you are the king of popularity!

Chandra: Then we are of a bond no force can sever,
Brothers bound by love to die together!
With contempt for the evils of mankind,
Wanting but the benevolent gaze of God's eye,
To look upon our acts and in loving shine!

Ashara: Chandra, we need know how to order our ranks.

Chandra: Then to work, with main strengths in squares of phalanx,
With spearheads of elephants in the central van
To propel the main thust of salient attacks!
And cavalry in main support as auxiliaries,
With spear and bowmen, supporting on the wings!

Silesh: Such order of force we have already tried
              Such was our form, when most the army died!
              Our main weakness feeds the enemy's strengths,
              Our slow mobility 'gainst their immense speed,
              While we are as swift as elephants in stampede,
              Infantry we are, whilst they bring up cavalry
              And maneuver like leopards on our periphery!
              Spying the chance that we open a weak flank,
              Then, they pour in depth in the prone crevasse!
              Means of our advance must adapt, it's clear,
              For in war, we're not permitted twice to err!

Ashara: With respect, Silesh, in two hours' interval
              How may we remold all our forms of battle?
              We are tied to the post of experience,
              And must fight as we can, without variance!
              Besides, we haven't the necessary horse,
              To match level with theirs, force per force.

Ashwin: Our course is the same, so shall be our end,
              Destined we are, then, to die together friends!

Chandra: We may prove overcome by their speed and steel,
              But in the throes, we'll put such sting in their heel,
              Our virulence will make their advance yield!

Mahedhara enters with a guard onto the promontory

Mahedhara: I am come, Chandra, from the Hun encampment.

Chandra: Mahdu's hearfelt plea! I had forgot it!
              How fared Madhu? Did the Hun accept it?

Mahedhara: They greeted his plea and person with contempt,
              In this sack I bear his head, his heart they kept!

Chandra: Lambs may take such a shearing of their life -
              But lions won't suffer meek beneath the knife!

This act carves a breech in my sanity!
I would the settled order of the world cleave -
To forge a path, to make these butchers bleed,
Who desecrate the frame of our peaceful priest!
I would fill the green arable world with their blood
And laugh, as I starved, swimming through the flood!
Oh! That we may breach their bristling lines,
To wreak revenge on children and women kind
And kill them as unweaponed, as my dear friend,
Who in act of kindness, met such evil end!

Darshan: Calm, King! If we in action our souls lose,
What of ourselves escapes the Hun's abuse?
If we become like them in this storm's toss
As we're vanquished, we'll suffer greater loss:
The essence of what we defend will be lost!

Chandra: Mahed! Take this relic of my slaughtered friend
To temple, for his beloved brethren to tend!

Allow that in the battle's drawn order,
I will occupy the front rank and center!
To Tomara I'll carve a narrow corridor
And in his ambitions - I'll bury my sword!
I have in remaining life but one design:
Dispatching that barbarian's merciless mind!

Ashwin: They begin to load some catapults at random,
Those same machines we left in cities abandoned!

Ashara: What once ours, will they not use against us?

Chandra: Even time, once ours, gives them obeisance,
We are all chaos and they all readiness!

I must go down to the edge of the river,
And secure exile there is in procedure!
Then will commence our wheels of revenge -

To roll on butchers of our family and friends!
Where the scope of our unquenchable redress
Will bear all killing means, with a rage limitless!

End of Act Four Scene Two

ACT FOUR
SCENE THREE

EXODUS OVER THE RIVER JUMNA

Place: On the shores of the Jumna River

Present: In the foreground: Ajay and his family and massed citizenry. In the background: Sita, Asunaya, Shekar, and soldiery at the royal barge. On the Ramparts: Atmaram, Gowind, and assorted Mathurans

Scene: *The scene takes place along a narrow channel of land between the eastern wall of Mathura and the banks of the Jumna River. The strand is swarmed by Mathurans waiting to embark on the few remaining floatables and skiffs tied to land. Sita, Shekar, and Sita's troops are aiding the people in leaving while controlling the growing frenzy. The royal barge is the last craft of the line. Overlooking the channel and the river upon the eastern wall are many old and infirm witnesses of the exodus, those deemed too old either to fight or take flight. On the river, amid the throng, are Ajay, his mother, and his young siblings, waiting passage over the rising current. The storm is at pitch force.*

Sita:　　　　All these infant wanderers of the dark
　　　　　　The tortured of mind, the broken of heart:
　　　　　　Plying this thin strand, to venture a watery path
　　　　　　On a river unsure, 'neath a sky of wrath!
　　　　　　Yesternight they were warm, safe in a soft bed,
　　　　　　This night they tremble between exile and death!
　　　　　　Girls and boys, who spent hours with simple toys...
　　　　　　Now they wail for peace of their former joys!

Asunaya:　　There are so many yet to put aboard ships.

Sita:　　　　We don't have any means to compass it!

Ajay:　　　　Mother! Isn't that old Raghu I see!

133

Over weak women and children trampling?
There! A soldier has struck his madness down,
Rightly! His madness will stay and bleed aground!
I had known him as a kindly and calm vagrant,
Whose tranquil eyes ever bore a friendly glint:
Chaos of the time unhinges the prone,
Reason by commotion is overthrown!

Shekar: On the city walls are the true sufferers -
Whose weakness prevents they be wanderers
Look at that wealthy man calling!

*A gem merchant, Gowind, is casting his wealth in rare stones over
the walls to the crowds below.*

Gowind: You striving!
The Hun may relish my impending death,
But they'll never savor these, my gems!

Catch them as they fall with an unburdened hand!
Or let them drown beyond the lust of man!
Let them descend into the murk of the stream,
Their glint and allure are all-destroying!

The catapults of the Huns begin bombarding the city with burning globes.

Atmaram: It looks as though the sky's stelled hosts and choirs
Were falling from heaven in these spheres of fire!
These balls crush the brows of statuary gods,
Toppling down, to drown in the churning sod!
Be wary the fall of these burning globes -
They may ignite weak flesh, when they explode!

Ajay! Get quickly aboard that barge, my boy -
Mathura, by fire, will soon to be destroyed!

Ajay: Come! Mother! With everyone hold on!

| Sita: | Keep the line quiet! Who are the next ones? |
| *To Ajay* | Come now! |

Ajay and his family alight onto the barge.

Sita:	Shekar, there's no more room on this ship!
	With the present number, she dangerously lists -
	My heart breaks at it!

Enter Chandra with Mahedhara and his guard.

Chandra: Sita! You must embark!
Temple fires are exploding in blazing shards -
Winds may shift and flames engulf this barge!
Every soldier! Put children on your backs,
And unto your sides related matrons clasp!
Take to the flood, swim the heaving river!
Become vessels yourselves for these survivors!

Soldiers begin to do swiftly as they are bid, to clasp children and their mothers and to leap into and swim the river's current, some clinging to rafts, skiffs, and barges.

Sita: We cannot leave so many!

Chandra: What remedy?
We crawl the narrows of cruel necessity!
The city begins to burn, her temples to sink!
Dogs knell her end with vibrant howling!
You cannot watch this bitter fate round us close -
You must board ship now or unwilling be thrown!

Sita: I'll go! Allow me these stranded to mourn!

Chandra: Take your rightful tears and shed them aboard!
Now is not the time by emotion to be moved -
Trifling with time will entwine you in our doom!

Sita: Before you go with chivalry to ride,
               To fall in war, your virtue's sacrifice,
               Cast a last glance of your unequalled eyes
               That I may feed on their image through time!

Chandra: Allow my love rest in your heart's deep recess
               There visit me, when you would own remembrance!

Sita: This parting brings two lovers to their deaths
               Though I... life in a moving tomb must accept!

Chandra: Bear my living love to the eyes of our child
               Now go, launch! The river's motion is wild!

Sita: Emotion chokes me... I cannot stand nor breathe...

Chandra: Sita! Bear all safely on! On to Ganges!

The ship sways away from the shore.

               All the light of my life hath left the shore,
               All that remains is ravening dark of war!
               He who loses all those souls who brought him bliss
               Cares naught of the gathering dark of an abyss!

End of Act Four Scene Three

ACT FOUR
SCENE FOUR

CHANDRA AT THE HEAD OF INDIA'S ARMIES

Place: Before the northern wall of Mathura

Present: Chandra, Ashara, Darshan, Ashwin, Jagjel, Silesh, Mahedhara and the assembled armies of India

Scene: *Chandra arrives at the front of the Indian formations to meet with his generals and commanders, then to address the massed army. The rains and winds continue to gust heavily. The catapults have ceased to fire on the city, though the city is now in various quarters aflame.*

Ashwin: Chandra, we have measured the Hun quantity.

Chandra: Numbers mean nothing, only proximity!
Even in the smallest hollows of the deepest seas
Nature forms breastworks of adversity,
'Fore us is the body of our mighty adversary!
They have set fire to our too-fragile haven
And surround our forces in circumvallation,
Are we not resolved to wound this predator?
To the extent his ambitions are staggered!

All: Resolved!

Ashara: And our arms are to their best prepared!

Chandra: Then their souls will want strength from what they'll hear!

Chandra ascends a tower to address the Indian Armies.

Dear Indians, brother Kyshatrians
Arms who uphold our defense, blessed Paladins!

Need I express what your eyes fully perceive?
Or would I your all-faithful souls deceive?
Before powers of a merciless enemy,
We stand at thresholds of our mortality!

We stand under Siva's implacable sentence,
Whereby the living are scoured of weakness!
Through the world's animate and fertile realms
The weak and unfortunate are overwhelmed!
Siva ferrets nature with strengths of the tiger;
To ferret Man, Siva raised these damned monsters!
We stand before the armed might of a scourge
Unlike any predators who haunt the world!
Siva arms the tiger with claw and fang,
While he arms Huns with metallurgies of man!
Tigers hunt their prey singly through the wood -
While Huns pursue peoples in multitudes!
Tigers cull the weak alone from the herd,
Huns consume hosts in bleeding massacres!
Tigers make lesser ranks of nature their prey,
Huns chase down nations and raze them to the plain!
Tigers hunt the weak within a scope of range,
Huns hunt kings across the world in their rage!
Tigers when feasted and sated soon repair,
To docile, lazy quarters of their lair!
The Hun, when grossly fed to a surfeit,
Feels more the longing pangs of insatience!

Equipped with the powers of human reason
The Hun uses God's gifts as a daemon!
These Devil's pawns, the grotesque, the hell-born,
Are monsters who feed in theaters of storm!
In fields of chaos where men most want justice
The Hun preys on the feeble and the helpless!
The Hun is a man more beastial than any beast,
One Siva elaborately arms to test our strengths!
Given his means, his will, his insatiation,
The Hun lays waste to all human creation!

Gaze behind you and witness Mathura burn!
The Huns will pour India in this common urn,
While Siva's sentence is implacably served!
Before us stand Siva's dread instruments
Caparisoned with darkness of a thousand sins
Propelled by the sole virtue of brute courage!

Within us live a thousand lights of goodness,
Which uphold the covenant of our justice,
Let it not fall by the lone vice of cowardice,
Rather, let's sacrifice our sole source of weakness!
We must battle here! If fate ordains to die...
That the soul of beloved India survive!
We must minister Vishnu's will to preserve,
All that is beautiful and ordered in the World!

If unto Vishnu we give our life in sacrifice,
'Tis best we mirror the Sky's harmonies,
More important than mass to yon luminaries
Is their consonant movement in sympathy!
Whereby the Lord of Heaven hears their praying,
In a constant and glorious symphony!
Thus, let's compose ourselves into a warlike choir
Bound together: a marching aegis of fire!
Moving to fulfill Vishnu's, not our own, desires!
Let our harmony thread the fabric of our ranks
Governing motion through our woven phalanx!
Let the mist of our souls in this great contest,
Rise to Vishnu's scent: a collective incense,
Purged of the bitter ash of mortal weakness!
Where better to battle, or for our lives to perish,
Than before the beloved Mathura we cherish!
Where better to sacrifice than before this temple,
That is our beauty's living womb and cradle!

Let us go forth now upon our enemy -
And on this altar of battle, fear not dying!
For either we will overcome the evil Hun,
Or win by grace of sacrifice, Vishnu's love!

The soldiery cheer their assent to Chandra's plea. Then to a soldier nearby standing,

> Sound the conch shell when I give you the sign
> Look for me to do so from our foremost line!
> Mahed! Go and free the rebels held prisoner;
> Leave them the choice of battle or surrender!

Silesh:
> They can do neither: your prisoners are dead.
> We had word while you were at the river's edge.
> Ashok heard the rebels were in silence to be cast
> And so muffled them - with an execution's lance!

Chandra:
> How could he have misheard!

Mahedhara:
> I gave the order
> Perfect as possible when they were handed over!

Ashara:
> Jailors are not known for wit or delicacy,
> Nor for the sensibilities of tender hearing!
> Having luminaries in his envious power,
> He warped your just will to his base desire:
> Justice is hard to maintain in an age of peace,
> And is a miracle when a war's unleashed!
> Indeed, tossed by the elements of chance and force
> Nothing, though of sternest substance, holds course!

Chandra:
> It's true, one can murder an ordered world
> If one errs in a word or his words misheard?
> Good gods! What next upon my soul may fall?
> My brother murdered, with an errant syllable!
> One that I, his lover in life, had uttered,
> How much further may my soul be sundered?

Darshan:
> This whirling environment of madness
> Spawns all manner of unseen accidents,
> Which collide and combine with falls of chance
> To produce greater progeny than promised

In the single seeds of their origins!
These seeming unconnected events of chance
Are the fracted glass of an indiscernible mask,
Coverting the form of Destiny's deep design:
Which evolves to the being and face of time!
With our slight means we can but act for the right!

Ashara: No one can be expected to reasonably act
In the tumult of this quaking cataract!
So densely does time crowd chance events
How 'scapes any of us from unwitting death?

Chandra to himself and addressing the Skies...

Chandra: Samudra! I am worthy of your just curse:
Darkness falls on the soul that ordered murder!
Oh Heaven! Plague me again with being reborn,
But make me a futile worm when you storm!
I am the actor of horror unforeseen,
Unintended, but of my soul's making!
Ashok, my factor, who solely I unleashed
Magnified the demons of my inner fiend!
The enemy stands more than before me,
He thrives within me, a visceral entity!

How am I different from the Hun?
We alike for pride destroy all I love!
All for the wants of a personal desire,
We fight over levers and keys of power!
To the desperate events of chance consigned
Who is the greater daemon, the Hun or I?

Oh Samudra! How are we come to fatality?
From the furthest radius of our empery,
To the sacred core and bond of family
All's been dissevered in this calamity!
The heart, the seed of all that energy,
Forged in our common womb of nativity,

Is shattered with the force of a bursting star
Whose embers drift to die in the cold and dark!
Siva has proved our inner avatar!

Siva, be my guide! While I've a grain of life,
Let you be my guide in this last act of strife!
Of what to preserve, let me think no more
But of what to destroy - in this knot of war!
Steeped in the blood of my sacred family
Let me forth with world-killing weaponry,
Let the world be free of these common enemies!

Let the conch shell sound through heaven and earth!
Siva! Stand aloft in your witnessing perch!
Watch as men rend one another for their pride
While with blood of men, this earth is dyed!
Let us end things in this last decisive strife,
Let it end the evils that we do in life...
End these chance events, this mutability,
As they solely end, with the end of our being!

To his generals...

Friends, let's forth to meet the scene's thunderer
With our arms steeled with hatred and horror,
Let's go forth panting for a wide revenge,
Revenge that will end only by our death!

Ashara: Bow and spear, arm and march!
Silesh: Skirmishers advance!
Jagjel: Forward darts and lancers!
Darshan: Cavalry to lance!
Chandra: Infantry in harmony! Move forth for attack!

End of Act Four Scene Four

ACT FOUR
SCENE FIVE

THE VIEW OF BATTLE

Place: Atop the northern walls of the temple city

Present: Atmaram, Gowind, and other Mathurans

Scene: *The forces of India begin their advance toward the center of the army of the Khan Tomara. The monsoon's crest remains at pitch force. The city of Mathura is burning in many precincts. Mathura's remaining citizens are gathered to witness the spectacle and outcome of battle.*

Gowind: Could there be a more vibrant, moving scene?

Atmaram: It bears appearance of a fantastic dream,
           All orders and forms, colossal and moving:
           The senses drown in the flooding panoply.

Gowind: The air is thick with the scent of sweating fear!

Atmaram: Horn's blast and dog's howl fill the atmosphere!

Gowind: In swift motion flow slingers, lancers and darters,

Atmaram: Like locusts swarm these forces of light armor!

Gowind: Advancing on the wings the spearman and archer:
           Readying bows with instruments of slaughter!

Atmaram: The Hun sets ahead the same contingents,
           Both massed bodies assume the offensive!

           Chandra moves at the center of his royal corps
           With elephants, chariots and titanic hordes;
           Cadenced to motion, sounds the beckoning horn;

143

Thunder follows the lightning to the storm!
Forth to glut the daemon of dread raven war!

Gowind: Stones, arrows, spears, lances, and javelins,
Launch, arc, career and crash in their descents:
Cleaving with fury the ports of unarmored ears;
While brazen cries of soldiers ascend the spheres!

Atmaram: The cadence of brass quickens, shields start to rattle
Sounding the call of encounter to battle!

Gowind: The phalanx lowers spears down to the level,
Scything the Hun front with a gross upheaval.
I hear echoes from the front and hear a tune,
Our soldiers sing a faithful hymn to Vishnu!

Atmaram: Look! The orbit of flailing short swords
As man to man, strengths are matched in war!

Gowind: Desperate strokes strike for a foes ruin,
As force and fortune lord over confusion!

Atmaram: Victory is vouchsafed to the stronger advance,
Lest strength's outweighed by slights of chance!

Gowind: Moving in waves, ride surrounding cavalry
Of Huns closing round our corps periphery!

Atmaram: Look upon the valor of our united army:
A vast isle moving through a spreading sea:
With Chandra, advancing for India's soul,
He now descends... on Tomara's stronghold!

End of Act Four Scene Five

ACT FOUR
SCENE SIX

AT THE CORE OF BATTLE

Place: To the north of Mathura at the center of conflict.

Present: Chandra and Tomara, Ashara, Darshan, Uldin, Mahedhara and other fighting soldiers

Scene: *At the center of the Hun encampment, the Indian Armies have arrived, having broken through the central front of the barbarian forces. They have achieved an open space, as if in the center of a hurricane. There stand before Chandra, unaffectedly, the Khan Tomara and General Uldin, their surrounding guard having been defeated en masse.*

Ashara: We've won this encampment with divine ease!

Chandra: Such the might of virtuous unity!
                  Such is our strength when it is well-ordered!
                  Bring up forces, in impassable cordon,
                  Give us room to howl, to fight - to roar in!

Uldin: Your ambition's confined to corners, Lord.
To Tomara

Chandra: Here your grotesque enterprise ends - Hellborn!
                  Welcome to bloody mud and bloating flies
                  Who drink deep in your wrathful paradise!
                  As I through these countering forces ripped,
                  So I'll tear bloody passage through your ribs,
                  If in your chest you have a mortal heart,
                  I'll treat these diners to culinary art
                  And prepare their feast, tearing you apart!

Tomara: Did wheels of your stately carriage break?
                  You finally show me your soft, weak face!
                  To the deciding fray you arrive late,

But may join your father and brother's fate!
You and yours proved unequal to the test
Of better battling my tribe's armaments!
Certain, I have cut this kingdom's fabric
Unweaving the legend of its covenant,
Defiling its foundations of Justice!
'Twas easy keeping your forces divided;
It had been different had you united!
Now the gold crown is down, so is your throne!
Comes now pandemonium, comes the volcano!

Chandra: Aye! You have raked life from our provinces,
And laid waste virtues of our covenants;
You've eclipsed the light of my father's star
And condemned a great empire to the dark!
Aye, your force split even brotherly ties,
Until the madness of my wounded pride
Turned these bloodied hands to fratricide!
Yea, you burst the Guptan filial hearth,
Till its energies severed in a curse;
More, you invaded into my sacred core,
And break my soul, in a fury of storm!
You flood us like the ever-shifting main
Assaults shores through every nook and cave!
You so drown the kingdom with your horror,
In the end I turned, to become your mirror!

As you have murdered Vishnu's model son,
Feel Siva's instrument: that I am become!
As you have harrowed my innocent soul,
On your frame feel its darkest force explode!
As you carved the core of my heart's empery,
Face loosed powers of its unreined fury!

Tomara and Chandra exchange several parries of sword, with Tomara taking a grave wound to his side. Both combatants part, exhausted.

Tomara: It's true, you may stop my person even here
But my son will advance in his career:

146

Driven by hunger, fed by your despair,
Till the rim of the world will disappear!

Chandra: No, no, not so, your wheel too will be broke,
Cracked by the sharp steel of this raging stroke!

*There are again several exchanges with Chandra wrenching his
sword into Tomara's abdomen.*

Tomara: While time and change move and swim like the main,
With varying currents and shifting face,
There will ever come my kind again:
Grazing the world, probing points soft and weak
Attacking for power and spoil with strength!

Chandra: Doubtless in future you'll be born again,
To rage through the Earth with Ruin and Death,
Then we a laborious birth will endure
To defend the beauties of that novel world!

Chandra approaches the wounded Tomara and savages a mortal stroke.

Know this also in your time of dying,
Though you have worn yourself out with hunting,
We've succeeded at something! Our best womb
Has 'scaped your grasp, and evaded this tomb!
Seed survives that Siva could not divide:
Seed of my own, with my Sita, will have life!
It's proved: you are of mortal, limited kind,
You'll stride so far in arms, but then will die!

At Chandra's feet, Tomara dies.

Darshan: Chandra! What a show of valorous greatness!
This mighty warlord's arms had not a chance!

Chandra: How easy to strike with a pointed blow,
When the terms are of man to man opposed;

How much harder to wrangle one's own soul,
To spy the enemy and keep control!

Mahedhara: What to do with this Uldin?

Chandra: Behead him!

Mahedhara takes off Uldin's head in one motion.

Ashara   Fight on men! For the King! Hold cordon!
Rest, King, while you may in this environ.

Again to himself and to the thundering skies

Chandra: I'm come, Vishnu, closed in by awful truth,
Enlighten, Vishnu, my final pursuit!
To know the awesome frame of your design
Whose greater justice holds us here confined!

Oh! For the peace of nature's softer moods,
When her vast being soft and slowly moves,
Whence faces of earth and ocean are calm,
Breezes sweep the features with supple balm;
Whence fingertips of differing elements,
Interblend in a quiescence of balance;
Whence the difference in opposing poles
Dance in harmony, subtly and controlled!

Why ends foresense of splendorous heaven?
Why does balance shift to breed contention?
Why do rifts erupt in wombs of nature
Which makes war invade every fissure,
Admitting chance to weave in the mixture
While poles plunge, colliding in the equator?
What causes the elements to coalesce
In ranges of mad, fisted opposites,
Which confront our strengths with this horrid test?
Such twisted seasons come to humanness
Through rifts of our pride, desire and weakness

148

'Whelming the balance of human justice:
Till vice is loosed to recruit barbaric toils:
Which overtake weak prey to devour their spoils!

Tossed in this chaos and cascade of time
I have behaved unwittingly and blind:
Allowing vice to enter me like the main,
With currents impossible to contain!
Lest we keep out vice 'midst shifting times
We're engulfed by sin's overwhelming tides!
To defend a kingdom I killed brethren,
Assaulting the primary will of heaven:
Justice that bid brethren be protected!
Out of proportion were my acts of pride,
An angry king, I left my brother die.
Yes, my brother betrayed his rightful king;
I betrayed you, Lord - a far greater being!

Kingdoms stand in lists of temporal things
Whilst justice survives in eternity;
Empires are of lines and of boundaries,
While you occupy time through infinity;
While the polar basis of this earth shifts,
Your rule of the universe is constant;
While all within the world rises to fall,
Ever standing, remains the word of your law!
Before this law, I should have knelt in awe!
What's more important than law on this stage?
Where everything born is born to change!
And where slight changes can loose chaotic rage
Like rifts in caverns, deep in Earth's membrane!

Mayhap the Hun deserves greater pardon,
Of unformed wit, they're ignorant children!
They move to desires like Sivan engines,
Drawn ferrous bits to magnetic objects!
What hope have I, who killed brethren for pride,
Knowing the difference of wrong and right?

In this end, I've been no better than them,
The beasts, who for appetite, prey upon men!
To clutch and uphold the gold Guptan crown
I let your greater law in my soul drown!
To uphold our name, clutched in measured sounding,
I betrayed Justice's profoundest meaning,
And stood by, while Ghandhara lay bleeding!
It was to your law my faith was first owed,
Which bade me to care and preserve all souls!
Here I've murdered my brother's, and my own!
By virtue of arms, Tomara's life's gone
Now Siva's fury from my heart must be drawn,
Which infects like a cancerous agent my corse
Gathering, growing 'till it becomes the corpse -
Vishnu, my self's end is my soul's last resort!

Men could end this butchery and blood flow
If each defeats enemies of his soul:
Sacrifice pride and desire from mortal forms
Cancerous Sivan agents! Feeders of War!
Let there be sacrifice for ends of justice!
Come, Huns! Kill the sins my soul is clogged with!
Time for this theatrical king[52] to take wing
To shed his weighty sins, to fly this scene,
Come, deathly instruments, descend on me!

Mahedhara: Chandra! Mihirakula advances this way….

Ashara: Come stand and join the fray…

Chandra: Aye! To slay and be slain!
Ride, Sita! Ride for the right to live another day -
Fight for that justice, which from me escaped!

End of Act Four Scene Six

---

52 Theatrical king: A reference to the short span of the character of a king in a stage play.

ACT FOUR
SCENE SEVEN

FROM A PROMONTORY

Place: A crest of the eastern vale of the Jumna River, opposite and just north of Mathura.

Present: Sita, Asunaya and Shekar, with the Royal Guard and Ajay.

Scene: *Sita and her royal guard view the battlefield and the city from a promontory on the eastern side of the Jumna River. They are transfixed by the varied scene, while disconsolate streams of refugees are passing. Ajay stops, exiting the stream of survivors.*

Sita: Was e'er an instance of such sacrifice?
                    Oh Husband!   So's given the remains of life!

Asunaya: Ashara! I should be at your wondrous side!
                    By the death you give, you have saved my life!

Shekar: They've given grave injury to the enemy
                    Chandra has crippled their force with this scheme!
                    This attack was courageous in attempt,
                    But our arms are folding in envelopment!
                    Descending Hun cavalry make a seam,
                    Cracking the sphered cordon of our army!
                    Our valorous forces, the Huns divide;
                    Our pent arms surge forth, dissembled and wide,
                    Our force parts 'fore the foe and are too slight,
                    It slows to stop, in the Hun's closing might!
                    Our bright banners drown and descend in the flood!

Sita: In a tide of fury! An ocean of blood!
                    So sinks the aegis of all that we love!
                    Opposition's down, now comes the final wave,
                    When the city will fall by the sword and stave!
                    Their time is out! And they've nowhere to run!

Our poor subjects, in a world blazing down!

Ajay:
I hear cracking temples fall to ruin,
And people run through fire and confusion!
All hope is gone with the fall of our arms,
All hope bursts in this severing of hearts.
Mothers part from daughters, fathers from sons -
Where to go when there's no more room to run,
For the weak, the wounded, the woebegone?

Sita:
Our hope lies in strengths within ourselves,
It's we who make the world a Heaven or Hell!

End of Part One

"They fall upon me where I am most weak,
In the undefended realms of my dreams!"

BUT BY THE CHANCE
OF WAR

PART TWO
"NIAGARA"

CONTENTS
PART TWO
"NIAGARA"

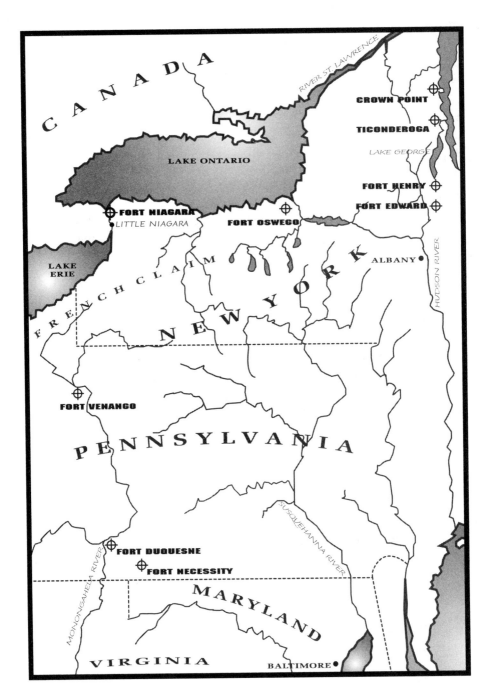

CHARACTERS
PART TWO
"NIAGARA"

THE SENECA:

Lone Bear	Seneca Chief
Captain White Hawk	British Empire Officer
Grey Swan	Seneca Matriarch,
	Mother of White Hawk & Lone Bear
Red Fox	Seneca Warrior
Day Star	Wife of Lone Bear
Mink	Son of Lone Bear
John Hawkins	Son of White Hawk

ENGLISH:

Brigadier General John Prideaux	Head of British forces at Niagara
Brigadier General Thomas Gage	Under Prideaux
William Johnson	Leader of colonial militia,
	Liaison to the Five Nations
Major John Slattery	Master of Ordnance
Major Robert Rogers	Leader of Rogers' Rangers
Captain Ogden	Ranger
Lieutenant Dunbar	Ranger
Private MacDuff	Ranger

FRENCH:

Captain Pierre Pouchot	Commander of Fort Niagara
Captain Chaubert Joncaire	Leader of French Seneca

OTHERS:

Half Moon	Abenaki Emissary

Others (mentioned but not appearing):

Whispering Waters	Wife of White Hawk,
	Mother of John Hawkins
Francois Bigot	New France Quartermaster
Abbe' Piquet	French proselytizer to the Seneca

ACT ONE
SCENE ONE

BLESSING ON LITTLE NIAGARA

Place: Little Niagara Falls

Present: Lone Bear and Day Star, later Mink, Grey Swan, Red Fox and a retinue of the Seneca people

Scene: *A small, renegade band of a few hundred Seneca, who are allied with the French, live near Little Niagara, which is situated on a bend of Niagara River, two miles north of the Great Falls and two miles south of the French fortress of Niagara. The Senecan grounds consist of several native longhouses and a French chapel. The homestead sits on a vast level area adjacent the lesser falls whose precipice is twenty feet in height. Behind the expanse climbs a wilderness of wooded cliffs. The falls emit a constant thunder of rushing waters. A mist rises from the confluence of the waters meeting at the turbulent convex of the river base. The scene opens within the main longhouse and moves outside, beside the river.*

Day Star:	You have slept too late, over long; The world has altered from the forms of dawn. Even the lustrous light of my namesake Over the horizon's crest has escaped.
	We have refrained from the morning's blessing, For of your voice in song we're wanting.
Lone Bear:	My frame feels rigid: immoveable sore, Unliable to motion as the sycamore, Whose fixed roots fold deep in Earth's floor: Twined with our fathers' bones forevermore.
Day Star:	These deep wounds in your back are mottled blue: Swollen, bruised, with infection imbrued.

Lone Bear: I know not what to expect from such fissures,
                 Made by the sweep of fiery missiles,
                 But I've faith in the mercy of your salve,
                 Am I not shamed, though? The wounds are in my back!

Day Star: Your chest bears enough of hardened scars
                 That valor's borne in these truceless wars!
                 The shapes of all weapons there impressed
                 Evince the strength of surviving prowess.

                 Tell me! What chanced at Ticonderoga's fort?

Lone Bear: A fight unfought, one we were made to abort!
                 Damn the French! Before ever a shot was fired,
                 They turned their tail and like weak runts retired!

                 Enough! Allow me Niagara's blessed mists
                 To feel her embrace and view her countenance;
                 Then we've Mink; this is the day he inherits
                 Communion with our ancestral spirits!

Day Star: I know it is Mink's time, but have you time?
                 You've just now returned from the latest fight!

Lone Bear: If Mink and I wait more, for an end of war,
                 We must wait further, and wait forevermore!

Day Star: Can you not tell your wife of the matter?

Lone Bear: Leave it all until after, let us speak later!

Day Star: Very well! The blood is stopped, the wounds dressed.

Lone Bear: Then let's on to the sacred river's bed.

Lone Bear and Day Star exit the longhouse and stride beside the river, meeting their son Mink and Lone Bear's mother Grey Swan.

Mink: Hello Father!

Lone Bear: How is my dearest son?

Grey Swan: Lone Bear! Say! How succeeded your mission?

Lone Bear: These words venture deeper than my wounds!
                 May I have peace? May my soul be soothed?

Grey Swan: Into what war within yourself, do I intrude?

Day Star: Forgive him, Swan, he is in a darkened mood.

Lone Bear: My women! The whole world is full of ire!
                 Wherever I turn, I move through vales of fire,
                 Give me peace on these waters, by these shores,
                 Where 'twas you Swan, saw fit to have me born!
                 Allow sight and sound of my native home
                 To heal the deep wounds carved throughout my soul!

Grey Swan: Come, my son, sit beside the living stream
                 That's been, since birth, your wider nursery,
                 In whose waters flows your second being.

Lone Bear: Leave me to see the otter and the mink
                 Play carelessly on fringes of the stream;
                 Let me hear leaves of alder and willow
                 Flush in my ear with the winds gentle flow;
                 Let me scent the bristles of the pines:
                 Whose topless heights adorn the skies;
                 Let me hear the river's haunting gulls,
                 And aloft, view cliff surrounding eagles;
                 Then shall I feel peace in this wondrous home,
                 Then calm will take root in my burning bones!

                 Thereafter, Mink, you and I will take a journey
                 To forests where we'll take time for talking,
                 Then I'll leave you in wilds for a night's passing...

Day Star: Mink! This morn when dawn's light unfurled
              And wakened the hills and rivers of the world -
              I strode supple fields of caressing dew
              Left by the fallen tears of the Moon,
              Suffused with gilt hues of a rising sun,
              As thoughts in my soul revolved of our love:
              This day and night you are to spend afar,
              To commune with Sun, Earth, Moon and Stars
              Discovering their essence, of whom you are!

Mink: Father, when you are rested, I will be ready.

Lone Bear: Let's rise, son, and proceed with the blessing.

To All   Let us convene at the communal flame:
              Join voices with mine, before the Falls we pray!

The retinue of the Seneca, led by Red Fox, gather beneath the sun, at the edge of the falls, before the ever-burning communal fire, the sacred Calumet.[53] During the song, smoke drawn from the festal pipe is issued to the Sun, to the Earth and Waters, to the four points of the compass and to the four winds.

All: Aereskouy,[54] Spirit of all Life
              We adore you, dearest Lord,
              As author and giver of light
              Whose great impartible orb
              Seeds wombs of the Earth and the seas,
              Suffusing through the multitudes
              The constant fire of your being.

              Aereskouy, spirit of beauty,
              We adore you, our fair parent,
              Author of Earth's aerie streams,
              Moving life through every breast,
              Animating life's diversity:

---

53 Calumet: Sacred central fire of northeastern Native American settlements; also refers to the pipe smoked on ceremonial occasions.
54 Refers to the Great Spirit.

Your breath, that moves in the breeze,
Stirs the vast birth of your being.

Great Spirit, our common fire bless -
Whose single flame and varied mists
Reflect your Sun and sacred breath!
Help your children know your spirit
As Over Lord of nature's aspect;
Aereskouy, take from we, your kin,
This praise to your Sun and Wind!

Respire our varied words of love,
Rising through many sighs as one!

The gathering of the Seneca loosens with Red Fox advancing to Lone
Bear, Day Star, Grey Swan, and Mink.

Red Fox: Lone Bear, I need speak with you of events
Whose catalogued affects begin to press
Here upon us, in our natural fortress,
So far do virtues of English arms advance.

Lone Bear: What more? Mink, go dress and prepare yourself!
Well, Fox, if my ears must bear it - what else?

Red Fox: Since you left, General Prideaux's force
Have environed great Niagara's fort
With twelve hundred Iroquois warriors
Aside two thousand of his regulars.
They've been burrowing advancing trenches
To within range of the French defenses.
All the air round Niagara Fort is ashen
With fume from firing muzzles of cannon;
The bombardment has continued sans cease
Till the fort's walls tremble at a breach!
And General Gage comes from Albany,
With more battalions to join the fray!

Meanwhile Pouchot, the French Fort's master,
Awaits new arms, to stave off disaster,
Such force is advancing from Ohio country
With fifteen hundred mixed troops under Aubry.

Lone Bear: All England's virulent, venomous bees
Abandon their many-nooked mansionary,
With regular and winged industry -
To impale Niagara with their stings!

Have we any new orders from the French?

Red Fox: To guard this natural port and fortress
To counter a southern British movement.
Or, to be prepared to march to the north,
Should they again need reinforce the fort.

Lone Bear: Aye, I trust the French spine will not waver,
As at Ticonderoga's surrender!

Grey Swan: Ticonderoga's surrender!

Lone Bear: She's down...

Grey Swan: She's gone! You say the whole fort?

Lone Bear: The whole town!
Nor tree nor flower is left on the place,
To elemental dust - the works were razed!

Grey Swan: Lone Bear, my son, tell me what has happened!
How can so strong a bastion have fallen?

Lone Bear: Ticonderoga was well-trooped and timbered,
Our muskets were full of shot and powder,
Our cannon were loaded in emplacements,
Our men were afire with great confidence:
We were ready to destroy the English!

When their troops had barely come into view,
T'was our captain gave us incredible news:
We were to leave the fort and northward move:
To reform a line and to defend Quebec,
Ticonderoga had to be - abandoned!
Thus, by a French order, the deed was done
Ticonderoga was blasted to atoms!
All the great works of Man are mutable,
As you could see from the diaspora
Of stone and beam 'twas Ticonderoga!

Red Fox: Where is great Blue Moose, our companion?

Lone Bear: My dearest friend died in the explosion.

Day Star: In every victory, loss or retreat,
            Our numbers lessen - we are vanishing!

Grey Swan: You had held him in your closest confidence,
            Like inseparable twins through existence.

Lone Bear: His swiftness could not run beyond the blast:
            He was consumed in indiscriminate wrath!
            He who was the strongest warrior living
            Chanced to fall in the fire's red scattering.
            I had to hear his last guttural cry,
            And view his Great Spirit abandon his eye!

Day Star: It is small wonder you did not reply.

Lone Bear: I'd rather with Blue Moose been left to die.

Grey Swan: Damn the English and all their hellish spawn!
            They're the same since my father was shot down,
            When their settlers despoiled our sacred grounds
            And we retaliated with attacks on their towns!

Red Fox: It was a French explosion brought Blue Moose down!

167

Should we not think to change our alliance,
And follow our brethren of the Five Nations?
This whole war now tends to the loss of France!
Downward she angles like a sickly tree,
Whose disease is seen in the blasted leaf!
This, another fall, another retreat,
Another petal's down from the Fleur di Lis![55]

Lone Bear: We gave our word and that is sovereign,
No matter our sacrifice or France's ruin!
The French allow us to honor our fathers
To live in the spirit of ancient elders;
The French honor our ways with loose reins,
While England offers only unyielding chains!
They hold in contempt our simple traditions
Proscribing them as acts of sedition;
They deny us the songs of our ancestry
Calling them Devil's chants of outlawry!
The English unforest the wilderness
For their monolithic church and villages;
They cut swaths out of our verdant paths,
Scourging the earth, leaving not even the grass!
And grounds where we entrust our fathers' bones,
Where they may have peace, an eternal home,
The English plow those bones to make their parks,
Without even respect for burial yards!

They scythe from Earth's nature all its variety
Forging the living into a single being!
They do not even reverence our dead!
And you would make them our sudden friend?

Red Fox: We must either have superior force
Or make a friend of the victorious!
Your roots may run deep, fixed, adamant and thick,
But you must bend or we'll break before this wind!

---

55 Fleur di Lis: A flower lily which became the royal symbol of the French monarchy and appeared on most French imperial banners.

Who is likelier to kill the other -
The running deer or the advancing hunter?
It's always a choice 'twixt England and France
We have always needed strengths of alliance!
You should care more for how our children fare,
Than for the bones of our long dead forebears!
It is time to join our other Iroquois brothers,
To join England and throw the French over!

Grey Swan: Fox! How dare you speak so cavalier
To one before whom you'd best bend in fear!
Lone Bear had more strength in his infant smock
Than you have in your whole family's stock!
Careful of the strong words you play with,
When his weakest motion can mean your death!

Red Fox: I have been well-schooled in Lone Bear's vast fame,
And were it personal valor that wins the day,
I would place my worth on Lone Bear's great back,
And bid him launch at Prideaux his attack!
But this isn't a contest of champions,
But war, testing the fitness of nations.
Through them, it is a test of alliance -
And this test is killing the friends of France!

How many ages has the world now grown
Since Iroquois and Algonquin were alone?
Our Wampum relates there was such an age
When war between the Algonquin and us raged
Much as it does even to the present day!
Certain we had 'mongst our own some conflict
As we ranged in battling tribes as opposites,
Yet, we didn't face loss of our whole clan for it!

Then it happened, that Earth's bowels groaned
The Moon, Sun and Stars together moaned:
The world's core broke in some depthless place
As her skies, seas and caves jostled and quaked!

And she lost balance for many endarkened days.[56]

There was the haunting cry of the death of an age!
Then began the onslaught of Death's cascade,
And nations of our brethren fell as they prayed:
The gods, they cried! The gods that signal sent
That our fate was wrestling with deathly events!

For then, too! Growing England began to move,
And France flexed to her present amplitude,
And our peoples were cloven into two:
Each had to choose from opposed magnitudes!

Four periods of wars have since ensued
And it seems, while the world has a frontier,
The Earth will bleed 'neath war's deathless career.
With no hope for peace or the end of the lance,
While our peoples fight to some new balance,
Or while England endlessly wars with France!
Till Earth achieves a new balance of power
'Twixt magnitudes that succeeds a passing hour!
If we cannot ourselves the best force display,
We must be the friends of those who may!

Lone Bear: Through this contest, its change and divisions,
Even we Seneca have suffered schisms;
War has severed the superior bonds of brethren,
While hatred fills the clefts of former union!
Is not our sole living source of unity,
Beyond our bond to a common ancestry,
This Niagara and her living domain:
A haven the English would certain profane!
By covenant with France this is all our own!
While France fights, we hold to our ancient home!

Red Fox: You hold to the frailty of failing order!

---

56 Endarkened days: Refers to the earthquake that occurred in the northern part of North America in June, 1638.

Lone Bear:	Can you tell me the English are any better?
	Or are the Seneca? Or the Algonquin?
	We're all born to die, all given to ruin!
	But we can hold to the French covenant,
	Hold against all, unless the French break it!
	We have given to the French our word
	Words are oft a war's sole survivors!
	Before such gusts of chaos we must stand!

Red Fox: Or prove 'fore such winds, that we may adapt!

Lone Bear:	I would that these green forests were cocooned
	And Niagara were some unfound womb -
	Wherein I might plunge an eternal root
	And so bask beneath Sun and Sky unmoved!

Red Fox:	I understand you're as firm as arbor,
	But it is wiser to move like yon river
	Whose waters, here now, are soon flown forever,
	Nimbly, like the spirits of our ancestors!
	Show more mercy to our flowing family seed,
	Than rootedness in dead bones of ancestry!

Lone Bear:	I am tired of this chaos and these thoughts
	Whose perpetual riddle assaults us!
	I owe to my boy Mink a far greater duty:
	To learn to enjoy the world for her beauty!
	I need one day, without thought of fighting!

Red Fox: It is more pressing to judge the war's course!

Lone Bear:	Are Mink and I to await the end of war?
	Then history's taught, we need wait forever!
	My son and I go now, we go together!

Red Fox:	*to himself as he is leaving*
	It cannot be that we: leaf, root and stem,
	Come to the future of some oblivion;

                 Such is the fate of rooted trees beside
                 A river's rolling force of time and tide!

Grey Swan: You should sterner answer such insolence!

Day Star: Perhaps Red Fox counsels to us what's best!

Lone Bear: Enough I say! For just a day, enough of this!

Day Star: Bear, your lunch is finished, rabbit with mint.
                 For weeks our hunters have seen no larger game,
                 Not since the armies of the English came.

Lone Bear: Would I had never in life's chance heard
                 A syllable of English or of French a word!

End of Act One Scene One

ACT ONE
SCENE TWO

PRIDEAUX'S TENT

Place: British Brig. Gen. John Prideaux's tent, which stands before Fort Niagara at the confluence of the Niagara River and Lake Ontario.

Present: Brig. Gen. Prideaux and William Johnson; later White Hawk and his son, John Hawkins, enter.

Scene: *The atmosphere is one of siege and war. Thick and high walls surround Fort Niagara, an immense edifice with earthen and timber outer embankments that surround the main stone structure. The fort consists of many barracks and storage buildings, all adjacent to the main canteen and central administrative castle. Loosely constructed temporary dwellings stand in a ragtag order among the more permanent structures. Freshly dug trenches weave between the fortress and the British bivouacs. There is a constant movement of men, cannon and munitions. The English encampment resembles a vast, systematic quadrant formation of white tents in regular lines, with communication passageways between rows. Prideaux's living quarters and administrative center stand prominently at the front. Although temporary, Prideaux's quarters are spacious, lofty, and well-organized. A small cot sits at one end of the tent, while heavy standing tables line the other walls. Scientific instruments, books and rolled maps of the Americas and the world rest on each table. The instruments are evenly spaced and meticulously cleaned to a gleaming polish.*

Prideaux: Send this message to Gage: I'll not hold
And wait his tardy march; we must go!
This is the hour that is advantageous,
The hour when fortune is poised to aid us!

Can you believe the leverage we have gained?
By the accident a French messenger has made!
Not recognizing one of our own recruits,

Mistaking his person, disregarding his suit,
And telling him, and so us, routes of Aubry,[57]
Even to the measure of his marching!

Johnson: An instance of the chances of accidents!

Prideaux: A disastrous chance for our foes, the French!
Had our sentinel not appeared a resident
Or been elsewhere before or after the moment,
Had he not then been casually dressed,
Had he encountered a lover or a lost friend,
Or stopped to play the Good Samaritan...
We would not so easy defeat these French!
It is amazing, that for all their energies,
Niagara will fall by accidental meetings!

Johnson: We'll engage forces of advancing Aubry
Within this hour in vales to south and east.

Prideaux: When the French learn we've sunk the frail craft
Which bares her last hope of reinforcement -
So sinks Niagara's harbor of power!
News will spread on winds of this fallen hour
Wide over flow waters of these inland seas:[58]
The massive weight of the French displacing
Will sound o'er waters: a detonation!
Tidal waves will rise against the French nation
Throughout the French colonial realms
Ramming the order of her dominions,
Scuttling wracked vessels of falling armies,
Submerging French America to drowning:
Like driftwood crashing through Niagara's cracks
And smashing into pits of her cataracts!

Johnson: To Gage then, I'll see the message is sent!

---

57 Aubry: Captain Charles Aubry, leader of the relief force, which marched for Fort Niagara via La Belle Famille.
58 Inland seas: Refers to the interconnected waterways of the Great Lakes of North America.

Enter Capt. White Hawk with his son, John Hawkins

White Hawk: How do you both, General and Johnson?
              May I introduce my son, John Hawkins?

Johnson: We know one another, how now, young John?

J. Hawkins: I am well sir, thank you, Mr. Johnson!

Johnson: I'll be off, General, and I'll bring word,
              If of the reinforcement, aught is heard.

Prideaux: See that you do! How do you do, young man?

J. Hawkins: Well sir, pleased to be in your company!

Prideaux: Have you been well, Hawk? Let me see,
              You're here to give me further instructing?
              To teach me vagaries of your speech?
              Or of medicinal herbs in this world,
              Or of the virtues of its grains and its corn,
              Or of the intracacies of wampum weaving,
              Or the best methods of hunting and tracking,
              Or may I learn your culture with more strides:
              Of the Iroquois and the Algonquin tribes
              With whom we are, or will soon be allied?
              For my greater education, what have you in mind?

White Hawk: I have more knowledge now than I had before,
              Of the whereabouts and varied numbers
              Of the French and Indian parties of war.

*Prideaux turns to speak to young John Hawkins, who, Prideaux has
noticed, is hobbled.*

Prideaux: Pardon, young man, is that leg of yours hurt?

White Hawk: He has been slowed since his difficult birth

> By a foot unlike what's ordained by nature:
> His right foot is fixed and its bones are fused,
> Therefore, the manner of his stride is altered.
> And, of course, it is a great hardship to run
> Or to do much, as would his companions.

Prideaux: And so you cannot hunt, as do your friends?

J. Hawkins: No, sir.

Prideaux: Do not be downcast, young Hawkins.
> We are all of us challenged by imperfections,
> But we advance by that which holds us back
> And strengthen, by adapting, for what we lack.

A cannon from Fort Niagara is heard misfiring, and the errant missile lands near but athwart of Prideaux's tent. The General moves to the tent's door and yells toward the fort:

> Have we taught you nothing, you French!
> After so many years, firing at a trench?
> I crave foes who are worthy of our steel!
> Pouchot![59] Among you, you've no cannoneer?

Then to John Hawkins

> As I was saying, you mustn't feel self-pity
> You are among nations of England's family,
> And with our justice comes also our mercy.
> We care for our own and tender you so,
> We'll do what we can to heal your poor sole.

White Hawk: Thank you, sir.

Prideaux: Exalt your other good strengths!

---

59 Pouchot: Captain Pouchot, Commander of Fort Niagara.

White Hawk: He loves learning, and is much given to reading.

Prideaux: Then wisdom runs sure, through your family!
             It was wise Ulysses, not brute Ajax,
             Who won the armor of Achilles - who's that?

J. Hawkins: Homer![60]

Prideaux: Close you are! We have a scholar!

Enter Johnson

Johnson: The French fire from the fort is lessening....

Prideaux: Take orders! Keep pounding! Don't let them breathe!
             Keep on them, until they send for mercy!

Johnson exits. Young Hawkins has moved over to a table and surveys one of the brass instruments on it.

J. Hawkins: Pardon, sir, can you tell me, what's this job;
             This collection of differing wheels and knobs?

White Hawk: Don't disturb the General, John, ye gods!

Prideaux: Hawk! You have for years been my best teacher,
             We've each a world to learn from each other!

Prideaux handles the instrument and demonstrates its use to John Hawkins

             This is a sextant, a means of measure,
             We English use when over seas we venture!
             Our frail vessels sail the tempestuous main -
             For undiscovered continents, without a name!
             We find guides through the fore horizons dark,
             Gauging on points of regular moving stars,
             Measuring to the horizon: there is an arc,

---

60 Homer: Actually refers to the work, "Ajax", by Sophocles.

> Then, as you see, plotting along Earth's rim,
> We gain our measure in degrees and minutes,
> And find our position on boundless oceans!
> To conceal things is one of God's glories,
> While man gains glory by his discoveries.[61]

J. Hawkins: Do the French also have such a sextant?

Prideaux: Yes, but the French have little need of it,
They follow us without use of instruments!
When we see them - we must be always ready
With our courage prompt and our weapons steady!

White Hawk: Why do English and French energies never tire;
Far away you leave the peace of your home fires?

Prideaux: I suppose it comes of our common sway
Of ancestors, or elders, as you say...

White Hawk: The Christian?

Prideaux: I suppose there's that mission -
To bring the world the mercy of Christ's teachings,
There is of that good hope, no denying:
To Christ's kingdom we're always climbing,
We always pray that his kingdom will come,
But that's the hearth's well-honed, warm cornerstone
We preserve for the edifice of our home.
I was speaking more of ancient Rome!
The last governor who made our world one...
The French and we are Rome's extant sons:
From which sire we build justice through empire,
By our elders we were taught never to tire:
To conquer worlds and bring them into our own!
Such has been the case since time's struggling dawn!
Before us there were the Greeks against Persians,[62]

---

61 Discoveries: Paraphrase of Psalm 25.
62 Greeks against Persians: The Greco-Persian Wars, 499-330 B.C.E.

Then it was Greece's sons: Sparta against Athens;[63]
Thereafter, it was Rome against Cathargo,[64]
Then Rome's sons: Caesar against Antonio;[65]
Then, it was the European 'gainst the Saracen;[66]
Now it's Europe's sons: we 'gainst the French,[67]
You see, if not for France... we might fight our friends!
It is ever so, two great powers battling on,
In hopes of making the various world one!

White Hawk: It sounds like the Iroquois and Algonquin:
We oft have suffered from some contention...

Prideaux: We contend between us for every prize,
To the loser goes envy, to the winner goes pride,
Neither having to do with the love of Christ!
We pattern, I suppose, on the beehive,
Whose walls are bitter, while all is honey inside.
We savor and save Christ's love for our own,
The proper place of love and mercy is home;
Thus we'll save the tender foot of your son.

Young Hawk has moved to a table containing a telescope, a micro-scope, a glass prism and several books. He feels the polished sheen and regular cylinder of the telescope.

J. Hawkins: Pardon, sir, these are odd-looking kinds of cones!

Prideaux: Those are my new scopes, micro and macro,
And that is Newton's "Principia" beside,
This cylinder is to observe objects that defy,
Owing to smallness, efforts of the human eye
To view composition or motility.
While the greater cylinder makes viewable
The vast, distant spheres of the celestials.

---

63 Sparta against Athens: The Peloponnesian War, 431-404 B.C.E.
64 Rome against Cathargo: The Punic Wars, 264-146 B.C.E.
65 Caesar against Antonio: Augustus Caesar and Marc Antony fought the last conflict of the Civil Wars of the Roman Republic, ending in the battle of Actium in 31 B.C.E.
66 European 'gainst the Saracen: Loosely refers to the wars between Islam and the Christian kingdoms from 700-1571 C.E.
67 We 'gainst the French: Refers to Anglo-French Wars, 1551-1763 C.E.

What Newton ingeniously discovered
Is that matter in all her sizes is governed
By like laws of motion and gravitation,
That there is no object so great or small
That is not by some attraction enthralled,
Adhering to great magnitudes that are near
Until that attraction subsides into a frontier.
Where other objects are held by other spheres,
His law makes the cause of all motion clear!
Beside, there's his optical invention.
Newton adduced from prisms, color spectrums:
Where light is fractured to her base colors,
Which one may view in the rainbow's auras!

Johnson enters again excitedly.

Johnson: Sir! The barrage has Niagara near a fall
We have opened a gap in the fort's south wall!

Prideaux: Will we win this most coveted ground of all?
Will Niagara, like Ticonderoga, fall?
A month ago it was deemed impossible!
Look here, Johnson, we must now be ready!
Tribes allied to the French will be unsteady;
Prepare for dwellers on the frontier to shift -
Rather than go off on their own as derelicts,
They are prone to join our own alliance!

Johnson: We are ready sir, to extend friendship,
To all who join our family of nations,
They may move like ready magnets!

*J. Hawkins has moved again to another table full of instruments
with a balance scale and weights.*

J. Hawkins: Sir, and this?

Prideaux:	By weights of measure and that register,
	We may mix large and small weights together;
	You may counterpoise an object and ascertain
	Its mass by the mass the dish contrary contains.

Johnson:	Niagara fallen, French honor will fold:
	Many of their present friends will revolt:
	And we may make friends of these former foes.
	France's equilibrium with us will be blown!

White Hawk: The Iroquois put much weight in gravitas.[68]

Prideaux: Is that the lesson, teacher, you have for us?

You know, Hawk, back home we live next the French.
Only a small stream divides the eyes
Of continental France from our varied isles!
From these two opposing shores we contend
In the ranges of all human creations:
From arts of elegance and strict sciences,
To our architecture and our churches;
From our manufactures and our inventions
To our domestic stocks and our horses;
From our table silvers and our dishes
To our gardens and our latest fashions;
From our music and our latest dances,
Even to the rudiments of our language!
Yes, we come together in all places,
Like fire and water, vying in void spaces.
We compete most in our readiness for war -
From ships, to defensive cities, to forts,
To all the instruments of invented force!
Like Rome's first sons, Romulus and Remus,[69]
Brother twins, the ever-warring wolf pups!

J. Hawkins has moved to another table and a clock.

---

68 Gravitas: Latin term for all the aspects of honor.
69 Remus and Romulus: Legendary twin decendants of Aeneas and cofounders of Rome. Remus, in derision of his brother, leaped over the original wall of Rome, and Romulus, in a rage at the act, slew his brother.

J. Hawkins: What's this hanging arm, holding a gilded sphere,
Which sways a measured arc through the air?

Prideaux: That is a collection of gears and levers
Made for the strict measure of days by hours.

White Hawk: Is it not sufficient to know it's day or night,
By the Sun's constancy or Moon's varied light?

Prideaux: Not when we measure time with industry,
For time by content is accelerating!

Johnson: Things will move swiftly and badly for France,
With this blow, they won't have a breath to catch!

Prideaux: Yes, I can sense the hour of France is waning.

Johnson retires again from the tent.

Young Hawk, what's that book you're opening?

"The Rise of Rome," Sibylline Prophecies[70]
Give it a go! Let us test your reading.

J. Hawkins: "Mankind's time will be of eight ages
Numbering rise and fall of epochal stages:
As one age ends and another approaches,
Wondrous signs will fill Earth and Heaven,
Auguring the advents of revolutions,
In man's life, his character and languages,
In structures of his institutes and customs:
All will revolve around time's great calends."

Prideaux: Excellent, your accent sounds as though born
Within confines of England's distant shore!

White Hawk: If given the means, he'll learn, General!
Who are these Romans this book heralds?

---

70 Sibylline Prophecies: A collection of oracles, which were consulted at times of crisis throughtout the history of the Roman Repulic and Empire.

Prideaux: A people of a city who vanished long ago.
                Everything's born to fall, even old Rome.

The clock knells the half hour, Prideaux points to the minute hand.

                You see Hawk! When this long arm aligns down,
                Then that knell will inevitably sound!

White Hawk discovers a tall pole standing angled in a corner of the tent.

White Hawk: My! What's this, a warrior's brazen spear?

Prideaux: Ah! What you have there has a novel career!
                By that weapon-like shaft of common iron
                We are capable of harnessing the sky's fire –

J. Hawkins: How can so slight a thing reach the distant sun?

Prideaux: It filches the fire from the heart of a tempest
                Where wind and rain contend, which rules the current!

                You might say we've raided a god's armories
                By forging a key to steal his lightning!
                It is one of our colonist's inventions,
                A man of Pennsylvania, named Franklin;
                He too is a studious person
                Whose mind and spirit ably serve England,
                More than rude strengths of his feet and hands.

Reports of cannon fire are sounding far more frequently, almost un-
interruptedly.

                French cannons are picking up their volleys –

Johnson re-enters

Johnson: From La Belle Famille, sir, we've word
                Aubry's force is fallen, its remnant scattered:
                We've a victory, after an hour's encounter!

183

Prideaux:	Hence we have this fury of the French power! French desperation will fire to the last powder; In hopes of driving us off, before their fatal hour!
Johnson:	What then, sir, should I order is your desire?
Prideaux:	As before, to quell their fire with greater fire! Hawk! Here's the hour of action you desire: The fall of this noble and long-held bastion Will unleash forces into an unruly vacuum: We must flush out all our obstinate enemies, And convene a peace, or make our foes to leave!
White Hawk:	Niagara is ours when victorious?
Prideaux:	Niagara will be the Seneca's! As we are grateful for our new alliance, As it's been the land of your ancestors, You have my true word, the land will be yours! I understand a group of Seneca soldiers, Some of your tribe's renegade warriors, Are to the south, camped at the river's bend: 'Little Niagara,' do you know this area then?
White Hawk:	Yes, General, you see, I was born there… I'm brother to that Seneca Chief, Lone Bear, Who, with his strong band, has followed Joincare,[71] They've long fought the English, during that truce, While our Five Nations[72] were not allied with you. Lone Bear's faith in the French will not give place: He's turned back the emissaries of our race, Since our alliance with England has been made.
Johnson:	I too have tried to move the Seneca of Lone Bear But they remain with him, and in France's sphere.

---

71 Joincare: Chaubert Joincare, a half-Seneca, half-French soldier who worked actively to recruit the Seneca to the armies of New France.
72 Five nations: The Five Nations of the Iroquois League allied with the English only at the end of the French and Indian War.

Prideaux: I did not know this, White Hawk, all these years!

White Hawk: I've been the crown and England's faithful subject,
                Since my dear son was born with his defect.

Prideaux: Dear God! How brethren can be driven to divisiveness?
                Especially in war, when they must come to grips,
                And take to the fields, as fisted opposites!

                        End of Act One Scene Two

ACT ONE
SCENE THREE

THE WILL OF THE BEAUTIFUL

Place: Atop the cliffs overlooking Little Niagara

Present: The Sachem Lone Bear and his son Mink

Scene: *Father and son have scaled from the falls via obscure and winding cliff paths to an ascent above Little Niagara, from which prospect they see over distant mountain tops, surrounding the ancient domains of the Seneca. The sun is bright above a pale blue summer sky interspersed with high-reaching white clouds. In the direction of Fort Niagara, there are darkly hued columns which appear as clouds but are in reality the fumes of soundless cannons; their noise is imperceptible in the neighborhood of the muffled thunders of the cataract which reverberates through the vales. Gazing down on the lesser falls, a double rainbow glows from shore to shore of the river by the misty vapors which continually arise from the agitation of the river depths and currents.*

Lone Bear: Is that not the finest of exercise!
               Hurdling upward through courses to this height,
               Where nothing stifles the air or subdues the light?

Mink: I, now and then, near slipped on a morass!

Lone Bear: Does that not strengthen your balance's sense?
               In the mist rising from the churning deep,
               There's wind-borne dust become mud on the steep.

Mink: A worthwhile run no matter the hazard!

Lone Bear: Aye, the climb is hard, but we the harder!

Mink: I'm just glad we're together!

Lone Bear: So am I!
I sorrow, Mink, my life has been so tried…
For a year now, I've wanted to spend this time
The world herself has been a slippery thing,
By my labors, I pray for remedy.
Let us take this morn to spend on this shelf,
While time serves and we've peace among ourselves!

As I reckon, you have known fifteen summers:
Life changes, unveiling novel wonders!
You have of life's bounty thus far much learned
Of forms and habits of fellow creatures,
Who inhabit the world's living vestures:
Of armored beetles, tireless ants, limp worms
Who labor in the Earth, her sleepless miners;
Of sleek minks, jocund otters, bustling beavers
Who marry earth and river as their engineers.
Have you not learned of their varied potencies
Which evolve into a being with their ancestry?
As of the husbandry of the squirrel
Or the elusiveness of the whip-poor-will,
Or the swift, leaping beauty of the deer,
Or of the custodial vigor of the bear?
Have you not noted in this abundancy
The scope of life's spectral diversity?
Have you not studied colors, sounds and forms
Whereof all creatures are variously adorned?

Mink: I have sat in tree limbs from dawn till dark
Till I became a vein of their still bark
To study the wondrous wing of the skylark!

Lone Bear: Yes, it is of value to study the sky borne bird,
For to do so, we must look heavenward!

Mink: Tell me, Father, what is it you wish me to learn?

Lone Bear: You have done well through your ambling childhood

To learn life of the waters, skies and woods:
But it's time to conceive of life's sole source,
Her profusion and her ultimate course!
And 'tis fit you should do so at your age
When, tiring of play, you enter a somber stage.

Mink: Yes, I have been somber and have a tale
That I must tell you, for it made me pale!
Just after you had parted to the war,
My peers and I upon a hunt went forth:
'Twas the first time we had gone unattended,
Our spirits were high, our manner exalted!
We came upon the traces of a great elk
And gloried we should take such trophy ourselves!
We followed his signs and soon sensed his odor
And found him alone in an umbered cover.
I let fly first with my strong bow and pointed shaft
And full through the elk's upper neck it passed!
A groan issued from him as he went down;
We came upon him as he writhed on the ground!
'Twas the first time I saw death's agony:
In this elk's wan crying and bloodletting!
He tried to rise, but found his body confined,
And we proved too timid to use our knives;
Thus he laid there and labored for an hour,
Before death's growing force subdued his power.
As we neared him, to harvest his frame,
We heard keening of a sorrow beyond name!
We looked silently for these hidden mourners
And spied the elk's young, hid amid the arbors.
They had watched their father die, these orphans!
They witnessed my shaft cause their sire torments!
My band and I left our fallen trophy;
We found suffering in our quest for glory!

Lone Bear: Our conversations the more apropos
That you've survived the gauntlet of these throes:
Life is a vast gauntlet to be endured,

From whose painful throes - we are the stronger!
Such the reason for life's difficult birth,
And 'tis from these pains our beauties emerge!

Let us speak of Aereskouy Soutanditenr
Life's author, whose order formed the world:
Of his Spirit's will to diffuse his glory
By fragmenting into myriad renderings!
Of his marriage with Ataensic, Earth's Mother:
How his seed fragments on her earthen shores
Forming a diaspora of metaphors;
How his spirit suffused Earth's clay and waters
Spawning endless forms of sons and daughters!
And of the Sun, Aereskouy's minister,
The vortex and hearth of original fire,
Whose light suffused Ataensic's womb with his warmth
And gave all of life the fire in their forms:
His light is cradled in every earthborn eye
As in the numberless stars of limitless Sky!

This light mingled in the earth and water,
While Ataensic formed her nascent wonders:
Earth's creations sprung from Ataensic's womb,
Her grasses, mosses and sensitive flowers
Her maizes, brushes, and lofty arbors
And all the animals of multiplied powers
Of our family, headed by human brothers!
A vast, involved, teeming, breathing empire
At whose apex we ourselves have been sired -
That we, sons of God, might to God's strength aspire!

Mink: What's in us magnificent or special
That life around is made so bountiful?

Lone Bear: We are among principals of God's design,
Born of the benevolence of his mind:
To bear children who could stand distinct,
Capable of love, of fealty, of strength,

And of independent will in all things:
Hence, most like God in his divinity!
More, made capable to apprehend God's beauty:
Thus able ourselves to create the beautiful.
In love of God, we flourish on God's earth,
That for love of him, we may to him return!

Mink:

All creation created to be our bread,
When by God's hand we'd be easily fed?
All this sacrifice but to see us follow,
When he might hold us in his hand's deep hollow?

Lone Bear:

Would we be better off to lay supine
In soft, all-caring hands of the Divine?
We'd be weak, clinging jelly, a parasite,
That would eat and breathe, and have no spine!

How would we form an independent will
If a sycophant, living to eat our fill?
What fealty would we know but its show:
Not fealty but its immaterial shadow!
And what love? Our love would be thin veneer,
If but to eat and beg were our whole career!
And what powers would we have to create,
If we were an all-embraced - chainless slave?

Mink:

What, Father, do you mean to say to me?
How can one see into the works of divinity?

Lone Bear:

As with finding any hidden quarry:
To discover it, attend the treading.

We are blessed by all life's opposed burdens
Of generation and opposition
Which move us to rise as God's children!
God gifted the living with that potency
Of fecundity, born of loving pairings,
Between sensitive sexes of a harmony

To bear children of shared heredity!
So to engender that parental love
Which Aereskouy and Earth must feel for us!
That as parents we must attend the young,
With nutrient and love, as flowers new sprung
Are nurtured by Earth and drawn by the Sun!

Does not a child's presence probe our hearts
Giving it pulse in all its harbors and parts!
A child's slight smile or laughter employs
Our deepest sense to multiply our joys!
And does not a child's brow, when in furrow,
Serve to bend our spirit and magnify sorrow:
Children serve to token every emotion,
As the wellsprings of virtue and devotion.
Children are fountains of love's education!

What is learned from a child's constant needs
But virtues which attend on filial duties?
What is learned from children who are rash
But the virtue of a mature temperance?
What is learned from a child's errant actions
But the virtue which attends steady patience?
What is learned if a child lies in his word
But the virtue that lives in speaking the truth?
What is learned from faults inherent in kinship
But the healing joy of complete forgiveness?
And what, for all, is love's greatest reward:
It's love's reflection, in a child's lucid orb!

These emotions and devotions form a frame
Of a sacred relation that's beyond any name,
Teaching God's sentiments for us are the same!
These lessons reach us from God's soul
That we, rooted in Earth, always feel his hold!
That we are capable to feel and reflect that love
That he, through generations, must feel for us!
And that relation is the everlasting bond,
Which, through all life's assaults, binds us to God!

Mink:	If Aereskouy loves his varied children
	Why does he allow injury and harm to them?
	Why does he not fashion us as his extension,
	Why does he not form us, at birth, to perfection?

Lone Bear:	Such a perfection would be statuesque:
	But perfection set in just one dimension
	Such perfect form would be calcid bone
	Capable of one form and one form alone!
	In strength not greater than its single element,
	Of capacity no more than an inert sediment!
	There is no entity as a living statue,
	With no capacity for change of attitude,
	Whose whole corse is of stone: cold and fused!

We are the better with tense opposition imbrued!
We are bone and breath, blood and sinew blent
Protean and fixed: a mechanism resplendent,
For we gain strength by our freedom of actions:
As God seeks our perfection through our relations!
Consider again to view Aereskouy's treading,
His seeding this life with bursting variety,
Within which the elements are ever-changing
Strengthening by adversities and beautifying!

Mink:	How comes this change to make better selves?
	How so? How can harm and adversity help?

Lone Bear:	Remember, Aereskouy made the constant Sun,
	Skybound, reflective of his constant love.
	Thence he formed Sun's alter, Minister Moon,
	Moving on the wheel of time inexorable!
	Through the night she moves in her pale career,
	Nor ever does she two nights the same appear,
	But ever-changing light pours from her sphere,
	Until a phase of time has passed and life altered,
	And Moon comes 'gain in familiar pattern,
	Reflecting the death and birth of the seasons
	By whose revolving folds we knell the years in!

Such are the ministers of day and the night,
One constant, one changing bearer of light:
The world is polarized, like their contrarity,
Assuming at extremes a duality:
As with fire and water, so with air and stone,
As with sweet and sour, so with hot and cold!
As with day and night, so with dark and light;
As with joy and grief, so with death and life!
So we know love and hate, weakness and strength,
The poles of good and evil, of war and peace,
And all the subtler measures lying between
In a perfect spectrum of diversity!

Beneath the aura of these great ministers
Is Earth's life which flows like yon rivers:
In flux and ferment between shores opposed,
Ever moving and chafing in shifting course,
That what survives the currents has strength in life:
And that greater life rises from turbulent strife,
While the weak and enfeebled are sacrificed
In the hard trials of time's passing rights!
Life is a river passing through cataracts,
Strengthened by obstacles which hold it back;
And the issue of this gathering of force,
Is life's rising order from the collisive course!

Thus the hangings in trees of grains and fruits
Serve small reptiles and insects as foods,
And those who crawl are pursued by those who walk,
Who are by those that can run swiftly stalked!
And they who can run are plucked to the sky
By the strength of eagles in majestic flight...
The lesser to the greater are sacrificed,
While renewing the spectral body of life!

And there is adversity yet to percieve
For 'neath the Moon moves a discreet energy!
Bouyant in the chance meandering winds,
Which rise unseen, we know not where nor whence,

In woven layered motions, like the currents!
And when wind and current adverse contend
Effects of things unforeseen interblend:
As when dust winds convolve with river mists
And wed to create on the rocks this morass
Which very nearly felled you from these clefts!

Mink: Always? Everywhere? Life is challenged?

Lone Bear: Yes, with life's physic greatly strengthened,
            Nothing lends more to virtuous strength
            Than this living gauntlet of adversity!

Mink: I admit a deer's flight is made swifter
            By the stealthy tread of the panther;
            And the wolf that threats a bear's cubs
            Gives strength to the bear, to defend his pups.

Lone Bear: Yes, that's a relation of special order:
            Strength engendered by the predator!
            Nothing cures a rabbit's meandering faults
            More than a swift lynx's precise assaults.
            Nor does anything make furtive the whip-por-will
            More than a hawk intent on an easy kill.
            These adversities are wellsprings of strength
            Which every free living thing must needs!
            The skylark's flight lifts on an airy surge,
            Better so, when winds 'fore him are adverse!

            As much as love teaches through generation,
            Adversity instructs through opposition!
            While change and chance add to the burden
            Of fortifying blessings upon Earth's children!

Mink: While that's true of all Earth's other children,
            Man have few predators, we've only brethren!

Lone Bear: Our burden is of a much higher realm:
            For the true predator of man is himself!

Man contends with a double adversary
Rising from his own inborn liberty.
Of another order of power are men:
Given a near-divine apprehension
And capacity to act over a spectrum!
It is the cost of man's will of independence,
The price of our near-divine essence,
That we live in quadrants of opposites
Which prey on strengths of our consciences;
And scourge mind and soul of weaknesses!
Therefore, our sacrifice is of another kind:
Not solely of sinewy might, but of mind:
For we sacrifice our frailty to sustain life!

You see, men face a unique condition
As it is inborn in our disposition
That we collect and divide by opposition:
Note the collections of our enemies and allies
Note the divided counsels of our own tribe!
Ever dividing oneself from the other,
Rending the tribes, some brother from brother!
There is the adverse in each congress of man,
From imperial alliance - to our clan!
The adverse lives in each person we know:
For there is an indwelling seed in Man's soul
Of a contrary, to its own self opposed:
We to ourselves are an enemy we know,
As much as the one with whom we come to blows!

Mink: Then we must sacrifice inner weaknesses
             As nature does, with loss of her feeble ones?

Lone Bear: The weak being in the world must perish
             That weakness in the world does not flourish.
             Yes, the office of our soul is as the world's:
             Of our feeble vices, we must be scourged!
             This is the composition of the gauntlet of man
             Who is assayed by motives, resolves and acts!

Mink:	How is weakness judged by a man's motive?
Lone Bear:	We need ask: to what is a man votive?

Some men live by the soul: the holy men,
Content to pray in a hermit's wilderness,
Feeding on the raw root of bloodless plants;
Ever without comfort, yet ever giving thanks!

Others are of the calm, calculating kind,
Who move by the reasoning of the mind!
Discerning from choices what most is right,
These, if wise, are just votives of the tribe!

Then there are numbers governed by hunger
Who feed to the full, but never fill desire!
They graze like beasts who never raise their eyes
So much seduced by desire's weak device!

Then there's those blindly led by temptation:
Their whole world is condensed to sensation,
Their strengths are misled by any change of whim,
Like weed spores adrift, propelled by the wind!

Last, there are those whose motives are hybrids
Blending some measures of the four incentives:
Wherever mankind is congressed,
These four motives of men are present!
In the copse of Man's inner soul and mind
These motives, like combatants, ever vie:
What is to one the highest immutable cause?
Do we serve the cause and that cause above all?
Do we serve our vice, to our own betrayal?
Beyond one's motives there is one's resolve:
Are we as constant in our will as the Sun's light?
Or changeable as the Moon in the night?
Are we driven by the flux of a river's current?
Or worse, by whimsical winds, lazily swept?
This is the scope of man's inner gauntlet!
This is how Man is his own opponent!

Now let's move to man's other opposition,
It is himself, again, but by reflection:
Having mirror inner fallibilities,
Having mirror inner capacities,
Collectivized in camps of vast armies,
Functioning as two predatory bodies!
Like our French battling the English empire,
Battling for the world, through the world entire!
They each possess their armored corpus
And look to the gaze as mirrored opponents,
From their men, to their clothes, to their armors -
Each 'broidered similarly, but of differing colors.
They are no more than vast living predators
Each seeking to be the other's overlords,
Each feeding on the weakness of their foes,
Each taking vantage of the other's throes,
Each waking the other's slumbering strengths,
Each purging the other's numbers of the weak;
Like the hare's frail members purged by the lynx!
Though unlike the war of the hare and lynx,
The strengths of men are mirrored and linked!

Mink: What purpose is gained by this symmetry
Of forces gathered, endlessly battling?

Lone Bear: The great issue of this gathering of force,
Is life's rising order from the collisive course!
The lesser to the greater are sacrificed,
While renewing the human body of life!
For this battle not only scourges feebleness
But inspires man's soul to its most virtuous!
In the defense of the hearth and the home
And all the issue of love's generation!
Man's love heightens in face of opposition
Creating unique fields of heroism,
Where sacrifice is made in battles of devotion,
By men and women moved by love's motive!
If Man fights solely for himself or a whim,

How long his resolve? How weak his motive?
But if for the magnitude of a higher law,
If to a cause a man may devote his all,
Then the mind feeds its sinew great resolve
To aid man in his most imperiled hour,
Then are forged mosaics of majestic valor,
And the courage of man becomes his hammer
'Gainst which frail motives and resolves scatter!
It's free men and women, who are right-minded,
That survive the whims of self-serving tyrants!

Man's strengthened, ennobled by this dual force,
Of contraries, within and without, at war!
Man must of himself be strictest overlord,
Or his vice falls before his predator.
Man must suffer through this opposition:
To excel by the power ...of his reflection!

Mink: I understand, then, how man is fecund
Through the generation of heavenly love...
Also, how our liberty gives us strength
By our resistance to adversities;
But how do we express divine beauty?
Didn't you call it one of our blessings?

Lone Bear: Between the generation of love, our ecstasy,
And the gauntlet of opposition, our agony,
There lives the light and shade of artistry!
Thus we sing to Aereskouy with prayers
Sung to the sun and stars, his shining heirs!
We return his breath in heartfelt cadence,
Wafting to him on prayers of reverence!
Shown before him by acts of obedience!
Thus our song is delicately beaded and strung
Along interwoven strings of wampum[73]
As orisons threaded with our dearest love,
Colored with devotions of God's faithful ones.

---

73 Wampum: Beads which were often woven systematically to relate history of peoples or treaty agreements deemed sacred by northeastern Native Americans.

Thus we dance to Ataensic's divinity
Moving like her creations, rhythmically,
Spinning concertedly with Earth's single being
With deference and reverence in our weaving!
Thus, we adorn hide and feathers of her forms,
With enameled totems of her children inworn
In testament to the sacrifice she has done,
In symbol that all of her children are one!
With man the blended Son of Earth and God,
The Sachem of her terrestrial synod,
For whom the sacrifice of Earth is given,
As man, among brethren, is a Son of Heaven!

Beauty also comes of acts through relations
We form with our elders and the nations,
Of being upright ones 'mong Earth's creations
Of prizing our Father's will above all temptations!

Thus, as God formed this order in the world,
Man must not deform it with any falsehood!
The breath of life given us must remain pure
For life to be just and for justice to endure!

Our sacrifice for all the gifts of our Mother
Be that we sacrifice weakness for our brother;
As Earth sacrifices the feeble of her children,
We must sacrifice our sins for our brethren!
And we must be true to our ancestors,
Maintaining virtues of our forgone elders,
For we are the flower born through their calyx!
Do they not yet live in these rising river mists?
Does not the bed of this river hold their bones
Mingled in the colored veins of the stones?
Does not this canyon sound their living moans
Whereby we still hear their soul's moving echoes?
Does not Sun's reflection on the river's surface
Glare with the emerald remnants of their spirits?
Does not the rising glory of their pure souls
Light azure Niagara's eternal rainbows?

Mink:	I see the rainbows from the canyon below There are two, with their colors opposed:[74] Inverted perfectly in their arced orders Are the progressions of their like colors.
Lone Bear:	It is the same source of Light, of course But whose reflection is oppositely bourne.
Mink:	When shall these teeming contrarieties end?
Lone Bear:	When man faces his opposition without weakness, And he stands strong enough in his relation To be a proper son to the love of heaven! For when we lose all this sinew and bone, We become of light and relation alone...
Mink:	You know, the elk I killed should not have died; He was powerful in his frame and stride.
Lone Bear:	Had the elk been of a bright strengthful age He would have heard your approach through the glade, And survived by a swift, timely escape!

End of Act One Scene Three

---

74 Rainbow colors opposed: When two rainbows appear together, the order of the color spectrum reverses.

201

ACT ONE
SCENE FOUR

THE SURRENDER OF FORT NIAGARA

Place: Prideaux's tent

Present: Gen. Prideaux and William Johnson, representing the British Empire and Capt. Pouchot and Capt. Joincare representing New France.

Scene: *The French have come to Prideaux's headquarters for the purpose of surrendering Fort Niagara, after a twenty-one-day siege punctuated by unrelenting cannonades. The scene opens with the conference of surrender held around a central table, adorned for dining.*

Pouchot:	Health to you General,
Prideaux:	Sit, gallant Captain!
Pouchot:	May I present Chaubert Joincare, my second, He may speak for our Indian allies: His mother descends from the Seneca tribes.
Prideaux:	This is my second, William Johnson, He's a soldier, who once was a merchant, One must adapt through these rugged forests! You're both welcome, if a bit past your time, Come sit down, and as brethren we will dine.
Pouchot:	How came you to know the course of Aubry, That you could engulf our designs so swiftly? For though his forces were insufficient, We'd have challenged you with reinforcement.
Johnson:	By an accident, Captain Aubry's messenger

Mistook the rustic garb of one of our soldiers,
And conversed with him as to your designs:
Of Aubry's relieving arms, their course and time!
The numbers of the troops and their munitions
Down to the horses being ported with the columns!
When your messenger this news had finished,
Our colonial flew to us, as upon the winds,
And our counter plans were put to motions.

Pouchot: When we considered our present position,
The nearness and scope of your trenches,
Your reinforcements of men and cannons,
And ravages this abandoned post had sustained,
Without hope or means to communicate…

Prideaux: Your valor, if judged alone, was worthy of success
Your actions here only honor your Prince;
It is no cause of yours he's lost this continent!

Johnson: His loyalty to you is the profligate!

Pouchot: This revolution passes my comprehension.
This edifice and fortress form the central defense,
And intersection of all the French possess,
To Louisiana and the equatorial gulf,
And here she stands, abandoned with insult!

Prideaux: I marvel there weren't more reinforcements
And greater effort made to save the fortress!

Pouchot: France lurches, like Rhodes, beneath a Colossus!
A crown overbuilt, rusted, cracked, corrupted,
Ready to crumble with a vigorous wind -
Then shall the Earth tremble in her depths!
While in Paris there is mindless revelry,
At the Empire's edges there's a bloodletting!
I daresay, Prideaux, you could end this war
At a throw, defeating King Louis' whole court,

With one attack on Paris' taverns and brothels -
You'd kill the whole host of France's nobles!

Prideaux: I thought better of France's noble court
               She'd been our good foil, our sharpener of swords!
               France has been the fount of English strengths;
               I'm amazed she's come to this senility!

Pouchot: How goes the larger war? We've had no word.

Prideaux: What has occurred that you may not have heard?
               France's remaining soldiers retire northward
               To Montreal for a final encounter.
               While our generals, Wolfe and Amherst, equip
               To march there and meet two hundred ships
               Advancing via means of inland seas,
               Sailing to engulf your force in its retreat!
               While of Ticonderoga's fall you know,
               And now, with Niagara overthrown.
               Thus, on no waters can French vessels thread
               But the waves whereon they sail are England's!

Pouchot: You deserve this triumph for England!
               If war is the foremost endeavor of man,
               And you succeed everywhere, by sea and land
               The English are the foremost of all men!
               You own victory by the most ancient law
               That the lesser to the greater must fall!
               France is rightly overthrown and beaten
               For its diseases of luxury and weakness!
               She's overthrown by a natural justice.
               As the British wheel of state accelerates -
               France in America will disintegrate!
               How long before distant Paris feels this fate?

Prideaux: Allow us show our quality of mercy,
               Allow our physicians your wounded to treat,
               Allow generosity to redeem your scarcity.

Your forces will be fed and well-embarked
For the journey you must take to New York.

But we are concerned with your alliances,
Tribes harboring in this depthless wilderness:
We would seek to spare them unneeded throes
As we see this war comes to a peace and close!

Johnson: Joincare, you know who remains that can fight;
              What native powers, about here, abide?

Prideaux: I won't go the hazard of moving our line,
              While leaving any such enemies behind!

Joincare: You will find some tribes not of the French mind...
              This injury wounds more than their monarch's pride,
              It brings eternal death to our source of life!
              Where the French lost position of a fortress,
              Our peoples lost dominion of the forests;
              Where the French lost the overlooks of rivers,
              Our peoples lost dominion of the waters;
              Where the English felled lofts of a wilderness
              Our peoples lost their sylvan gods and spirits!
              Destroying the lands by which we survive,
              Threatens us beyond our corporeal life!
              You will not easily unseat my native kin
              From the patrimony of their interest:
              For all that we are or conceive is found
              In these lands whereto we're eternally bound!

Prideaux: I don't seek universal imprisonment,
              On peoples whose chance of long residence
              Long ago placed them in this wealth of lands!
              England's justice will extend equally upon
              Territories and peoples our strengths have won!
              With that, accept our embrace of your kin,
              In the spirit of brotherhood and friendship!
              Yet! Do not wish to excite those enmities,

	Reserved our Crown's unrepentant enemies!

Reserved our Crown's unrepentant enemies!

Joincare: For my clan, and by this emblem of wampum
           I pledge my faith to your father's kingdom!

           There are French allies who with these losses,
           Will meander in some loose circumference...
           Some will attach to your gathering strength,
           As the aura of France is felt diminishing!
           The Algonquin are of a country between,
           Who'll bend to your Crown's growing gravity,
           But there's those I know will not be tamed,
           Who consider England's presence profane!

Pouchot: Speak you of the Seneca Sachem,[75] Joincare?

Joincare: Yes, my friend, with whom I've had a long career,
           The "Overlord of the Western Door," Lone Bear,
           Whose family has for centuries been
           Protectors of Niagara's wilderness!
           For years he has made battle for the French.
           He beheld in them - Niagara's best defense!

Pouchot: His valor's unmatched in my experience:
           From his earliest youth to his present age,
           Unending war this noble Sachem's waged!

Johnson: Is it true Lone Bear's hundreds of followers
           Live by Little Niagara, along the rivers
           And vow to burn in sacrificial fires,
           Before swearing faith to England's desires?

Joincare: Your numbers of his devoted is avowed.

Prideaux: If they are so numerous and so proud,
           Why weren't they fighting at Fort Niagara?

---

75 Sachem: Synonym for king.

Pouchot: They were seconded to Ticonderoga.
             Lone Bear was head of the native militia;
             He was since ordered to hold the lesser falls,
             Rather than be prisoned in yon doomed walls!

Prideaux: He holds the merits of a noble hero!

Joincare: The guiding principle of his daring soul
             Is defense of Niagara, his ancient home!

             Is it not predictable someone would be
             Determined to enforce his own liberty?
             Is not the slight and weak fluttering wren
             Furious in his own freedom's defense?
             There is always one stolid and unimpressed
             With any greater power's eminence,
             Who will ever pose an untamed threat!
             For he remembers what once it was
             When his ideals were free and uncorrupt!
             Niagara will provide you no resting place
             While Lone Bear wanders free and unafraid!

             Yet there is greater danger in this diaspora
             With the French loss of this vast area,
             'Tis as though one overturned a central hive,
             Razed their lodge, but left some of the swarm alive!
             Even if the heralded queen has died,
             Another will ascend to rebuild the nest,
             Survivors will gather there, for defense!

Prideaux: How wide are Chief Lone Bear's resources?
             Can he raise any power of substance,
             With relics of a shattered resistence?
             What number are his total present forces?
             What number could his authority engage,
             If these Seneca remain free renegades?
             Can he rally power and a new magnitude -
             To which the loosed Algonquin might be moved?

Joincare: Is it not the will of like things to collect:
              Is not your alliance testament to that?

Prideaux: There's more, for Lone Bear battles for his hearth:
              'Twere as if I were in Bristol, cornered,
              Battling all the powers of the Infernal!
              The spark of my ineffectual anger
              Would metamorphose to flaming valor!

To Pouchot and Joincare

              You gentlemen will form an embassy -
              This word of peace to the Sachem carry:
              He may hold his ancient authority,
              He may maintain this native home and clan,
              If he obeys the greater laws of England
              And admits that his authority must move
              In harmony with England's attitude!

Joincare: I don't know, Prideaux, if this plea for peace
              Will leave the courage of Lone Bear appeased.
              Among thunders of cataracts he's been raised;
              His life has been one of hardship and the chase;
              He has singly battled the panther and the bear -
              Do you think such a man feels a sense of fear?
              He's ready to do or suffer anything
              To uphold his rightful home and liberty!

Prideaux: As high office is best reserved to the wise,
              As Lone Bear is the Sachem of his tribe,
              He must know the world round him is fallen,
              The French weal in America is in ruin,
              And his home, though mighty, is surrounded!
              Though he is strong, he is opposed by all,
              The bravest, when so overmatched, must fall!
              No matter where he may flee or tread,
              Every measure of this land's now England!
              It is in his and his people's interest

To adapt, not engage this circumstance!
His strengths were better spent being phoenix-like:[76]
As he must grow from ashes of his former life!

He must consign himself to take up his lance;
With his followers, he must willingly advance
To this camp, to lay down their ordnance!
Or I must make him the object of my chase,
And make Lone Bear mindful of this phrase:
Panthers attack bears singly, with fang and claw,
But I come in hordes with fire and cannonball!
And beneath my guns, his strongest will fall!

Pouchot: He will need time to consider.

Johnson: Three days?

Prideaux: He has that time to see his people are saved!

Pouchot: If he comes in, you will show lenity?

Prideaux: My whole hope is to afford him mercy,
As to a member of the British family!

Joincare: Can you reconcile with someone whose kind
Put so many of yours under the bloody knife,
Or suffered them to burn - a living sacrifice?

Prideaux: For men to embrace a friend, it is easy;
The greater obstacle is to embrace enemies:
To reconcile with those whom one stood against,
And make of one's opponents - new friends.
In order to live in peace and composed,
We must embrace those whom once we opposed.

---

76 Phoenix-like: Mythical bird which regenerated itself from its own ashes.

Joincare:	Do we have your solemn word as to terms?
Prideaux:	Yes, you have it! The offer: and my true word, And I am mindful, he that lies, murders worlds!

End of Act One

ACT TWO
SCENE ONE

EMBASSY OF JOINCARE AND POUCHOT

Place: Little Niagara Falls

Present: Lone Bear, Grey Swan, Day Star, Red Fox, Chaubert Joincare and Capt. Pouchot

Scene: *Lone Bear has returned from the mountain heights to his home, and the embassy from Niagara is arriving.*

Lone Bear:	Mink's fine, if there's trouble, he knows to fight.
Grey Swan:	Does he not know what Englishmen look like?
Day Star:	He is so young!
Lone Bear:	Weren't we all young once, And the world's safe as it was, and perilous!
Red Fox:	Sure that's Joincare and Captain Pouchot!
Lone Bear:	The French need a general for that fort!
Day Star:	If they are free, must not Niagara be?
Lone Bear:	No victory's won by their slow limping: The quality of their gait is of defeat!
Red Fox:	Better news is always borne by running!
Lone Bear:	I can hear them from here before they speak, Their eyes tell the tale their wampum would sound.

Joincare: 'Tis good to see you, Lone Bear, on sacred ground.
              Brothers, I've wampum bears heavily on me.

Lone Bear: Unload your words: mumble, speak, shout, or scream,
              I've heard nothing good since France's last defeat!

Offering wampum to Lone Bear

Pouchot: The same has fallen on Niagara's defenses!

Lone Bear: The fort lost and you alive! What's amiss?
              You pledged your life to defend that fortress!
              Here, Joincare! I thought you only half French
              Yet, you retreat with shame as well as their best!

Joincare: Though your derisive taunts befit me well -
              Hear us! We have not come to save ourselves;
              I would rather bleed beneath English batteries
              Than suffer such loss again, giving it speech!
              Since we last met in council and congressed,
              The English, in great numbers hereto have swept:
              They attacked Niagara from all directions!
              The world as once we knew it is in ruins.
              Overcoming French force and fortresses,
              Matron Nature herself and her wilderness,
              England subdues the elements to her uses,
              Mastering even the rivers to her purposes!

Pouchot: 'Tis true, the English show incredible strengths,
              In swiftness and discipline: thus in her victories!
              All her armies descend united as limbs,
              Moving in the single body of a Colossus!
              Of forces at Niagara, half are perished,
              Of our reinforcement, all were lost us!
              And after three weeks of pounding cannon,
              Niagara's defense has been abandoned!

Joincare: Nearby posts of strength also surrender:

The whole river's been lost to the invader!
Wherever the Fleur di Lis have been brought down,
There arise banners of the English Crown!

Lone Bear: All has altered in the span of a moon,
Since I moved for Ticonderoga and doom?
And you French, don't you move nimbly?
Always down and away to hollow sloping!
And where is Piquet,[77] the reverend father,
Who reads the Bible as he bids us pass the powder!
Bids us whom we love, or whom we slaughter,
Where is the eminent preacher of the French?

Pouchot: The precincts of Niagara, he has long since left,
Despairing that it could afford no more defense!

Lone Bear: Our alliance with you French, your kingdom,
Sealed with indissoluble words, with wampum!
That's the true fortress that you've abandoned!
Did not every Frenchman assembled promise
That this, Niagara's sacred confluence,
Would be defended to France's last breath!
Even if the whole Earth shook at its core
And fire issued in rivers from her pores
Or the atmosphere poured waterfall storms
And sky burst with lightning in swarms,
And floods filled the globe to her mountaintops,
Crowning minnows the world's new monarchs!
You said our sacred Niagara you'd defend
Till the last man fell beneath his last breath!
Yet, here you breathe? Yet, here you stand?
Such are false promises of broken France!
Yet, the word of man alone can withstand,
When the whole world slips away like the sand!

France gave its word to my ear to sway my soul,
But does not give its word the acts France owes!

---

77 Piquet: Abbe' Piquet set up a mission with Chaubert Joincare to recruit the Seneca to the cause of New France.

With the passing away of your solemn oath
The covenant chain that bound us is broke;
And we're alone, beneath England's fatal stroke!

Red Fox: We were once knit within a bundle of sticks,
While bundled, there could be no breaking it!
Alone it's a question if we can persist:
A lone clan against England's alliance?

Joincare: The English have sent us to plead with you:
Niagara's fall need not involve your doom.

Grey Swan: How can it not? A man lives by the land,
If the land is fallen, so must be the man!

Pouchot: The English would allow you keep this land -
Circumscribed, no doubt, as they will give out -
But your customs, your dress, your dance, your hunt
Your longhouses, your manners and prayers,
All these you may keep as being yours,
So long as you abide laws of England's wish.

Red Fox: Can a victor leave more to the vanquished?

Lone Bear: Yet, they ask the sole thing we can't relinquish!
Pouchot, you know not what France has broken;
Nor Fox, what you sacrifice as a token!

One's customs, manners and woven raiment
One's hunt and dance and habitation
Are but the housing and dress of a nation!
This world was authored by our Great Father
'Twas his breath which wove nature together,
By his will, our peoples derived our law
'Tis the central law - that relates us all!

What's custom worth without the kindness of it?
What's the longhouse without its inhoused spirit?

What's dress absent the inner fire it protects?
What's dance without the harmony it reflects?
What's manner without elegance of beauty?
What is left is not worthy of the hunting!
Nor skinning, nor cooking, nor the feeding,
For we'd lose the central worth of our being,
Towards which life moves by its laboring!

I'd rather the English would unhouse us:
Leave our bare heads to a tempest's triumphs;
Let the English take every stitch of our clothes
Leaving us to die slow in a winter's cold!
Or hang us in fires till sinew slips our bones,
Rather than lose the law which forms our souls -
I'll not lose the essence of what makes us whole!

Joincare: Lone Bear, we speak of our people's existence,
Of the simple matter of continuance!
You must show our people worthy mercy
You must adapt to the present necessity:
Join with the other Five Nations finally,
And survive to be of England's family!

Pouchot: I know Prideaux, he is as fair as firm!

Lone Bear: Think you he will give me his word as to terms?
Do you think he'll keep it as you did yours?
When our homes, longhouses and dances
And manners and customs depended on it!
As to our prayers: they sound in the sacrifice
We daily abide observing the law in our life!
In the compass of life, what is more sacred
Than the word by which peoples are related?

Yet you broke yours when you broke covenants
And surrendered the strengths of our alliance:
And left us prone to the marauding English!

Day Star: You murder us! You murder our world's hope
                When you murder your word and the truth it holds!

Pouchot: The truth is, the English hold the upper hand!
                They are superior by sea and land,
                And we French are wounded and on the run:
                We have just room to maneuver to prison,
                Where breathless and bruised, crippled and helpless,
                We can but hope for English mercy to us!

Joincare: Lone Bear! You're no less at mercy in this place...
                The British will find the paths to these caves,
                For all-discovering war will find weaknesses
                In the cliffs and forests of these approaches!
                And as nature lays siege to flaws in her children,
                England will make you suffer the same burden!
                They'll move like nature, an implacable engine!
                Or she will be given to lenity as she is tempered;
                England will show mercy, if you will surrender!

Pouchot: Adapt to the conqueror, for that she is now,
                Can you not move within weal of her crown?

Lone Bear: Our law is the soul of the Seneca
                Its ancient seat is here in Niagara!
                I'll consent to part beloved Niagara
                If it saves the exiled soul of the Seneca!

                We'll fly to the Abenaki[78] of the north,
                Following the Saint Lawrence by her course!

Joincare: You will find that course a haunted passage,
                Teeming with arms under British manage.

Lone Bear: Then we'll run for the Ohio valley
                To join the Algonquin there and rally!

---

78 Abenaki: One of the Algonquian-speaking peoples settled throughout New England and southern Quebec; they were among the tribes held responsible for the massacre at Fort William Henry.

| Pouchot: | All French and Indian armies on those forks |
| | Have surrendered to the British all of our forts! |

| Lone Bear: | Then we'll walk the long trek to Mackinac... |
| | So far the British won't follow our track! |

Pouchot:	They have taken Michillimackinac!
	All the forts of the lakes they've taken intact,
	They're known to circle the continent,
	And the English have seen to their investment!

| Lone Bear: | Nor fly, nor run, nor walk - must we crawl? |
| | After all our labor and loss, is that all? |

Red Fox:	It may be time to believe and admit:
	This vast victory is no accident:
	That the British are composed of excellence,
	An excellence attended by providence.
	Nature herself upholds the majestic
	Whose native worth achieves a summit
	Attended by signs of greatness and genius!
	Their law is the source of this strength displayed;
	Perhaps to this great strength, ours should give place?

| Day Star: | Certainly it's time, Lone Bear, to listen! |

Grey Swan:	Listen to this counsel of cowardice!
	No, Son! Not while life's flame is in your limbs!
	Our birthplace and home must be defended
	Even though weak France leaves us abandoned!

Lone Bear:	England I honor, for manifest strengths,
	She has won justly, overwhelmingly!
	Such does not happen by serendipity
	But with health, prowess, and by acuity
	By courage, sense of duty and unity!
	All of these virtues England's displayed
	And is the more reason we've war yet to wage!

For the successful tread of England's nation
Measures the swath she makes of devastation!

Do they not roam the earth like a black giant
Or demigod careering in gross defiance?
Raking the world, tearing her sinew and skin -
Not an ungentle lover, but a wrathful rapist!
Who rips up the womb of gentle Ataensic
To fill his stomach with overgorged harvests!
Who mines her mineral to feed the blacksmith
To metallurge weapons, sickles and scythes,
Wherewith to heave down defenseless forests -
To give them over to the farmer and the plow,
Putting under chain and hoe our sacred ground!
And doth the giant not bellow over us,
Screaming words from monolithic pulpits:
Condemning our atmosphere-dwelling spirits!
Tell me the truth! Are they not then a scourge
Who change what's under, of and above the Earth?
We Seneca are proud sons of Ataensic!
As she suffers, we will stand in her defense,
In our prayers we gave to her our word,
That we would ever love and defend her!
And that we will! For it is truth to tell:
One's word is the only indestructible,
Even when crushing change is inevitable!
Here we will maintain the Seneca soul,
By gazing in death's face and holding our own!

Joincare: I believe, Lone Bear, in what you defend
But do you truly defend what is best?
England has won in every contest,
Has not nature herself crowned the mightiest?

Pouchot: If England can vanquish France with her allies,
England can defeat your undefended tribe!
There'll be nowhere left to go, what will you do?

Lone Bear: Where shall I run, now I am loosed?
              Upon the English, from every ambush!
              I'd rather die beneath a blasted forest
              Or bleed my swimming blood in river depths
              Than accept the world and ways of the English!
              I'll fight for Aereskouy and Ataensic!
              I was born rigid stone from my elder's loins,
              To be through fields of war, England's counterpoise!

Pouchot: You need to think what is best for your clans.
              Take the time given, think on alternatives!
              Take the three days to weigh and consider
              Pyrrhic[79] defense for you, amounts to self-murder.

Joincare: Think to surrender or to flee while you may,
              After three days, Prideaux will not be late.
              Fly, if you will, to avoid a worse fate,
              Time and war will crush you, if you hesitate!

              Where would you keep this gift of wampum?
              It's the tale of war at Niagara done.

Lone Bear: Put it with our Seneca chronicle,
              Under the altar, in the French chapel.
              Would the English, you think, burn their God's house?
              No! Their faith must be strong, I do not doubt,
              Otherwise we wouldn't be at their mercy,
              But celebrating our own vast victories!

              Mind, Pouchot! To speak is humanly unique,
              But God reserves to speak truth in his speech!
              Anyone among deluded multitudes
              Can speak eloquently with falsehood -
              France! You lied! And murdered our world!
              And now you can't lend us...even a soldier!

---

79 Pyrrhic: Refers to Pyrrhus (319-272 B.C.E), king of the Greek Molossian tribe, as well as Epirus and Macedon; some of his victories against Rome were as costly as defeat.

Grey Swan: Seneca women are blessed, it is deemed
With the gifts of future-seeing prophecy!
Turn, Pouchot! Hear what fruits grow from these seeds:
France! We may die, for here occurs the first quake,
Of world-shattering events which will radiate,
Consuming your empire's crown in our fate!
For this quake emits destabilizing waves
Whose crests bear death like a pestilent plague!
Over the vast ocean, horror will be borne,
To drown your kingdom in an all-leveling storm,
Whose survivors will feed on their own brethren,
Till high and low are crushed in one oblivion!
Since nobility was broken in breaking your word,
Since you have confounded our world's order,
Nobility in your cursed kingdom will be purged;
And your settled order will suffer mutation
And like ourselves, be lost in some new creation!
For our revolution will spread unsubdued fire,
Becoming kindling to France's funeral pyre!

Pouchot: Yes! The world is everywhere on fire,
Would by its light we could see the truth entire.
Speaking of fire, Lone Bear, I esteem your brave act!
I understand it was you who braved the gauntlet,
Who lit the tinder at Ticonderoga,
And escaped, before the fort exploded!
I heard many who fled were not so fortunate.
Many unforeseen things occur in the world
When fortune and war are together hurled!

Exit Pouchot and Joincare

Lone Bear: Aye, but the word of man need never suffer it!
I should hang them both in fire for insolence!
Red Fox! See that those two really do leave!
Then return; we need to send our several leads
To call the warlike Algonquin to convene,
And find how many wish the English bleed?

Day Star:	Did you light the fuse that destroyed Blue Moose?
	Oh, dear husband, how could you?
Lone Bear:	It is through!
	The French asked who was the foremost in courage;
	Moose wouldn't leave me go, without an entourage.
Day Star:	Of yourself you lost in the blast - a half!
Lone Bear:	Who can foreknow a fire's uncontrolled path!

End of Act Two Scene One

ACT TWO
SCENE TWO

PRIDEAUX'S GATHERING FORCE

Place: Prideaux's tent, adjacent Fort Niagara

Present: Gen. Prideaux, William Johnson and White Hawk; later, Gen. Thomas Gage, Maj. Robert Rogers and Master of Ordnance, John Slattery

Scene: *Prideaux, Johnson, and White Hawk await the arrival of Gen. Gage's forces before the tent of Prideaux. There is a vital energy of motion: of men, horses and war materials, as the army of the British Empire prepares to move beyond Niagara. In the background is the fort, whose entrance is open with conveyances being made freely through her ports. Aside the doors, some French soldiers are gathered, reverentially interring those lost in battle, before their general removal to the prison ships, waiting at anchor, in distant Hudson Bay.*

Prideaux: While we await Gage's coming forward,
                What's our present forces?

Johnson: I have the number…
                Of Englishmen we have fourteen hundred
                And nine hundred of the Five Nations,[80]
                Less our loss of the fallen and wounded,
                From when the seige began, we've effective
                Twenty-one hundred troops able to go.
                More, the news of our victory swiftly roams:
                New allies arrive from surrounding tribes,
                Formerly with the French, as Wyandots,
                Delawares, Shawanoes, even Hurons!
                And from Aubry's late and fallen army
                We've recruited from among the refugees.

---

80 Five Nations: Refers to the Iroquois confederacy composed of the Mohawk, Oneida, Onondaga, Cayuga, and Seneca tribes.

White Hawk: Victory brings them, like planets round the sun?

Prideaux: Less losses than I thought and far more won
And natives coming over to us, well done!

Johnson: It may reach, if you'll believe it, hundreds.

Prideaux: France's thread is broken, her stitch vanishes!
If alliance they made with the tribes is breaking,
What remains of them will prove easy taking!

Johnson: We've word of other forces on the go,
Taking foot or bateaux[81] for Isle aux Noix,
And others are moving on the Ontario:
Bound for Fort Detroit and for Canada,
While others wander the surrounding forest:
The wounded, broken exiles of conquest.

Prideaux: It's foreseeable, this broken alliance
Of France will unleash a tempest of chaos:
Through the continent there will cascade effects
With her patriots scattered in a wilderness;
But as England's power grows on new subjects
This tract will reassume order and find rest!

Johnson: Meantime, we make ready for the advance!

Prideaux: White Hawk! Take charge of the natives to a man,
Including those newly come to our camp,
Prepare them to move north in three days' time!
Time is accelerating, upon us before we like!
Mindful! Time is the greatest ally we have,
If we move in the rhythm of her advance.
I've sent a peace embassy to Lone Bear's camp,
We will know how they've fared, they'll soon be back.

White Hawk: Heard and understood, General -

---

81 Bateaux: Shallow-draft, flat-bottomed boat used in the North American fur trade during the colonial period.

Johnson: Here's Gage.

Prideaux: Welcome, Gage! You arrive late in the day,
               Niagara surrendered to us this morning.

Gage: So goes the glory!

Prideaux: How comes your army?

Gage: Some degrees behind me, though soon arriving.

Prideaux: What's the aggregate?

Gage: Five thousand effective.

Prideaux: Good, we'll unite to move and join Amherst,
               Near Montreal, where he makes his approaches.

Gage: I've a dispatch sent to you from England
               Sent by messenger from Minister Pitt.[82]

Prideaux: I had been expecting that, let's have it!

Reads   "My Dear Prideaux,
               I hope this communication finds you inspired
               At the volcanic edge of far-flung Empire!
               I write to convey that our operation,
               Succeeds at all points of our ambition!
               Our plans to deplete the French in their home
               By challenging her holdings round the globe,
               And to deplete the French in her colonies,
               By financing Frederick's Prussian armies[83]
               Succeeds! We achieve sweeping victories!
               Hawke[84] met the Atlantic fleet of the French

---

82 Minister Pitt: William Pitt, first Earl of Chatham, Minister of England, whose strategy won the Seven Years War.
83 Prussian armies: England, by financing the Prussian armies on the European continent, was free to fight around the world
for the expansion of the British Empire.
84 Hawke: First Baron, Edward Hawke, a victor at the Battle of Quiberon Bay in 1759.

And sank or drove her vessels off of Brest;
While Boscawen,[85] near Gibraltar, encountered
Their Med fleet at Lagos, and saw them founder!
Thus, the waves are free sailing for our navies
Through Mediterranean and Atlantic seas!

And if this be not reason enough for you
To exalt the well-being of our fortunes -
Our forces and fleets have struck Senegal,
In Africa, they too on France turn prodigal!
And in holy India, in that ancient seat,
Clive,[86] our natural born general, won Plassey!
While Admiral Pocock,[87] sailing Seas of Araby,
Found and scuttled the French Cuddalore fleet!
Thus, we've opened channels, freeing our motions,
From the Atlantic through Indian Oceans!

Yet, there is more, for in the vast Pacific
William Draper[88] with the navy of Cornish,
Crushed Manila and the Philippine islands:
Fighting Spain, that other of France's allies,
Whom we've beaten by our daring enterprise!

Finally, in Caribbean waters we also succeed,
Taking Cuba, Guadeloupe, and Martinique!
Making all the Earth's vast oceans and seas,
Unto our Thames[89] - a system of tributaries!

Now I doubt the French will suffer Scottish winds
To attempt our isles with spurious invasions,
As she has done for a millennium![90]
Thank heaven we judged advantage and time

---

85 Boscawen: Admiral Edward Boscawen, victor at the Battle of Lagos, 1759.
86 Clive: Major General Robert Clive, victor at Battle of Plassey, 1757.
87 Admiral Pocock: Sir George Pocock (1706-1792 C.C.), commander of British naval forces in Indian waters, who sank the French Cuddalore fleet in 1758.
88 William Draper: Sir William Draper, British military officer who conquered Manila in 1762.
89 Thames: The River Thames, principal waterway from London to the English Channel.
90 Millennium: For a thousand years, England had been subject to invasions from France through Scotland, either directly or by alliance.

And reversed our composition of allies,[91]
Choosing over Austria, the genius Frederick,
Who seizes all the attentions of a continent!
Is he not the Atlas[92] of our alliance
On whose shoulders our further fortune rests,
As we gauge France everywhere the world crests?

I regret you do not fight beside Frederick,
And glory on fields of France, with his ranks,
Exhibiting all the arts of chivalry,
Which you uphold yourself, with idolatry!
But your genius for adaptability
Is indispensable to the colonies:
You're England's virtuous Alcibiades![93]
I wish you good fortune and good fighting
Now onward! Strive forth for England's glory!
                                    Your Friend, Pitt"

Prideaux: Mars himself is restless - awake! He stirs -
                Through every nook and harbor of the world!

Johnson: I've been too busy myself in America.
                I was ignorant that the world's on fire!

Prideaux: Is she not? The late War of Succession[94]
                Left swaths of the world in states of vacuum:
                With weakness in Italy and Hanover
                And in Silesia and Bohemia,
                As well both sides ever shifting Rhine,
                That contested river, since Roman times!

                Then France and Spain are weakly colonied,
                From the Americas to the distant Indies,
                And where there's weakness, there's a vacuum,

---

91 Composition of allies: The network of European alliances exactly reversed after the last continental war.
92 Atlas: One of the Titans who held the world on his shoulders.
93 Alcibiades: Athenian general (450-404 B.C.E.) during the Peloponnesian War; legendary for his ability to adapt to local custom and shifting winds.
94 War of Succession: The first war of Spanish succession, 1701-1714.

229

            Where there's a vacuum, there is motion;
            Where there is motion, there is contention,
            Or rather, twin advances: one harmonic
            And internal, in the moving wheels of empire!
            The other external, hard and fractious,
            Collisive, rancorous: sounding dissonance -
            Where there meet and engage the opposites!
            Like base elements at war, as fire and water:
            Pouring elastically through all pores
            Fisted, ferocious, ever at contraries,
            Until a war crowns superiority!

Gage: Here comes Rogers. Lord! What a filthy type!
            How they dress and paint themselves with those dyes!
            Aren't they more savage than Indian tribes?

Prideaux: They adapt to the fighting of this contest
            By feeding, living, soldiering in the forests.

Gage: I know that you esteem these things, Prideaux,
            Native leggings, moccasins, the beads and bows;
            But you adapt by addition, they by subtraction -
            Can they not bathe and keep a uniform on!

Rogers: Johnson and the General! Great to see you men!
            By looks, General, you still wash your own linen!

Prideaux: Why ya think we camp by so many rivers?
            Good to see you, Sarge, your hair's still together!

Rogers: We've been everyplace that's likely to lose it –

Prideaux: We may have work for you here, don't doubt it!

Rogers: Where the fightin' isn't fit?

Johnson: Rogers'll fight it!

Rogers:	How's our old shop clerk?
Johnson:	Still lookin' for safe work!
Rogers:	Well then, you've stumbled badly in your plans! What work is there round here fit for a man?
Prideaux:	We have a group of some fierce Seneca Who've gone renegade round Niagara, Whether they will surrender or will fight, We should know before the coming of night.
Rogers:	Who's it then?
Johnson:	Lone Bear, with his few hundreds!
Rogers:	You'll be stickin' your head amid the hornets, In Niagara's hollows and crags he's nested? Those Seneca to a man would slaughter us! Lone Bear is a fighter as fierce and strong As any a man as I've fought among!
Prideaux:	It could be a great trial?
Gage:	A trial I might ease. This officer is Major John Slattery, You've orders, Prideaux, this major's assigned, To make this fort our new center of supply, Through which we will feed all our forward lines. Among his ordnance, are some delivered, That are new cannon he calls howitzers, Which might just suit this very occasion: They'll remove those Indians from that canyon!
Slattery:	Gentlemen, good day, as General Gage said, In supply we've fifty howitzer bores They are short, narrow, wheeled for transport; They're compact, fireable from spaces enclosed;

231

For cannon of the caliber, they are accurate
As any we've had a field on this continent.

Rogers: I can blast Lone Bear with a few of those,
And his men, out of dangerous strongholds!

Prideaux: Well, gents, let's wait and see if we need go.
These are new invented guns, I've not known.

Johnson: We'll have to bring them up and field test 'em.

Slattery: I hear it's a crippled Swede's[95] invention,
And you won't believe from whom we've bought them -
Francois Bigot, the supply master of the French!

Prideaux: What!

Slattery: He says his French masters aren't paying
While his wife, kids and mistresses need feeding!

Prideaux: Such a traitorous man deserves hanging!

Gage: In war, one must seize on every advantage,
So long as his present need supplies our wants...

Prideaux: A French officer no less!

Johnson: How corrupt!

Prideaux: How out of harmony with virtue is this?
For wanting such supply, down came this fortress!

Looking over to the new graveyard in front of the portal.

Johnson: Are they not digging graves that bastard made -
Should he not be the first, beneath those spades?

---

95 Swede: Barron Menno Van Coehoorn, inventor of the Coehorn Mortar in 1673, was adapted for use in the French and Indian War a hundred years later.

Prideaux: Well, as it is, war discovers all faults
             And first invades cavities that are corrupt!
             Withal, Athens[96] was felled from her heights
             By Spartan valor, and by her own inner strife!
             Rome's fall came, it's surmised, by barbarians,
             But 'twas her softness too, her luxuriance,
             That felled her millennial walls to ruins!

Johnson: Here returns our embassy at a low ebb.

Enter Joincare and Pouchot

Prideaux: How fared you, gentlemen; have we a friend?

Joincare: He will ponder for the three days promised;
             He's desperate, with his few and last options.
             He may, like the Narraganset Cononchet,[97]
             Prefer dying himself, leaving the world ablaze!
             Or fight like King Philip,[98] whose self defense
             Saw him, with his comrades, die in the marshes,
             Rather than suffer to be England's subjects!

Prideaux: Everything had moved in ways predictable,
             Measurable up to now and governable.
             But there is always one that will slip the net,
             And move in a manner one does not expect.

Joincare: Lone Bear is entrenched, not easily shaken
             No matter what force it is would push him.
             We made every attempt of persuasion.

Prideaux: What is his condition?

Joincare: Badly wounded.

---

96 Athens: Resorted to exiling prominent generals of the Persian and Peloponnesian Wars, including Themistocles, Cimon, and Alcibiades, over political intrigue.
97 Narraganset Cononchet: Leader of the Narraganset nation (?-1676) who died in King Philip's War after refusing to surrender.
98 King Philip: Also known as Metacomet (ca. 1639-1676); chief of the Wampanoag tribe and leader of native resistence to colonial expansion in King Philip's War 1675-1676; like Cononchet, he died without surrendering.

Pouchot: He performed the blast of Ticonderoga,
And fell in the path of his own explosion,
A sweep of splinters, metals and loose stones
Pierced his back, with some lodging in his bones!

Prideaux: He is wounded, abandoned and exposed?
Such a man in such straits can do anything!

Gage: While on Montreal we've to keep moving!
Let's look to alternatives of what's to do:
If he won't surrender - he must be subdued!

Johnson: We could attack through these dim forest alleys,
The hidden paths to Little Niagara valley.
But that way is the bloodiest path to him:
It would be through passages well-defended.
Doubtless, he has positioned trusty lookouts
Along those paths, in series of redoubts.

Rogers: Have you a full month and a thousand men?
This channel of battle will consume all that!

Slattery: Were I you, gentlemen, I'd simply bribe him,
With whatever is handy of beads and trinkets.
Some walls and doors that cannot be taken
With months of time and hordes of battalions,
Swing swifter for seducers with temptations!

White Hawk: No, not Lone Bear!   He'll not be corrupted.
Would a man who feeds on walnuts and turnips
Want trinkets?   You could offer hills of bullion,
He would rather defeat the fools of gold,
Than be gold's fool himself; he won't be sold!

Prideaux: You know this?

White Hawk: His whole will is to defend this wilderness!

Gage: Why not do the obvious, the expedient:
Surround him in the night and loose these cannon!
Let the consuming fire clear the canyon,
As his people flee the fire, we can take them!

Rogers: And we can scour the area from there,
Leaving no enemy left to peril our rear.

Prideaux: I hate the idea! Attack from the shadows?
Like the Devil practicing his arts in darkness!
I'd rather live amidst hell's earthly children:
The spiders, toads, wild dogs and serpents,
Than commit to act as bestial as they,
While I may stand and fight by the sun of day!

I should prefer to meet this sylvan prince
On fields of Europe's ancient continent:
Where our fairest youth, in youthful ardor,
Are ranged in valorous thousands by order -
Into a single, breathing, living force
Of a mind and limbs, a soul and living core,
Composed 'neath the citadel of a general!

Or at least like the foes he knows in nature,
As when the panther meets the immovable bear
To contest possession of a cohabited lair:
Testing if good courage outweighs base fear!
All their strengths are bent in opposition
And that lair soon evolves to the strongest!
This contest, at least, noble Lone Bear merits -
His valor and his nature demand it!

Gage: What sense is it to wait on these few hundreds?
Attack, Prideaux, and let's be done with this!
You know how to win, but not how to use it.

Prideaux: We have the advantage in only this
We are free – not to be merciless!

Otherwise, let's leave this new, nether world
To be whipped for weakness by nature's scourge!
Leave this world to her gods and chieftains
To rule this place as her proper sovereigns!
Why do we engage in this world-circling war,
If not for the issue of superior law!
Why do we pass through avalanching seas,
Or dare the boundless desert's extremities
Or swim fetid stench of the densest marshes,
Or stride impassable, glaciered mountains?
Why do we dare these ferocious frontiers
While battling our foes everywhere?
For as God, in the midst of his creation
Sorted nature's discordant elements
And ordered them by his natural laws,
So we move through worlds of thousands of gods
Of differing peoples, customs and tongues
To bring them the order of one civil law!
We circumference the world for justice,
Extending the light and order of England
For it's this Justice that founds excellence
Not just in our England - but in all men!

Justice is to man what tillage is to the land:
Seamed by ordered, equal, parallel furrows
Such land receives throughout sun and water,
In equal measure without bramble or shadow.
The fruits which rise begin from an even soil,
But this requires vigilance and constant toil!
Some stalks fall by; let be, most will thrive:
Justice brings harvests of the fruits of life!
Now, should we battle for this lawful cause
Through unforgiving terrains 'gainst implacable foes -
Only to crush this sense of justice in ourselves?
One meets more justice in a wilderness
Than you propose with clandestine forces!

Aye, this tribe has been robbed, beaten, abandoned!

If we'd not burden this world, or be Christian,
We can, at the least, prove a Samaritan!

When from nature's law and bosom we trod
We may emerge as a powerful demon
Or rise by our actions to the heart of God!
Let us use the mercy shown in God's covenant
Leaving behind nature's dictates as merciless!
Such divine law is as above those of nature
As God is above the crest of the eagle;
Even England's law is above that of nature,
As the eagle is above the amoeba![99]
This victory ought not be merely over foes,
But a victory over our lesser selves!

I would make a friend of this noble chieftain,
Our charity and understanding extend
As props of a mercy enlightened!
We'll coax these Natives with benevolence
And attend them as a bee does the pollens,
By whose adroit prodding and caring,
Nature's diversity is brought to flowering!
While wresting from varied flowers, sweet nectars
The bee through his subtle, vigilant powers,
Distills in a single honey, the Earth's splendors!
So shall the empire be of a vast variety,
Honeyed by one law universally!
For mercy brings harvests of life's flowering!

Thus, we need a new and better embassy
To whom Lone Bear will bear good listening,
But whom do we know?

White Hawk: I would volunteer, sir.

Prideaux: I thought so Hawk!

---

99 Amoeba: A simple single-celled creature discovered in 1757 by August Johann Rosel Von Rosenhof.

Gage: *To White Hawk*
                    What recommends you there?
             Are you a diplomat by your career?

White Hawk: I know our cause as well as I know Lone Bear's.

Gage: How can you know Lone Bear's cause? You know him?

    White Hawk: We were raised on this river by our parents,
             I am Lone Bear's brother by our lineage:
             I am also of the Seneca Order of Guardians!
             I've never spoke of it; years ago we suffered a rift,
             Which we had over the life of my children.
             But this occasion might heal all the clefts
             Between England and my renegade brethren,
             As between White Hawk and his lost brother,
             If you choose me to take forth your offer!

Gage: He might easily warn Lone Bear of our strengths!

Prideaux: And this war's destroyed how many families?
            Hawk! For us you are the perfect messenger
            Reunite the Seneca by means of your brother,
            That you may both find peace here in Niagara!
            And you shall go forth openly, by day,
            To bear our words, spoken in your own way!

Gage: This is folly! How much time have we to waste?
            My troops cannot wait here for two days,
            My orders are to march up Saint Lawrence way!

Prideaux: While Lone Bear deliberates, we'll not move!

Gage: All right! I will see to the arriving troops!

Slattery: You'll excuse me, General, I must go too!

Gage and Slattery exit.

Rogers: We've our encampments to make 'bout here then,
               If it's three days, I'll rest my fighting men.

Prideaux: Do it, Sarge! We've victory to celebrate!

Rogers: We'll not be missing festivities anyways!

Johnson: Go on, Rogers! I'll find you about the place!

Rogers and his group exit.

Prideaux: Very well, Hawk! You'd best get ready to go.
               My former offer and my thoughts you know:
               See if we can avoid this bloody attack,
               Knowing it's not fear, but mercy holds me back!

White Hawk: I'll go prepare the necessary wampum
               And hope the best for this last legation.

White Hawk exits.

*There remain Prideaux, Johnson, Pouchot and Joincare. A guard
unit arrives to convey Pouchot and Joincare to batueax, then to
transport them to convict ships, at anchor, in Hudson Bay.*

Prideaux: Well, men, I bid you farewell, its time to go.
               But Pouchot! Do you know a Francois Bigot?

Pouchot: He is New France's foremost Quarter Master.

Prideaux: It is contrary to our vantage to give you word,
               But your supply master is a gross traitor:
               He's selling us goods from French magazines.

Pouchot: Bigot? Whom I petitioned unceasingly,
               That our needs of men and munitions were pressing?

Prideaux: He has betrayed you to the uttermost.

He's so opposed to your dutifulness
While your men were starving and alone -
Even when you were suffering most and prone,
For weeks shuddering under our bombardments -
How did Bigot repay your devotedness?
He sold us supplies needed for your defense!
He'd not lift garnish from the dish he fed on,
Nor suffer the loss of a plump capon,
Nor retreat from a table of smoked beef,
Nor leave his wines and powdered sweets,
To save Niagara's fort, or spare your defeat!
You lost Niagara and she was overthrown
For you were starved by a Devil of your own!

Pouchot: All the lost valor; all the men who died!
All the pain and hunger, all this sacrifice,
And he does these evils in the King's name!
We die for our faith and he acts the profane?
All the graves we fill with our army's dead!
France! How could you leave your own abandoned!

Prideaux: All faults are found through discoveries of war,
What mercy does war or nature afford?
They pour death on the weak without remorse!

Pouchot: France is lost! She is so feeble and corrupt!
How can she allow this evil of Bigot
To flourish, while he feeds on France's soul?

Joincare: Yours is a largely virtuous army
But in the shadow of so vast an underbelly
One's bound to discover some deviltry!

Prideaux: There are those of the like in England's, doubtless -
There's always those opposed to our better selves!
We and your France emerge as knights errant
From our home lists to contest for the world
And this quest determines who's victorious -

The concentrated vice of France's single crown
Or the diffused virtues of England's table round![100]

To Pouchot   I recommend to you the rites for your fallen,
Before you must take ship for the prison.

Pouchot: Thank you, General. Let's be off, Joincare.

Prideaux: One Empire has been made, another razed
Over the soil of those new, restless graves!

As they turn for the grave site

Joincare: Long life and long live your honor, Prideaux!

Prideaux   Any of us may join yon ranks on the morrow...
But one's honor need not attend one's marrow!

End of Act Two Scene Two

---

100 England's table round: Refers to King Arthur's table, symbolizing parity among members and equal justice.

ACT TWO
SCENE THREE

THE RETURN HOME OF WHITE HAWK

Place: Little Niagara

Present: White Hawk, Lone Bear, Grey Swan, Day Star, Red Fox, and assorted Seneca members

Scene: *White Hawk is introduced as the legate from Prideaux, with a further appeal for peace by surrender. The scene is as before: the sacred domain of the Seneca, though the winds are increasing in vigor through corridors of the canyon.*

Red Fox: From the cliff top camps we have downward strode
                    Myself and our brother, one-time chief and lord!
                    Hawk's returned to lands of his long-ago birth!
                    My dear friend is home! We need no longer search:
                    Our brother's here to sit at our sacred hearth!

Lone Bear: Fort Niagara is fallen to England,
                    France has retreated from our agreements,
                    We are near exile from ancestral lands,
                    And here, after many years, my brother stands!
                    I suppose it is fitting, on an Earth overturned,
                    That you should choose this moment of return!

Red Fox: He hardly appears to be Seneca,
                    Wearing this garb of the British militia:
                    So many stripes, medals, such decoration!
                    Are you the paradigm of your new nation?

Lone Bear: How are you, Hawk? Do you do well these days?

White Hawk: Aye, but it's young Hawk with whom you'd be amazed -
                    How he thrives in life, in both body and mind!

243

Grey Swan: Englishman! What brings you back to our kind!
I curse the day I was overcome with labor
And gave birth on the wrong side the river,
To the weak babe who became this traitor!
'Fore you wandered here, I wish your foot withered!

White Hawk: And it's very good to see you too, Mother!

Grey Swan: You! Who renounced laws and rites of our Fathers,
You! Who allied with my father's slaughterers!
Who betrayed his mother, brother and elders!
Who cracked the sacred unity of the Seneca -
You! With horrid England, invade Niagara!

Day Star: Grey Swan! Mother! How can you speak to him so
When his love of you is all you have known?
How can you gaze on your son's equal spirits,
Favor one, and show the other such harshness?

Grey Swan: I treat them solely as their strengths merit!
White Hawk! You showed our tribe a traitor's path,
Dividing your own, unleashing caustic wrath
That's destroyed our tribe and our family
And cleft the sacred hold of our unity!
Rather than witness us weakened by these throes -
At your birth, I should have left you exposed![101]

White Hawk: Why's it only Seneca women rule men?

Grey Swan: We're the only women who give birth to men!
And find worthy of life but half of them!

White Hawk: If I have left our family and our gens,
Was it not you who taught me abandonment?
Was it you who first commended me a father?
Then, seeing my son's foot, sentenced him to slaughter!

---

101 Exposed: European sources describe infanticide, such as exposing handicapped newborns, by some Native American tribes; historians debate the extent of infanticide among Native Americans.

I saw his foot, it wrought my sense of pity;
You saw it too, but felt no cause for mercy?
Thus you bade me: 'Take your new son alive
Atop the mountains and bind him on the heights,
For with this weakness, he cannot survive,
Or his weakness becomes weakness of our tribe!'

In his soul was bound the love of my wife,
A love joined with mine, I would not sacrifice!
What God had wrought as a whole and joined,
I wouldn't allow your judgment to destroy!

Grey Swan: I didn't want to see that boy hobble through life!
And crawl in a frame that was formed awry,
With every step and turn a grievous trial
And our having to support him the while!
Nature framed him unable to function;
His twisted wound begged for his destruction!
By nature's law such deformity's proscribed,
If witnessed, the babe cannot be left alive!

White Hawk: Nature, in her catalogue of operations,
Has not the time to attend one gestation!
She can't wheel the mass of her immense being
And devote mercies to our small miseries!
And with the constant motion of elements
She hasn't time for details and perfections:
Hers is a cool, well functioning engine.
You, Mother!   Need not be her reflection!

As to our beloved son, who is now grown!
The love was perfect that made him whole,
That gave a form and lodging to his soul!
He is of great spirit, character and merit
My dear wife and I are very proud of him,
Even if the Seneca have suffered for it!

I would not steal through sable paths of night
To find a cold crag on a desolate height,
And pinion my newborn's hands to jagged stone,
And hear his plaintive cries, as I left him alone!
Abandoning innocence to gathering broods,
Who by nature's warrant would devour this food!
I would not leave my son to the jaws of wolves!
To follow ancient rites of a useless law,
With bowed shoulders, a shrug and blinded awe!

Grey Swan: I will hear no more blasphemy!

White Hawk: She weeps!

Grey Swan: Not for the son you saved, but the one I see!

White Hawk: You're a mother! Have you no sense of mercy!
                  The British have better laws for humanity!

Grey Swan: Have you no sense of your own ancestry?
                  These English made your own grandfather to bleed!

Lone Bear: Enough! This wound is still open, still bleeding...

White Hawk: You broke my heart with it, we were torn apart!
                  You put me on a devil's path - into the dark!

Day Star: Can you two not calm yourselves a little!
                  Soften your words, and be not so brittle!

Lone Bear: Come, Mother, let's us go to the longhouse,
                  In the interval, Hawk, you know my spouse...

Day Star: Is it not the strongest bonds, when they're broken,
                  Which leave the deepest swaths of devastation?
                  She holds fast to the laws of our elders.

White Hawk: I know she does and I do understand her:

She but lives by the pattern of her birth.

You look beautiful, Star, but your eyes are tired.

Day Star: Time assaults first and wears at our ports of sight:
Those doors where through tread the sufferings of life.

How's Whisp'ring Waters? *(Wife of White Hawk)*

White Hawk: She misses her sister.

Day Star: We were like sisters before the deep rift,
When the light of the Seneca eclipsed!

You know Grey Swan is right in what she said,
Though it's not my place your actions to condemn,
When you left the orb of our filial soul,
Burst as it were the central sun did explode.
All the law that governed and held us together,
In moments, on your leaving, dismembered:
Our own chief, the son of chiefs, had decided
Laws of our elders should not be abided!

White Hawk: It was to save a chief, the son of chiefs,
That I decided our laws hadn't the mercies
Necessary to our tribes continuing!
Laws are too rigid that take life for a limb:
That for accidents - condemn an existence!
That for a weakened frame - betray a spirit!

Day Star: That is but one law among our many.

White Hawk: Only one law should be upheld by many;
Its foundation should be one of mercy!

Day Star begins crying uncontrollably.

I'm sorry…

Day Star: It's just the pain that I'm feeling,
How every one and thing's disappearing!

Remember the Festival of the Maidens
When Whisp'ring Waters and I were claimants
Upon yours and Lone Bear's youthful spirits,
How we danced to the romantic rhythms!
How our unions were blessed by the Sachem,
How we all stood in lines of women and men
All young, strong and ornamentally dressed!
How we pledged our loves in the ceremony
I had and have never since been so happy!

Recall, we ran after the moon along the river
While hearing the canyons echoing our laughter!
We were buoyant as the silvered current,
Until we found the peace of an embankment:
A place for Ataensic to provide a coverlet!
'Twas a time the silver moon was glistering
In the textures of every flower and leaf.
The loyalty and love felt on that night,
Was the foremost bond of my filial life...
Why must what is most beautiful fall first?
And only anger that lingers with its curse!

Remember our companions and friends,
Who were of our wondrous generation,
It was between wars, when peace abounded,
We were free, our relations were giving,
We were a family of universal caring,
Of those beautiful souls, youthful faces,
With us at the Festival of the Maidens -
Most are dead now, all but few of our brothers,
Most molder on raised epitaphs to our elders!
Those that survive know not whither to go,
They keep counsel, as we all suffer alone!
I would give my soul for a moment's converse
With our old troupe of maidens and warriors!

When you took your leave of us, when you said,
"The Seneca law, not my son should be dead,"
A wound burst through the seed of every soul,
Our faith broke and fell from its sacred hold
Since then no one trusts the laws that hold us
And we suffer, as from a disease's corruptions!

White Hawk: My dear Sister, stop this agonizing!

Day Star: We have been born to an age of dying!
We cannot stop Death, nor can we stop fighting!

White Hawk: All right... all right... we have all been shaken,
Everything has changed of how we're related;
But I love you, Star, and I sorrow, Maiden,
That like the river waters, we may not return,
To the familiar bosom of our lost world!

Re-enter Lone Bear

Lone Bear: Still here, are you? My brother, Chief White Hawk,
Your honor would not stay you in idle talk!

White Hawk: No, I've been listening to Day Star and Fox;
It is my sincere hope to improve your lot.
I've come as special envoy from Prideaux...

Lone Bear: I had no idea that the General feared me so
Two embassies of peace - on one day alone?
My friends, now my foes - came to me this morning,
Now comes my brother, my love - my enemy,
Surely, with counsel for surrendering?

Not content annihilating forests,
Does England want death for all inhabitants?
Aye! England's great inexorable wheel rolls,
Razing the verdant world, crushing her souls.
This half-god, England, has broke her asunder

And laughs and revels over the plunder!

White Hawk: I understand your passion and your anger.

Lone Bear: Did you ever understand our father?
We are his sons, Chiefs of the Seneca,
We're the born defenders of Niagara;
You've come in company with her destroyers!

White Hawk: Not so! Like you, I come as her defender!
Like you, my whole soul is wrapt in this place
This wondrous garden, this realm of our race!
It is for love of her, I've England served,
By the post I've earned, I come to protect her!

Lone Bear: You! Protect her and guardian her vesture?

White Hawk: By Nature's verdict, England is now victor,
Serving England, I'll be this realm's protector!

Lone Bear: Do you say Ataensic crowns her killer?

White Hawk: Not her killer, her manifest superior!
And in this war, France's conqueror!
It is Ataensic, is it not, whose laws decide
The weak are sacrificed to greater might?
It is by Ataensic's natural edict of relations
The mightier consume the lesser nations!
England is greater by Ataensic's measure:
She's more numerous, stronger and swifter,
She moves in a unison, she's disciplined,
And she is superior foremost for her justice!
And I've found Prideaux's word to be good:
In his motives, resolves and acts, he is proof!

Lone Bear: A wondrous thing, a good man among them stands?
When how many are about here now, thousands?

White Hawk: I know that this is hard for you to endure,

But England is paragon'd by the law of nature!
Unless some force of Atensic's disappeared,
Or some greater god holds her judgment in fear,
The English have been her darling in career!

Prideaux, as enemy, will use you better
Than either the French or Aetensic's nature!
In fact, Prideaux honors you very greatly,
Just today, he wished that all his enemies,
Behaved in the charge of war like the French,
And abandoned 'fore him their bravest and best!

Lone Bear: Aye, they have! European love and hatred,
               We have known them both, and both are fatal!

Grey Swan re-enters quietly to overhear

White Hawk: It needn't be so, listen to me! Observe!
               You've understood, woven in nature's vesture,
               To honor the forces arrayed against you:
               In the daunting gauntlet of the wild wood,
               You have honored your opponent's forte -
               Now honor what England's strength may generate!
               Justice, based on the root of peace: mercy
               Given with forgiveness and understanding!
               That you may join England's growing family,
               In a gathering Empire of humanity!
               England's society is strengthened by mercy;
               It follows, our nations may also be!

Lone Bear: That sounds sweet…

Grey Swan: Ye gods! He's become a priest!

Lone Bear: I admit, I mistook the soldier's clothing.

Grey Swan: When they say what they want, it is with their love,
               When you grant it not, they bring crosses and guns!

251

Lone Bear: I've seen the object of your adjuration priest!
His lifeless image hanging on a leafless tree -
The honor paid his ineffectual ministry!

White Hawk: You mistake the party who is at mercy,
Such as it is, mercy's given voluntarily!
Prideaux could treat you as would Ataensic
Leaving you broken, subject to scavenge!
Or have abandoned you like the French,
Leaving you to the colonial's revenge!
Rather, he would embrace you in your need,
With all honors paid your former strength!
You have but to follow England's good law
And Niagara is ours: river and spawn!

Lone Bear: We've spoken to this notion with Pouchot,
I'll not enchain myself for the sake of a bone!
We're not dogs, willing slaves, for a home!

White Hawk: The laws are few which you would have to alter,
Like to not expose babes, who need be fostered,
Nor to hang enemies in sacrificial fires,
Nor eat an enemy's heart, as your law requires!
From these practices, the tribe must retire,
Remind me, why do you do such anyways?

Grey Swan: For babes who are born weak are born slaves;
Enemies whom we hang on trees to burn,
Through suffering, have their living weakness purged!
For enemies whose chests we pry apart:
We eat the strength of their living hearts!

White Hawk: As for babes killed for what they may lack,
Tribes strengthen, carrying them on their back!
Enemies shown mercy give the victor strength,
More than it destroys what of an enemy's weak!
Lastly, the strength in the heart of humanity
Grows by lessons learned through the gift of mercy!
For the English, it produces their great unity!

252

It's easier to abandon than care for lame babes,
It's easier to kill enemies than to ease their pains,
It's easier to devour a heart than to embrace one:
Waken your understanding, this peace may be won!
Trust the victorious justice of England!

Lone Bear: England's justice is reserved solely for those
Who live within the knot and tie of her folds!

White Hawk: Brother, as my young Hawk was threatened once
So are you now, whether or not it is just!
In this canyon, you are wounded and exposed:
Before gathering broods, you've been left alone!
As I saved my son, so would I save you,
From being transfixed to your certain doom!
The English have guns which issue forth a flame,
Which through the canyon caves can penetrate!
If they move against you, who will be saved?

Do not prove the weakest member of our tribe!
Waken, Lone Bear! Adapt you must, to survive!
Survive as England's honored enemy displayed -
Don't die a beaten dog, a whipped renegade!

Grey Swan: Listen him trumpet our opposite's glories,
We need not their justice or laws or mercies!

Lone Bear: Of nature's children, who's deemed most happy?
The wildest!   For they die defending their liberty!

Bring through our approaches your brave English -
Never will more men together perish!
I will fill all of yon living corridors
With pain and horror-bearing warriors,
Who will battle in the manner we are bred,
Like the Night Hawk with the Eagle - to the death!

Day Star: Oh, stop it! Do you know what you are saying?

Our brethren descend on us with our enemies,
In every skirmish, two Seneca will bleed!
If we are to survive, we must stop dying!

Grey Swan: You, my sometime daughter, should be the strong one!
You'll soon lead this clan and choose our Chieftains!

Day Star: Yes, I am to choose the next Chieftains of our line!
It would help if a male among us survives!
Who will? In the next struggle we are to fight!

White Hawk: I have learned English music, which teaches
Consonance lives either side of dissonance,
But you must seek to meet elusive harmony,
You must reach for it, else it's noise-making.

You two have set yourselves as in corse stone,
You've ceased to listen, you've refused to grow,
You are as dead, it seems, as our elder's bones!

Is it worth it, Lone Bear? A fight to the death?
To be annihilated in your wilderness?
You are deaf from Niagara's turbulence:
Impenetrable of heart, as are these forests!

It is I who serve our father's wish best,
I'll survive to be Niagara's defense!

Lone Bear: I wonder how we can have the same father?

White Hawk: Born alike, we differently reflect his aura!

Lone Bear: Red Fox! Take White Hawk away, out of my sight!
Let him rejoin his own, while yet there is light.
Day Star! Say goodbye to our one time friend,
Nor you, nor I, will see his dark face again!
Unless your loyalties would take you with him?

Day Star: It's here I stay, even if for one more day.

White Hawk: Mother, you weep! Not quite all made of stone!

Grey Swan: Go as you have gone, go your way alone!

White Hawk: You have two more days in which to consider:
                I advise you to survive by surrender!

Day Star walks along with Red Fox and White Hawk as they leave

Day Star: Mink is on his Recession of Becoming;
                He is due until morning to be wandering.
                Please let the English know he's just a boy,
                See you take him, with you I want him joined,
                That our single seed will not be destroyed!
                You must raise him to the age of man for me!

White Hawk: I still hope to change Lone Bear's thinking.
                We have Prideaux's word for this present peace.
                Lone Bear still has time to do the better thing!

Day Star: If it's forever…

White Hawk: I can no further think,
                But ungovernable pain assaults me!

End of Act Two Scene Three

ACT TWO
SCENE FOUR

JOHNSON, GAGE AND PRIDEAUX

Place: As before, in the camp of Prideaux

Present: Prideaux and Johnson and later entering Gage and Slattery

Scene: *As before.*

Prideaux: How goes our progress?

Johnson: Steady and aright.
It is another matter beyond our lines:
Attacks are occurring beyond our cordon,
With looting and murdering going on.
Homesteaders in numbers are on the run!
Some latch on bands of retreating French soldiers,
Some surrender to us to gain safe shelter.

Prideaux: With the law of the French Crown fallen,
And before our militia's force is arisen,
That nether world's for wild dogs to range in!
All the dark paths and forest corridors,
Teem with opposed heroes and monsters,
As they fight where there be no governing laws:
Where what holds down the brute in man is gone!

We have the forces! Some we'll let go from here -
Break off a battalion to move up the frontier!
Following hard the French retreat with our arms;
Let's hope present force prevents future harm.

Exit Johnson

                    Enter Gage and Slattery

257

Gage: General, I come to entreat further,
To bring conclusion to this Lone Bear matter.
My troops are here, ready to march from this place
And link with Amherst. Why should we delay?
Why should this one chieftain cost us a day?

Prideaux: In the first case, I granted three days' time!
That he have pause for the calming of his mind,
I gave word we should observe a term of warning
And that word was delivered him this morning!
Our word is all-important in this chaos,
It's the order on which future peace will rest!

Prideaux walks before the ordered tables and points to a chronometer.

It's like this chronometer, this mechanism,
A series of wheels, springs, weights and balances:
Each interdependent and interwoven,
Even these large massy wheels in motion
Depend on lesser wheels keeping momentum.
If the interdependent motion is upset,
If even a small wheel is slightly bent,
This mechanism will never keep time again!
If our word once given is then corrupted,
Our relationship with the natives will be disrupted.

Gage: That is nonsense!

Prideaux: Did God not form the World?

Gage: Aye!

Prideaux: Did he not do so in the form of his word?
A mechanism interdependent made good?
Worlds great and small are destroyed by falsehood!

Gage: This is ridiculous! We have the armor
To move these prone Natives from their caverns!

We can advance and be at Amherst's shoulder
In three days: the prerogative of a victor!

Prideaux: We've the means of sending our whole martial corpus,
Six thousand regulars, munitions and ordnance,
To crush the last ambitions of these Natives!
But from their ashes will rise resentments
That will forever poison our relations!
We could enforce on them strict obedience,
And confine them in chains and prisons,
But such blood wounds will seed new rebellions!
Or mercy may find a better, easier way,
Through paths where lions ought fear to prey!
We will give to Chief Lone Bear his three days!
I will, and we must, keep England's lawful word,
For our law is the present order of this world.

Re-enter Johnson

Did I not see you six weeks past in Albany?
Were you not in the house of the Presbytery?[102]
It is not enough to take your soul to that meeting,
But you must take that house about in your soul;
It's more than sung songs and bent knees you owe -
You must act in accord with our highest law!

What from you, Slattery?

Slattery: Begging pardon, Lord,
But there's more to Little Niagara's fort
Than you may know; there've been couriers,
Heavy laden with satchels, seen traveling, sir,
From the fallen French forts, or their ruins,
And from capitals of the Algonquin nations,[103]
Moving swiftly, secretly, here, locally;
It must be something very worth transporting!

---

102 Presbytery: Refers to attendance at church services.
103 Alongquin nations: Allies of the French.

Perhaps some treasured, sacred reliquaries,
Perhaps gold or statues from French missions,
Cased in silver, studded with precious gems!
This much we know, these treasures are secrets,
Else, why send them here with such hurry and care,
To the still-defended stronghold of Lone Bear?

Prideaux: Yes, if we don't kill him, how do we rob him?

This Niagara is a sacred area,
And will remain so, under rule of the Seneca,
While subject to England's overarcing will!
If White Hawk's mission of peace to Lone Bear fails,
I will go, confronting what danger there travails -
And I'll not kill Lone Bear, nor will I rob him,
At the worst, I'll prove the best Samaritan!
You may leave now!

Exit Gage and Slattery

Johnson: I have some select men here
Will soon be ready to move up the frontier.

Prideaux: Even in fellowships, always an opposite!
Be wary of those two, will you, Johnson?
This Gage has been my constant contrary
Engaged since long past in subtle rivalry.
He's always thinking, a man of stark ambition,
His mind is subdued, by delusive goals driven,
Thoughts of the undone haunt his restless hours,
With untaken actions and unassumed powers!

Johnson: I've noticed he's a man narrowly focused.

Prideaux: And he has formed this natural alliance
With the base wants of that supply sergeant!
Whose dangerous desires may prove fuel to flame:
Together they might focus and concentrate
On powers they may grasp and things they can take!

Johnson:	You and this man Gage, always at odds, eh?
Prideaux:	The momentum of the spheres in contrary directions Balances motion in whole solar systems, And as two poles hold a world together, There are opposites, even among brothers!
Johnson:	How 'bout we get to work testing the new cannons?
Prideaux:	Let's check it, and labor to make no use of them!

End of Act Two Scene Four

ACT TWO
SCENE FIVE

ARRIVALS OF ALLIES

Place: Little Niagara

Present: Lone Bear, Day Star, Grey Swan, Red Fox, and Half Moon.

Scene: *The scene is one of activity, with warriors coming and going and some emissaries of the Indian nations arriving and leaving. Lone Bear is in discussion with an emissary of an Algonquin-affiliated tribe, the Abenaki.*

Half Moon: We will stand with our brother Seneca
And do battle for sacred Niagara!
I may pledge three hundred warriors
Will be readied, and we will return to here,
Before light fills through the Moon's silver sphere.
Our men will fight well, this place will be saved,
By our warring spirits and our souls of flame!

And herewith Lone Bear! Honorable Sachem!
We've brought this vessel of Seneca wampum,
Restored to you, to fill your treasury,
With the woven word of your people's history!

Lone Bear: I thank you, Half Moon, and the Abenaki!
For attending brethren in extremity
Your fidelity is measure of your glory!
And thank you for fulfilling our request
For that wampum which over time we've sent
As faithful record of our elders' action:
We lose ourselves, with lost memory of them!

Half Moon: I wish you well until our time of return!

Half Moon exits

Day Star: The Sun is down and shadow drifts through the world,
              The wind rises over the waters, through the trees,
              While Mink remains at dangerous liberty!

Lone Bear: I've sent men for him. We'll send another group.
              The English would be fools to break their own truce!

Red Fox: Of those who fight with us, what's our number?

Lone Bear: Six hundred join our band of warriors,
              And we've yet to hear from many nations -
              My hopes rise with every legation!

Red Fox: It is not enough to match with their men and guns!
              Six thousand more men would not be enough!

Lone Bear: Were I to fight alone, like the blind boar,
              I should fight as fiercely, forevermore!
              My patience with counsel begins to wear down!
              I tire that my hope must always meet your doubt!

Day Star: It is not Fox alone who voices the painful truth,
              But Fox and White Hawk, I and others too…
              Your noble obstinacy may mean our doom!

Red Fox: The foremost warriors of our noble kind
              Cannot withstand this crushing change of time!
              From riverbeds to forests to the firmament,
              In the waters, the Earth and sky, it's evident -
              That the pattern of our existence has shifted
              Since England took her discovering steps
              On the paths of this once-virgin wilderness.

              Look! To the signs that appear all around you
              From the stars of heaven to the Sun and moon,
              From the topless pines, to the earth bound herbs

All Earth's creatures scream to you their words:
The storm comes Lone Bear! Have you not heard?

Lone Bear: My courage surpasses that of our brothers!

Day Star: It's your wisdom needs prove superior!

Lone Bear: Soon, I will surpass all things living in anger!
Virtue is immoveable and so is my valor!

Red Fox: Your valor will blaze like a night's meteor,
Which fills the sky with ineffectual fire.
Swiftly he flames, as quickly he transpires,
And space where his flame of glory was alight
Is soon o'erveiled in a gathering night!

All these portents that we presently see
Aren't waverings of changeable things,
But the carved form of evolving destiny
'Fore which there's no winning or escaping,
Only the agile virtue of adapting!
I plead once more! Listen better than the stones,
Don't prison living flesh in our elders' bones!

Grey Swan: Where are the brave Seneca whom once I knew?
You two! Like White Hawk, would surrender too?
Oh! Why could I not leave my fatal child
To the indiscriminate wrath of the wild?
Or why could I not have drowned him 'neath this tide
That 'midst these roaring waters he had died,
Rather than he led a generation to suicide!

Red Fox: Perhaps to war with the inevitable
Is futile action and battle suicidal!

Lone Bear: What will you do? I want no more arguing!

Red Fox: As I must! I will do what's necessary…

Lone Bear: That is all that I have an ear for hearing!

Exit Red Fox, Day Star now comes close to Lone Bear as Grey Swan departs in anger.

Day Star: This is the first time I have felt my fears,
It wakes my sense, the horror of war nears!
I feel a wrenching in the depths of my soul
As the unknown bursts through custom holds:
Our world is fragmenting beyond our control!
They are here, Lone Bear! At the impenetrable -
About to separate, the inseparable,
Soon to surmount the insurmountable,
We are about to know…the unspeakable!

These impassable cliffs were not high enough;
This forest not thick enough that shielded us;
These sacred waters were not deep enough;
These turbulent waves afford no harbor for us!

Niagara, the womb and cradle of the world,
Where the seed of all mortal forms were figured:
The unpolluted foundation of the Earth:
From whose waters all life first emerged,
Is about to be crushed by an uneathly scourge!

Lone Bear: The world may alter, fall or die as it will,
I'll remain true to myself and our elders still!
Though all the fiends with knives convene at my throat,
I'll battle, at that edge of life, to the last stroke!

Day Star: Where else can I go? What else can I do?
None of my pleas have any import with you!
We were born and bloomed together in life;
Unless you change, together we will die!

Lone Bear: It's you alone who try my rightful resolve,
I would save you and save you above all!

This time makes even my strong frame to quake -
Are my pains and sorrows leading me to mistake?

Day Star :   We should not all die for one decision made,
Only a law that saves life should prove so great!

Lone Bear: What is more important than how we relate?
It is the law by which we live that is at stake!

Day Star: It is the law of Ataensic's that has us cornered,
That's put our predator on our border,
Perhaps we perish here - for a lesser order!
Lone Bear, what good are even our highest laws
If our strongest cannot survive its flaws?
A law whose weakness threatens our strongest -
Should be abandoned in face of such events,
Replaced by law that protects even our weakest!
That protects the weak, the prone and abandoned -
As France has left us…on this penetrable island!

Lone Bear: I've never noted such law being England's!
I will take the time that the English give,
I will take the time to give more thought to this.

Day Star: Thank you, husband, at least to sleep on it.

Red Fox re-enters.

Red Fox: There's a group arrived from that reinforcement
Who were destroyed in the march for the fortress.
These few are survivors of the massacre…

*A breathless French soldier and three Algonquin warriors enter the
area of the fire.*

Lone Bear: Cowardice or strength allowed you to endure?

Fr. Soldier: No sir. It's chance alone that we've survived,
It's only happenstance that we're alive!

267

Day Star:	Come and seat yourselves beside our calumet, This eve, early autumn sits chill in the wind.
Lone Bear:	You've come from La Belle Famille? Speak!
Fr. Soldier:	We were marching for the fort under Captain Aubry…
Lone Bear:	Haven't the French a General fighting?
Fr. Soldier:	We marched with thirteen hundred souls at first.
Lone Bear:	So your column was dispersed?
Fr. Soldier:	Aye, it burst! The attack's suddenness created panic: Like a wave, each person the next affected, No one in the riot held his temperament - Once brave souls were driven to madness!
Lone Bear:	You found your way here?
Fr. Soldier:	Through pathless forests! The surrounding wilderness is teeming now, With British and allied parties on the prowl!
Red Fox:	We have heard some of yours took to bateaux For nether Canada or for the Isle aux Noix?
Fr. Soldier:	Those fortunate enough to have made the boats. The British scour every crack and hollow, To imprison the brigade's wayward stragglers! The English thread through this forest maze, Like an hundred-eyed panther of winding gaze!
Lone Bear:	We'll soon renew the war with the British!
Fr. Soldier:	You may count me out. I've had enough of it. If you don't object, I'll retreat with my friends.

Lone Bear: As you choose.

Fr. Soldier   Today has offered enough abuse!
               But what is that moaning and dirge-like sound,
               It's a melodic whining, whose pathos is profound?

Lone Bear: It comes from our Calumet, from the burning fume:
               Ants in the wood perish, singing that mournful tune,
               Having chanced to nest in the wrong knot of wood.

               End of Act Two Scene Five

ACT TWO
SCENE SIX

GENERAL GAGE MEETS WHITE HAWK

Place: The administrative chamber within the Castle of Fort Niagara

Present: Brig. Gen. Gage, Maj. Robert Rogers, William Johnson, Maj. John Slattery and standing guards. Later, White Hawk arrives.

Scene: *The Administrative Office of Fort Niagara is a darkly lit, large room with a broad wooden desk at the back wall. There is a stand for muskets and sabers and one for coats near to the entry door, beside a full-length standing mirror. On the walls are artistic renderings of past French commanders of the fort and framed notes of French nobles and administrators, as well as the Royal Charter. The French flag stands in the corner behind Gen. Gage, who is seated rigidly at the desk, while Rogers, Johnson, Slattey, and a lieutenant stand before him.*

Gage: Lieutenant! I want these relics of the French
      Out of my office! And out of my fortress!

Johnson: They will be expecting to share in our grief,
      And out of respect to attend a ceremony.
      They shared his battles, they shared his victory!
      They ate of his cold meals and bled where he bled:
      To them, he's the face and soul of all England.

Gage: We are marching in the morning, all's ready,
      I won't be stayed, by the gods, for ceremony!

To Rogers

      Now you're good to go? You've all necessary?
      The men, guns and munitions?

Rogers: Ready.

Gage: You'll go with the guns and Major Slattery;
                    You can steal in, and make it thorough and swift?

Rogers: By noon you'll have a free road, no problems!
                    We're clear.

Gage: You're the proper sort for the frontier.

Lieutenant: Pardon sir, but the Seneca, White Hawk's, here.

Enter White Hawk

Gage: Very good, White Hawk, let's know, how did it go?

White Hawk: I've a response, to be given to Prideaux.

Gage: Three hours ago, our friend Prideaux was killed
                    Testing the cannon; one misfired during drill.

Johnson: A part of a missile struck Prideaux's face,
                    Through there is his broken frame, lying in state.
                    A moment passed, no more, and he met his end,
                    By the chance of war, he suffered an accident.

Johnson walks close to White Hawk to whisper.

                    White Hawk! With this man delicately tread!

Gage: I repeat, what is there worthy for me to hear?

White Hawk: The matter stands as before with Lone Bear:
                    He is considering his alternatives.
                    I made strongest arguments that he come in,
                    That he give up arms and join our alliance!

Gage: He'll have his chance to renounce his defiance.

He'll surrender now - to be in compliance!

White Hawk: You... what?

Johnson: Gage orders a march to commence
On Little Niagara, two contingents,
Whose armed force departs one hour from hence!

Gage: They're ordered to request Lone Bear's surrender,
Or his forces will be forcibly sequestered!

White Hawk: That is not Prideaux's promise! We've three days!

Gage: Yes, it was three days, look up, the Moon's phase!
It is ever night when so glows her changing face.

To Rogers

So, you're certain, we can march by noon then?
Note the moon's full, she is luminescent.

Rogers: Forest shadows will conceal us certainly,
While the moon's strong beams will light the clearings,
We will see any of their warriors moving.

Gage: After the march, and preparations you make,
See that the call for surrender is raised!
If they fire on you, begin your cannonade,
Your fire should be contemporaneous,
You'll shock the inhabitants with suddenness.

White Hawk: What!

Johnson: Gage speaks with authority of England.

White Hawk: Which one? One on whose law the Sun never sets?
Or one I see here, conspiring in darkness?
What future is wrought by this perverse chance?

Like night and day, England shows two aspects!
The face of England's noblest is interred,
And in shadow, this guise of murder lurks?
Prideaux was the luminescence of the British
While you are her virtue's darkest eclipse!
Gage! You act as though you're victorious
But your vice feeds on Prideaux's success!
Your vice parades in virtue's cloak and name,
But a whore, in vestal clothes, is still the same!
The profane that hides behind virtue's name!

And in England's name, this evil's to emerge?
Where round our sacred fire will butchers lurk -
To commit this stealthy, murderous work?
Do you wish to view a true savage figure?
Come, Gage! It's here! In the depths of this mirror!

Gage: Captain! I suggest you remember who you are!
All I'm doing is preparing for our march!

The Lieutenant returns

Lieutenant: Sir, we've captured an Abenaki warrior,
With beads of wampum, he is a courier.
His people prepare to war beside Lone Bear,
Their war party will soon be marching here.

Gage: Those who massacred our people, the Abenaki,
After we'd surrendered Fort William Henry?[104]
The same Abenaki who murdered our women!
Who massacred our settlers and their children!

Rogers: Aye!

White Hawk: The Abenaki aren't an Iroqouis tribe!
They're not Seneca! We weren't at that fight!

---

104 Fort William Henry: Site of the 1757 siege by the French and their Native American allies; in a massacre following British surrender, many survivors, including women and children, were killed.

Gage: Which Indians do we face then, in this contest?
The merciful? You, too, have two aspects!

White Hawk: You cannot break Prideaux's good given word,
Battle, if you will, forthright as a soldier!

Johnson: You are addressing your commander, Captain!

White Hawk: If you proceed, I will find ways to warn him!

Gage: That, Captain, is an offer of sedition!

Johnson: Captain Hawk! I advise you to listen!

Gage: I've heard enough, the Captain's bound for prison.
Prison this man, Lieutenant! Do it at once!

Rogers, get you moving on your commissions,
If they do not surrender, fire upon them,
While mindful to spare the women and children!

As he is being subdued and dragged away

White Hawk: Prideaux was the flower of England's promise,
While you're the seed of her future nemesis,
With your blind, merciless expedience!

Gage: In war, we must seize on all advantages!

White Hawk: What is the virtue inherent in a higher law,
If those who should uphold it, don't hold it at all!
Where is the fabled English justice and mercy?
I'll tell you! With Prideaux it will be buried!
A broken cannon has broken the law of England,
An accident has killed England's best champion,
And who remains serves in contempt of him -
For you would fall on the prone and abandoned!
You and Prideaux could not be more opposite…

Gage: Please! I must prepare this army's movements,
            And this present time is expeditious.
            While moving for England's forward positions,
            I will give no more ear to tribulations!

End of Act Two

ACT THREE
SCENE ONE

ON THE CLEFTS

Place: At mid-height of the mountain above and overlooking Little Niagara Falls, the habitations, the chapel, and the calumet.

Present: Lone Bear

Scene: *Lone Bear, as he stands against a backdrop of dense trees, gazes over his homestead. Darkness has fallen. The moon avails to shed some light through the interspersed hollows of the forest. It is reflected on the river, and illuminates the longhouses and chapel of the Seneca homestead with a subdued white silver light. The ruddy flame of the Calumet relieves the night's colorless surroundings. The flames are amplified and stirred as the winds have heightened to a gale through the canyons.*

Lone Bear: Red Fox is right. We've not seen the embassies
      Whose promise would relieve our necessity!
      Damn the weak French for breaking faith with us!
      In war only their wish, not their strength, was just.
      Will without strength, strength without will's not enough!
      So after all these trials we are come to this,
      We stand at the brink of a precipice.

      Aereskouy, I have always loved you best,
      When you descend here with your strength-filled wrath!
      When your winds bend the majesty of the pines,
      When clouds hang darkly low, menacing the skies,
      When waters burst in flood, drowning the shore,
      For then I have felt you near, my Over Lord!

      Now these forces of nature are changing:
      I'm the object, not the witness of their fury!
      There comes a force 'pon us overwhelming -

Force that falls like your seasons... unrelenting!

But you know beneath winter's coldest ice,
You allow your children the breath of life,
That they might their lives and loves sustain,
Through the gauntlets of seasonal change!
If I'm to keep faith to your living order,
I must do so, as I perish from nature!

If it's the end, let me not misuse your breath;
Let's die before I say aught unlike myself,[105]
Let me die true to you, Aereskouy,
Let our relation not change, nor be destroyed!
For there's no force can pry my will to change,
I, whose virtue no earthly pains can break!

Lord, is there something yet that I do not see
In the folds of your emanating beauty,
Whereby you might otherwise have led me?
Would you not rouse me with ferocious warning?
By fires of sky-shattering lightning,
Or by cracking Earth's ribs and quaking,
Or by some other fearful summoning,
To acquaint me that your law is changing?
With a spirit beneath of every leaf,
Could you not have sent but one - to move me?

Or has some greater god manacled you,
Into the slavery and silence of servitude?
I hear not the war cries of your Thunderbird![106]
Is it that the true monarch of the forest arrives,
From some nether outpost, unknown of the skies,
And your thousand lesser spirits flee his guise?
Has the great god impressed the forest spirits
To some necessary metamorphosis?

---

105 Aught unlike myself: Cononchet of the Narragansets said he preferred to die "before I have spoken a word unworthy of Cononchet."
106 Thunderbird: Bird found in Native American myths that posseses supernatural power and strength.

Perhaps your body comprises many tributaries
Winding many forms through a single being,
Who now flow in course of one divinity?

Fact is, the English kill your multitudes
While the free and various Forest is subdued!
I don't envy your spirit's eternity:
Which feels life's passing, and death's agony,
In a sorrowing soul, that's everlasting!

Maybe the English are stronger, thus their law,
But how does keeping the weak make one strong?
What did Hawk say? They are stronger for the weak
They carry on their back, though their back would break?
'Twould make them stronger from love's generation!
Our law treats differently of imperfection:
We purge weak members as 'twere vices.
Perhaps in addition to purging ourselves of flaws,
Mercy for the weaker than ourselves is greater law?
Perhaps it's true, one's strength magnifies,
By supplying strength to those Nature denies!
By extending the love one owes one's children
To derelicts of nature, who bear undue burden.
Perhaps by this sacrifice, a people are strengthened!
I know that my strength has had to expand
As I have filled the loss of every man!
Perhaps we strengthen by gauntlets we take ourselves
To help those who by no fault cannot help themselves?
Wouldn't man's love heighten serving those in need?
Wouldn't one's love strengthen, serving selflessly?
And what cure it would be for our own weak vice,
This healing impulse of virtuous enterprise!
Greater life would issue from accepting such strife
As our own weakness would be further sacrificed!
And by expanding the scope of love's generation,
By expanding the wellspring of virtue and devotion,
Would we not be stronger facing opposition?
A people by a loving law so entwined

Would battle harder to protect their common life:
They would brave acts of supernal sacrifice!

England's vast victory does put me in awe -
As people are only as strong as their law!
Think how the French were casually swept
From all the strongholds of this continent!
But there's the block: these two are of one stock,
Brothers in opposition, interlocked!
How do these two turn love's golden key
Which adds to generation, empires of strength?
They nailed its prophet to a leafless tree,
And since, they love and ignore him faithfully!
If that is how they treat their Lord and King
How then will they treat a steadfast enemy?

Have they shown us any true lenity?
They save it, as do we, for our families,
Filial love is known to all, even the beasts.
There generation's empire has its frontier -
Where family meets the unknown stranger,
Or worse, when one counters an estranged brother!
The French and English, brothers in divide,
Like to the cleft between White Hawk and I,
Whose love was fractured by a changing time!
White Hawk is like these others of mankind;
I find them all dubious of word and mind.

The French did not keep faith or their word;
For this vice they're lost and are accursed!
Nor do the greater English keep to love's word
No, Aereskouy! In war, they keep only yours!
They always return to your uttermost law,
When in the fell passes of war enthralled:
The weaker before the greater will fall!

From their God and his ways I avert my eyes,
Faith in the God of my fathers I consign!

To the end I'll obey nature's hardest edict -
That life is reserved first to the mightiest!
In the test of war it is ever the same:
Therein, it is only this law which reigns!

I'll give as I expect to take, nothing,
In way of weakness or the way of mercy!
I'll battle till every injury's twisted sting
Winds within me to form a living armory,
And revenging wounds, gauge my ferocity!
I will battle on to my own extinction
And die the brightest flame of our nation!
Come then, Aereskouy, usher me…
My life's battle is in your honest keeping!
I am ready for my final trial, the last test,
The last issue of our native prowess!

But let's first hear the last rush of these waves;
Feel the cool impress of your Moon's last rays;
Apprehend the last breath of Thee in the breeze,
And hear the Swan sing a final melody…
I am but the last of native spirits to go,
The straggling exile of a world overthrown!

End of Act Three Scene One

ACT THREE
SCENE TWO

AT PRISON GATE

Place: The Castle Gaol

Present: White Hawk and a Guard; later William Johnson

Scene: *The confine White Hawk inhabits is a small room containing one cot with no blanket or cushion. The surrounding walls are whitewashed. There is a very small aperture to the outside, in the east wall, allowing air and the moonlight into the chamber. One wall consists of criss-crossing iron bars with a central door bolted by a massy iron lock.*

White Hawk: Damn the English and their broken promise!
              Whose laws are here broken? England's justice!
              Like any people, are they not given to corruption?
              Yet they claim the name of justice, Englishmen!
              This morning I was honored, a friend and ally;
              I was ambassador to rebels of my tribe,
              Future rule of Niagara I was consigned,
              And by this eve, all's been devoured by time!

              One cannon misfires and the world explodes,
              For with it fractured Prideaux's binding oath!
              They keep their word, as long as it self serves,
              It's otherwise protean as the waters!
              The sky's million stars could unseat themselves
              And descend through a limitless void pell mell,
              Each a rebel meteor, borne through confusion,
              In an unexampled revolution,
              Leaving not a single star's light left behind,
              To remind how 'twas the once-peaceful night;
              All this fall of a universe or a world
              By chance and time must some time occur,
              But a man, or a nation, may keep their word!

Empires of men can have their rise and fall again,
With peoples, customs, histories and legends,
Their discoverers, adventurers, traders and militias,
Their towns, cities, states and constitutions,
As they can all arise, so can they descend,
Like the French, to a well-trod oblivion:
All this fall of a nation or of a world
By chance and time may chance to occur,
But a man, or a nation, may keep their word!
Everything that lives and breathes is breakable,
But a man's given word - that's sustainable!
And Gage breaks England's to keep a schedule!
And I have served him? I have played his fool?
Serving England, I'm become a criminal tool?
I've misled Lone Bear and my people to their doom....
In time they had to flee, they will be consumed!

What have I sacrificed? I sacrificed all
To live with my son by a higher law!
But you may build walls round the strongest law
And it may not survive its human flaw!
Prideaux! You were the foremost man I've known
But by your brethren, your glories are blown,
The golden vessel you bore, they would not hold,
The vessel of peace is broken, blood will flow,
I would, by the gods, the first were my own!

My warning screams could crack the intersky
If I thought it could sound over the river's tide!
Nothing I can do here will save the prone lives
Of Day Star, Lone Bear! I would give my eyes!

Johnson: Guard!

Guard: Yes, sir?

Johnson: Report to the watch officer!

Guard: Sir!

The guard exits

Johnson: Well, we cannot leave you here, can we, Hawk?
              You all right? Here, let me unclasp the lock.

White Hawk: As your honored friend and brave companion,
              I was chucked down here in this damned prison!
              Now you free a renegade Native?

Johnson: You want a sad tale to make you want to die?
              Far worse than this happens all the damn time,
              When the hordes of human vices combine!

White Hawk: I raised myself by wings of constancy,
              Like a skylark, on winds of adversity,
              I overcame obstacles, all opposition,
              To be cast down, stumbling on this accident!

Johnson: Would you rather be with Prideaux, our friend?

White Hawk: He was the luminescence of England!

Johnson: We drew a bad lot: Gage's arrival chanced:
              The wrong time, wrong man, wrong circumstance!
              His like can sure cause hell for a long while,
              But he won't long survive the fruits of his guile -
              Justice and he, late or soon, will reconcile!

White Hawk: Set me free an hour and I'll see to it straight!

Johnson: I don't care to see three funerals this day.
              You must fly swift now and save those you can -
              You'll have to move fast, Rogers sure as hell has!

White Hawk   He's already threading the forest's maze?

Johnson:	Be sure you make straight for him, he knows your face!
White Hawk:	Can you care for my kin, for John make such claim, Until such time as I have something arranged?
Johnson:	I'd be honored, and Whisp'ring Water?
White Hawk:	Oh Lord! What has war left... unslaughtered?
Johnson:	I will see to her care too, be assured. My dear Hawk, you have from me, my good word.
White Hawk:	You've brought me a musket and tomahawk too?
Johnson:	You'll need 'em. After battle, what will you do?
White Hawk:	Outrun the widening scope of your England And find peace, some unpenetrated island.
Johnson:	There's always been peace and respect between us.
White Hawk:	Damn pity that can't be said of all of us!
Johnson:	Ambition, ambition, ambition, huh? Go by the side gate, you still have friends there.
White Hawk:	Thanks, my dear friend, I'll see you when all's clear.
Johnson:	Aye, we will. Those will be some beautiful days. Farewell, stay safe, and survive to celebrate.

End of Act Three Scene Two

ACT THREE
SCENE THREE

FORTIFYING LITTLE NIAGARA

Place: The Seneca homestead of Little Niagara

Present: Lone Bear, Day Star, Grey Swan, Red Fox, the French and Indian exiles, and assorted warriors and maidens.

Scene: *Some two hundred Seneca gather for a hurried council at the central location of Little Niagara's embankment. The moonlight, the calumet, and many torches illuminate the area. The wind is high, and the moon is perched over the river, making it a bright and churning channel. There is a rise beside the calumet that persons occupy as they speak to be better heard.*

1st Warrior: We looked everywhere within a day's stride -
                Nor Mink, nor his signs, were evident to our eyes.

2nd Warrior: But there was much to see: patrols are moving,
                Investing through Niagara's surroundings.
                Nor could we walk, nor run, nor take a turn,
                Without some contingent came through our wood!
                They move in manner swift and unconfined,
                Sweeping the forests and capturing our kind.
                There are many battalions moving round us
                Searching us out, capturing our stray ones!

1st Warrior: 'Twas yesterday we ruled all these forests -
                Now we tread like lost, criminal vagrants!

Day Star: I will go. I can go to find Mink now.

2nd Warrior: You'll have to ask leave of the British crown!

Lone Bear: *To Day Star*	Mink knows how to escape anyone's notice - Was he not bred on the paths of this forest? Or he can fight off their best combatants!
Day Star:	Yes, bred here, but not he nor we can stay here!
Red Fox: *Audible to all*	Lone Bear, your wife voices a sensible fear, Should we not embark women in the bateaux; And set them a course for the Isle of Noix?
2nd Warrior:	The British infest on the north embankment: They'll be sailing through a hostile gauntlet!
A Maiden:	If we cannot leave now, nor can we stay, When may we go? And what will be our way?
Grey Swan:	I see dress and ornaments of the Seneca, Sure that's our calumet, and this Niagara! Yet I see not one Seneca among you? Or maidens who know what's necessary to do? We must ratchet up our courage to its best, Let the bravest of us circle this calumet And give our sacred wampum this defense: That no matter odds, we fight to the death!

Since when do the Seneca accept chains?
We will not! Not while I'm member to our race!
Since when do Guardians of the Western Gate
Allow others to choose our people's fate?
Since when has any other than ourselves,
Ruled the woods and waters of this realm?
Then let us take up the hatchet and musket!
As they seek easy going through these forests,
Let's make bloody hell of Britain's descent.
Let's make her pay death for their conquest!

For love of Aereskouy and Ataensic,
Let's fight and die for life of the wilderness!

For us is there anything greater to serve?
Is there a higher cause in this passing world?

Warriors: Let the British find us ready –
Heatedly   Die fighting!

I'll swim in blood before I'm stopped…

                                        Die riving!
Better to die!

                        We will not be bent slaves!

Let them be slain!

                        Who would live another day?

Red Fox: Brothers and Sisters! Please hear my counsel!
Grey Swan has rightly just asked if there be
A greater cause for our fighting and dying,
Than this news that British arms are arriving?

I think we must first ask: what have we fought for?
And who was our ally throughout the war?
We fought for liberty in our Niagara,
For the ancient stronghold of the Seneca!
But as we plainly see by our surroundings,
Securing this land is beyond our ability,
For our chief prop and ally turned weakling!

We thought the French, and their Kingdom
Comprised of valorous and worthy brethren;
Yet our hopes were the first cause they abandoned!
We were wrong to fight beside the French then:
Such are effects of imperfect councils of men,
When even life's issue on perfection depends,
And we are left to ask, what's best for our nation?

In memory of our forebears and their laws,

We are asked for our lives, and that is our all!
We are asked to overcome our fear of death,
And die to honor our forebears' cerements:
A perfect sacrifice requiring our last breath!
Ought sacrifice's cause be of perfection,
If we're to fight to our annihilation?

Where do we turn for the perfect messenger?
Who or what is perfect in action and word?
The stars are stolid, and they are also voiceless,
Perfect in their motion, as in their detachment!
We may beckon and pray to their crystal spheres
But they obtain beyond, ne'er venturing here.
Then there are the thousand earthly spirits
Through which the Spirit makes itself manifest,
Who speak in their thousand various voices!
In the mix is there not much that's ambiguous?
Perhaps the essence of law has been missed?
It's possible our thousand laws amount to naught
And the highest law, to our memory's lost,
And we are asked to die for a lesser cause!
We are good servants to our ancient customs:
In our raiment, our dance and in our wampum,
We obey the thousand laws given to our sires
But can we be sure we know - no law is higher?
Are our laws worthy that we all presently die?
Or should we not question: What's the law of life?
Is there a greater law by which we may survive?
A law by which we may walk with all mankind?

Perhaps we need not make life our sacrifice,
But the enchaining vice of unmoving pride!
And the blindness which becomes life's confine!
Perhaps it's now we need adapt to a new time
And leave the wounds of ancient battles behind!

A multitude of contrary shouts arise from the assembly, then Lone Bear ascends.

Lone Bear:	Yes! We follow in the course of our fathers!
	Nor we, nor the British know any law higher
	Than to pursue virtues of our forbear's desire:
	Ours is but to defend home, theirs is for empire!
	We have heard time and again of this discourse
	And I say! There is one law, life has one course,
	One Aereskouy fulfills without remorse:
	That life's reserved to those that are mightiest
	And the weaker left, are from life rightly swept!
	And that it matters not when but how we die,
	For we must show faith in defending God's right -
	That we die and die bravely beneath his eye!
	Not fearful! Rather facing that obstacle,
	And proving fear, by faith, is surmountable!

Affirmative shouts drown out Red Fox initially, then he is heard.

Red Fox:	Brothers, Sisters, yet hear me. Do not deny me!
	No one in his heart and sinew is more mighty
	Or brave or more beautiful or more stubborn
	Than Lone Bear, the greatest of our chieftains!
	He will defend our thousand laws with his virtue,
	But the might of his virtue will destroy you!
	Have a thought for the future of our sons
	Before you lose your life for a forebear's love!
	Perhaps life's not always reserved the mightiest,
	Perhaps to survive, we need also be wisest!
1st Warrior:	Red Fox! Lead us 'gainst the British or leave us!
2nd Warrior:	Kill first the Seneca that are rebellious!
Red Fox:	Peace! I am willing to commit, like you,
	To what we find it necessary to do!
Lone Bear:	Peace, brethren! There's always two views of the world,
	But only one way our fathers are best served.

Red Fox, we thank you and you have been heard.

Now we must discern all this cove's approaches
And fill them this morning with men and weapons,
The periphery will be assigned the bravest!
Watch to the north, when dawn will be rising
For the coming of the Abenakis!

Among Lone Bear, Day Star and Red Fox alone

Day Star: Dear gods! I know not what to want of it,
To find Mink, to bring him home through the gauntlet?
He cannot aid our defense, only suffer it!
Lone Bear! Has not enough of us been cleft,
Since England and France severed the continent?
Did we not suffer enough by the rebellion,
Disuniting us from our near relations?
That made the Iroquois a fractured nation!
War's taken enough warriors and maidens,
And now threatens even our seed most sacred?

My husband! Mink is the only life we have,
You must let our one son survive the attack!
Leave one thing undivided, unmolested,
Someone to survive beneath the heavens…
Something so fundamental and blessed!
Our virtues so combine in him - let him live!

Lone Bear: Like all things that live, he must take his chances
And dance in sympathy, as nature dances.
To survive, he must show his mightiness!

Red Fox, you and yours defend the high plateau -
If you see the English, give warning halloa

Day Star: What more will come of this appalling night:
To my dearest love, I might never say goodbye!

Grey Swan enters exultantly.

Grey Swan: The spirits of the brave will strengthen with rage!
                Once such violent spirits are in motion,
                They will career on their own momentum,
                They will meet at a point of acceleration:
                Nothing any longer can hold the fury back
                Any more than you can calm the cataract!
                We'll become the perfect genius of attack
                And rip wide, bloody paths through England's ranks -
                The bear will face the angling panther
                And we'll die or thrive at the point of danger!

As Red Fox exits, he speaks to himself.

Red Fox: No, it's the lone bear against a swarm of bees -
                He stands in the way of their fertilizing seed
                And empire that will flower with their honey.
                Here they will descend on their industrious wings
                And bring death, Lone Bear, by a thousand stings!

Grey Swan: I am proud of you, Lone Bear, in this great cause,
                You fulfill the ancient will of nature's laws.

Grey Swan, Lone Bear, Day Star walk by the Soldier, refugee of La Belle Famille.

Fr. Soldier: There's no way out of it, there's no way clear,
                Far from home, I am to die alone: it's here!
                I'm between two blind, deaf ambitions at war;
                I'm to survive but till there comes the storm!

End of Act Three Scene Three

ACT THREE
SCENE FOUR

ARMING THE HEIGHTS

Place: The cliffs above Little Niagara

Present: Maj. Robert Rogers, Capt. Ogden, Lt. Dunbar, Pvt. McDuff, Pvt. Ogden, John Slattery, and assorted Rangers

Scene: *It is the hour before the dawn. The men of Rogers' company are assembling in the wooded clefts, after their march from Fort Niagara. They are attired in their usual manner: replicating the style of the Natives. The moon is still above the horizon; by its light and that of the calumet, outlines and shadows of the structures of the lodgment are well-defined. There are two warriors seated quietly beside the fire; the remaining Seneca, numbering some two hundred persons, are asleep in and around the longhouses. One hears the sound of the river's turbulence and of the men's nervous voices as they assemble.*

Rogers: Shhhh, we're near as many as three hundred warriors,
        We must play the Indian by their barriers,
        Stay quiet!

Dunbar: It doesn't look like much.

Rogers: Doesn't it?
        Nor do the muddy nests of the hornets,
        But they hold many a rude inhabitant,
        And when shaken?

Slattery: Right! In range for Brown Bess[107]
        Bring up the Coehorns,[108] we've one per five men.

---

107 Brown Bess: Musket favored by British soldiers during the French and Indian Wars.
108 Coehorns: Relatively small, portable mortar cannon developed in 1674 and used into the nineteenth century.

So take the cannons, your pistols and muskets,
Powder and balls, your swords, knives and hatchets!

Ogden: How are we to arrange for the onset?

Rogers: I'll move to the right of the line - two hundred feet.
Dunbar, you and your men come behind me,
Form to my left, and Ogden, you remain here;
Soon as you find your place, load and prepare!
I'll yell 'surrender' and see if they'll be spared
If I fire once, let it all go - fire and load!
Take out their trivial fire, make it smoke!
That out, they've nothing to see, nowhere to go,
Until roof to floor, the longhouse is laid low!
I want our best sharpshooters on the flanks,
Let your fire focus on any escape pass!
While the rest of us will venture into their dens
Where we'll have at it, with knives and hatchets!

Slattery: Pardon, Rogers! But can our men spare the chapel?
It seems little to ask…

Dunbar: It might house some relics!
We wouldn't want to fire on a house of God!

Slattery: Surely not, surely not!

Rogers: I doubt the chapel will survive the confusion.
Do what you can!

A Seneca matron is viewed moving from a longhouse to the calumet.

Ogden: Below, is that a woman?

Rogers: Yes, and according to order, have a care!
Women and children are to be spared.

Ogden:	It's hard to discern in the chaos and the dark When one's blood is up.
Rogers:	These are of the part That massacred innocents at William Henry,[109] These peoples allied to the Abenaki. Spare the innocent, but spare the braves caring! I won't quibble that we owe them mercy: Not after their chronicle of atrocity - We've known at firsthand their savagery!
MacDuff:	My blood and bones are on fire with fury!
Rogers:	It is the hardest thing in such extremity To keep your calm in a universe of violence…. You've not just your foe to fight, but mischance! Resolve, men to fight bravely and together, Soon all that we have will be at the hazard!

End of Act Three Scene Four

---

109 William Henry: Fort William Henry, supra.

ACT THREE
SCENE FIVE

DELUGE

Place: Little Niagara

Present: In the central cliffs: Rogers, Slattery, Dunbar, Ogden, MacDuff and Rangers.
To the east: Mink
Later around the calumet: Lone Bear, Day Star, Grey Swan, assorted Seneca, and Frenchman
From the cliffs to the west: arriving separately, White Hawk and Red Fox

Scene: *The scene is the same, with widened scope. Mink is just returning home, descending the clefts to the east of the calumet. Roger's Rangers are in the cliffs to the west. Other than warriors beside the central fire, all the inhabitants of Little Niagara are sleeping. It is an hour before dawn, the deepest of night. The winds are high and make a moaning sound as they move through the hollows of the canyon. The turbulence of Niagara is high as well, with mists being swept by the winds off the crests of the waves.*

Mink: Yet there she lies! Home's familiar flame,
                  One thing, in a world overturned, is the same!
                  The central home to which I may always come,
                  Where changeful moon meets a flame of the Sun.

                  I've seen in the forest so many of the British:
                  The many my father will soon make regret it!

A single gun fires from the darkness.

Rogers: Too soon! Who fired that shot? We are not ready!

A barrage begins.

299

Dunbar: Once begun, who can stop it!

Rogers: Damn! Fire steady!
At the best it will be scattered shooting:
Pell-mell havoc, beyond our controlling!

Lone Bear comes furiously out of the longhouse.

Lone Bear: A canopy of flames are Niagara's clefts,
The same clefts that had been our defense!
So this is how the great English relate:
They breathe a peace their acts take away!
By Joincare and White Hawk I am betrayed -
They fall upon me where I am most weak,
In the undefended realms of my dreams!
You fall upon my weakness, you predatory scourge -
What or who was ever different in this world!
For advantage, upon the prone the fighters fall -
England! You profess to be of a higher law,
But by your acts, you follow your words not at all!

White Hawk: Too late! Their fire's opening while I'm struggling!
There's a darkness and bramble intervening
Between my strengths and our hope of surviving!

There's ripping through trees the balls of muskets,
While arcing through the night, fly globes of death!
The dull thud they make into our earthly mother
Is followed by explosions of fire and thunder!
Watch the swift arc of the flaming iron globe,
As she dives in Earth, cleaves her and explodes!

Lone Bear, with rage of death, the scene ascends,
The mightiest can't withstand this force congressed:
These graduated powers of the English!
The greatest hero of our nation, our kind,
Can't withstand this wave, this all crushing crime!
Does nothing hold? Nor spirits of our mother

Nor the French covenant, nor English honor,
All are fled, fled upon the wings of an hour!
All's sacrificed at war's convulsive altar…
They all charge into a vortex of slaughter!
From longhouses warriors emerge, exposed,
Whose native might and prowess are overthrown,
Firing with ineffectual rifle and bow
Unto the obscure dark, filled with unseen foes!

In the blanket of arbors, I see the glimmer
Of unhoused pistols and unsheathed sabers!
They're readying attack on the encampment –
A cannon has found its mark, our calumet!
Our sacred flame cleaved to embers and ash!

Mother! Do not come out in the flashing light!
From these damned weapons, there's no place to hide!

Grey Swan emerges from the longhouse.

Grey Swan: You shoot my son as you shot on my father,
             So you have treated us since days of our elders!
             Upon them, advance, my true Seneca warriors!

Day Star emerges and screams above the din at Grey Swan.

Day Star: Do you see what comes of your blind attempts?
             Do you see what comes of your hate and revenge?
             When you demand we charge blindly into death,
             Behold, Mother! We will all blindly find it!

Lone Bear: A truce as strong and good as England's word!
             They break it the day it's breathed, as it serves!
             Aye England! You and the French are true brothers:
             My faith chokes on you both as my life smothers!
             Vanished like smoke are hopes of mortal promises,
             They are breathed by men and end in nothingness!
             Fire, warriors! On our unseen enemy,
             Who haven't the honor to face us openly!

Come! Pull down the lofty cliffs 'round my ears,
I will fight! Defying you without fear!
Plunge me in the deepest of this river's depths,
Yet I'll search your hearts and hold them in contempt!
To fight is all - fight on! Battle to the death!
Rally your Spirits: Aereskouy! Ataensic!

Grey Swan: England! You've come with your far-firing guns,
Not daring enough to face the strength of my son!
You don't face my son but cower in fear:
So you subdue him from a safe frontier!
You dare not fight the foremost of my children,
So with subtlety engage to murder him!
My son! I viewed your birth through blood and water,
And now I see your death in a sea of fire!

Day Star: If this is the manner in which we relate,
Then self-massacre will always be our fate!
This law of nature costs us so very much -
That we must lose everything that we love!

Husband!   You pay the price of your sacrifice,
Your great virtues served to uphold your pride,
But look, Lone Bear, how all around you have died!

Lone Bear: This fire is too great, this smoke is too dense!
Come, Seneca! Defend the sacred calumet!
Her sacred flame is near to extinguished;
Let us perish in embers of her fragments;
Farewell to you, Mother! Your son retreats
They won't grapple with me, but post their stings!

White Hawk: Grey Swan! Which of the hundred swarming bullets
Winged its unerring path to bring you death?
The great Swan is down, she has sung her last,
With her, forever goes the glory of our past!

Red Fox suddenly appears at the side of White Hawk.

Red Fox!

Red Fox: Hello, old friend, here we are met,
                              To witness from a gallery - a Hero's death!

White Hawk: Why are you not with him, standing in defense?

Red Fox: His great strength was the weakness of our tribe.
                              His pride, with himself, had to be sacrificed,
                              That our people have a chance of future life!

                              I attempted every form of apology
                              From founded argument to beggary:
                              I prayed him listen, but he would never bend;
                              He preferred, to humble life, this prideful death!
                              While he lived, his strength filled the world with awe
                              But he could not win 'gainst England's higher law!
                              He would not bend his unmoving, stone knees,
                              To the highest law known - of necessity!

White Hawk: Look! He prostrates his majestic cadaver
                              And bows quietly 'fore the sacrificial fire!
                              His frame is rent through with a hundred holes
                              But they never made a tear through his soul!
                              I would that we both a higher law had known,
                              How we would have fought for that divine fold!

Red Fox: So our Chieftain descends without a tear....
                              His sorrow, his loss is left for us to bear!

                              There is Mink! He descends the east cleft,
                              And there! Day Star goes to meet his descent!

At the other cliffs, Rogers views Slattery descending the ridge.

Rogers: Where goes Major Slattery at such speed?

Dunbar: Slattery moves at speed, propelled by greed!
                              His desire breeds a false, errant bravery.

Rogers: Their warriors are most killed or swim the river -
       It's time for us to move upon the survivors.
       Men! We had been led by chance and confusion -
       From now, it's mercy to women and children!

The scene shifts to Mink on his descent.

Mink: My dear Father! Why have you entered the flame?
       Once consumed, I may never see you again!
       Oh the pain! It comes, insupportable!
       My Father, your loss is unalterable!

*As Slattery makes for the chapel, he clubs Day Star out of his way,
and she goes to the ground.*

Mink: Who has the gall? Who's this English monster
       That without a thought assaults my mother!
       There he goes, the cur, into the chapel,
       I'll move on him, until his breath's disabled!

Slattery: What have we here, I can't see in the dim glare,
       Watch! You don't want to fall in this dark lair!
       Or in the pits my own artillery's made:
       They yawn everywhere, such ready graves!
       A statue! It must weigh ten pound!
       Of silver well-wrought, the virgin and babe son!

       What's this stuff, damnable beads, it's wampum?
       Here I'll give it a heave into this fire,
       That it might light what there is here of worth!
       Ah! A sack of coins, hundreds! A treasure!
       Maybe a hundred…but is that all? More beads!
       That's all! A statue and a hundred guineas!

Mink enters the chapel.

       Back off from here lest you come to harm, boy,
       For if you try me, sure you'll be destroyed!

Mink: Leeches cling on prey for as long as prey bleeds
             And cling they do, no matter else, until bursting!
             Are you prepared, glutted leech, to keep feeding?
             Even as round you, your host lay dying?

*Slattery drops the sack of coin and statue but it is too late, Mink has
the edge, though he is a smaller man, and subdues Slattery to the
ground, fiercely fighting until Mink hammers him with a tomahawk.*

             May you all fall as easily - you damned fool.
             You held on too long to a worthless jewel!

Slattery: What can I give you that you'll allow me live?

Mink   You ought have lived life by another motive!

*Mink carves Slattery's chest and pulls out his still-beating heart.
Enter White Hawk and Red Fox, later Day Star.*

White Hawk: Hold, Mink! You'll find his filthy heart poor eating;
             From such foul disease, prefer your liberty!

Mink: Red Fox! What do you with this Englishmen?
             Stand by or take part, I will kill him!

Slattery expires as Day Star enters.

Day Star: This is your uncle, Mink, Lone Bear's brother.

Mink: This man's in the dress of the English, Mother!

Enter Rogers, Dunbar and other Rangers.

White Hawk: Hold your fire and sword.   He's no warrior here!

Mink: Come nearer, fool, and I will prove my career!
             Assemble English! Walk in my living fire!
             I will down you all round my father's pyre!

305

Red Fox: Drop the hatchet, Mink! It is time to mourn!
It's true! This is your Uncle! Stand down - be warned!

Day Star: You see the cost of hatred and blind revenge?
Would you have me also grieve for your death?
Come, son! Do not be over bourne by the storm!

Mink mourns as he views his father and embraces his weeping mother.
Rogers faces White Hawk.

Rogers: I'm glad I saw your uniform, it's all torn.

White Hawk: Aye, as I am, it's you who's wrongly dressed:
You look the Seneca and I the English.

Rogers: Well, it spared you getting shot to messes.

White Hawk: Am I under arrest? What is my status?

Rogers: No, White Hawk, you and Red Fox are free men,
As are the rest of the Seneca warriors.
We want this war post, not her survivors...

White Hawk, Red Fox and Mink move to the calumet and the bone
and ashen remnants of Lone Bear and his attendants.

Mink: Oh, Father! Have you not taken your last breath?
Is not time's end lying on the calumet?

Day Star: He'd not choose another or a later grave,
He died as he lived, in the manner most brave:
He died in his wilderness, his spirit unchained.
But Mink! Your time is to come, you have survived,
Allow the future of the Seneca life!
Our brother, Hawk, will take us by his side.

Rogers: There's no returning to our camp for you, Hawk,
Sure, if you tried, you'd suffer Gage's assault.

White Hawk: With Mink and Day Star, I will move on!
                 But I've a prayer to sing yet to the wind and Sun -
                 There is prayer to Aereskouy to be done!

White Hawk sings as Mink, Day Star and Red Fox bow together.

                 Here, Lone Bear and Grey Swan's flesh and bones
                 Will fill the veins of these monumental stones!
                 Here, their voice will live forever in the wind,
                 With our ancestors' breath, theirs interblend,
                 To sound prayers heard through the canyon echoes!
                 Here, the light of their lofty, wondrous souls,
                 Will fill radiant colors of yon arced rainbows!
                 Here, their spirits will inhabit forever
                 Along the sacred river of our ancestors!

Day Star: Well sung, White Hawk, and in Lone Bear's accent.

White Hawk: Mink! We need find a place beyond this contest,
                 Where we may meet my wife and your cousin!
                 There is such a far-off place that I know,
                 The Potawatami call Kishwauketoe:
                 It is a crystal lake, whose deep blue waters
                 Are free from these adversary encounters!
                 It is only a mild and variant breeze
                 That unsettles her waters from their ease:
                 A place full of friends, where we can find peace,
                 Where we'll be far from war's destroying reach.

Day Star: Though it is a very far way that we must go.

Mink: It's well, Mother, we'll be better for such throes
                 If we can learn who it is that we ought to know.
                 And through such gauntlets, we're given to grow!

End of Part Two

"There is nothing left there, but the wake of wrath!"

BUT BY THE CHANCE OF WAR

PART THREE

"AMIENS"

CONTENTS
PART THREE
"AMIENS"

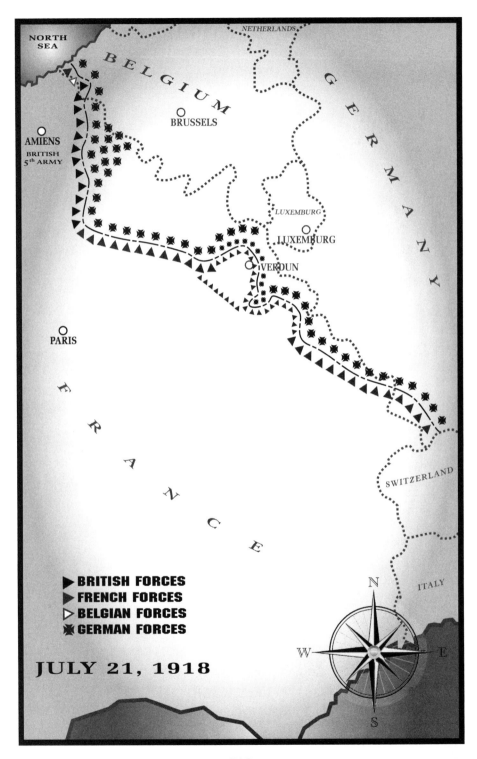

NORTH SEA

BELGIUM

NETHERLANDS

GERMANY

BRUSSELS

AMIENS

BRITISH 5ᵗʰ ARMY

LUXEMBURG

LUXEMBURG

VERDUN

PARIS

FRANCE

SWITZERLAND

ITALY

► BRITISH FORCES
► FRENCH FORCES
▷ BELGIAN FORCES
✷ GERMAN FORCES

JULY 21, 1918

N
W   E
S

CHARACTERS
PART THREE
"AMIENS"

BRITISH ARMY OFFICERS:

General Hubert Gough — Commander Fifth Army
Colonel Byron Blunt — Requisitions Officer
Major Gavin Blunt — Leader, Ranger Unit
Major Richard York — Fifth Army Officer
Major Henry Lancaster — Fifth Army Officer
Doctor Henry Meacham — Serving Physician
Lieutenant Pierce Blunt — Son of Byron Blunt
Captain Marcus York — Son of Richard York
Captain Geoffrey Reilly — Royal Flying Corps Officer
Lieutenant Ambrose Marshall — Driver

OFFICERS OF THE EMPIRE:

Captain John Hawkins — Canadian Seneca
Captain Blair Devlin — Australian
Captain Dylan Connor — Irish
Lieutenant Chandrahas Rana — Indian
Lieutenant Dumisa Zulu — South African

ENLISTED SOLDIERS OF THE EMPIRE:

Private Henry Gaines — Private Peter Weller
Private Jim Reiss — Private Patrick Shelley
Private Donald Potter — Private Ken Mahaffey
Private Robert Lemley — Gunner O'Rourke

OTHERS:

Father Condorcet — Priest of Amiens Cathedral
David Kupfer — Vickers' Representative
Major Gerule Bergman — German prisoner

Others (mentioned but not appearing):

Lady Patricia Blunt — Mother of Lt. Pierce Blunt
Henry Blunt: First son of Byron and Patricia Blunt
Adrian Blunt: Maj. Gavin Blunt's son, a prisoner in Babylon
Elena and Andrea: Love interests of Pierce Blunt

ACT ONE
SCENE ONE

THE GAUNTLET

Place: Southern flank of the British Fifth Army before Amiens, France on the 20th March, 1918, two hours before sunset.

Present: Gen. Hubert Gough, Lt. Ambrose Marshall (Driver), Maj. Richard York and soldiers.

Scene: *After a meeting with the Field Marshal Douglas Haig and Lt. Col. Winston Churchill, Hubert Gough arrives by car to the southern flank position of the British Fifth Army, before Amiens. The surrounding area is notable in that there is not a living thing beside the gathered humanity; not a blade of grass, not a standing tree, but as far as the eye can see, a landscape of mud with meandering, cavernous trenches, which appear like the borings and tracks of giant serpents. Above the trenches and following their wavering lines are stands of barbed wire twisted into helixes interspersed with machine gun nests and some medium-size cannon. Everywhere men are in motion as a skirmish has just begun between British and German lines. The two sides exchange rifle, machine gun and mortar fire. Reconnaissance and bomber planes fly overhead. Gen. Gough's car abruptly careers to a stop after a German bullet wounds his driver. Maj. Richard York and some of his men jump from a following car and run to assist the General and his driver.*

Gen. Gough: I wonder what we've done to stir the hornets!
                 Let's us help Ambrose - he's taken a bullet!

As he is helping his driver to the ground

                 Ambrose, son! You've been hit in the shoulder,
                 Try not to move, a medic will soon be over!

Maj. York: Well, sir, it can be said you make an entrance!

Gen. Gough: I'd hoped to take some time for an inspection
              Of the works on these unfinished trenches!

The General looks over the hood of his sedan as two bullets pierce the metal.

Maj. York: That's the rifle fire of a German sniper!
              They strike swift and sure, the damnable vipers.
              He must be able to see your car's ensigns.

Gen. Gough: Just how my dear brother met his demise[110] -
              Sniper's bullet, from a thousand yards away,
              That had the power to kill, after it ricocheted!

Maj. York: This has all the earmarks of a shock troop raid[111],
              But it makes no sense, who would dare it by day?

The General has opened the shirt of Lt. Marshall to inspect the wound.

Gen. Gough: I've just come from a meeting with Douglas Haig,
              The Germans prepare for an advance today.
              Hence the probing troops, reconnaissance planes -
              They'll search our weaknesses systematically
              Before scourging our faults with their artillery,
              Then they'll search for open pores with infantry
              Until they sense the evenness of our skin,
              And find that open pore, through which to pour in!
              Ambrose! You're lucky! It's your upper shoulder.
              I know it's painful lad, but you'll soon be better.

Lt. Marshall: I had hoped to continue on with you, sir,
              We should be together to face this danger!

*Mortars explode as medics arrive and gurney the wounded driver,
preparing to take him to the rear. Gough turns to his driver.*

---

110 Brig. General Sir John Gough (1871-1915): Killed by a sniper's bullet, believed to have ricocheted, at Fauquissart, France.
111 Shock troop raid: Swift attacks at the enemy's weak points conducted to assess strengths or take officers; such raids normally took place under cover of darkness.

Gen. Gough: There, Ambrose, you've earned the right to lie down,
              You'll soon enjoy the comforts of yonder town.
              I'll come to hospital and see you on my rounds!

*The medics lift Lt. Marshall and run to the rear, amidst continuing
sniper and machine gun fire.*

Maj. York: If this skirmish is an attack's prelude,
              We've not time to see this half-trench improved!

Gen. Gough: Damn it! We've just been given this area,
              Without the time to build sufficient barriers!
              In this horrid war, these brave men face enough;
              We must at least have the time to shield them!

              These men have death in droves to contend
              From the sniper's bullet, the machine gun nest,
              Or the silent night raider's bayonet!
              Never any rest, there is never a respite,
              While their minds contend with constant threats!
              When any time our bravest along this whole line,
              By just raising his too curious eye,
              May meet a bullet barreling through the sky…
              And, in moments, no more, bid his life goodbye!
              And these are merely death's subtler means,
              Which pale when a full attack is unleashed
              And human senses are shredded by artillery!
              When one's organs quake with one's senses,
              Until Earth itself has no sense of firmness!
              And we shudder with fear in these narrow caves,
              While brief hours crawl like an unmoving age!
              We send as many to an asylum's cage,
              As we do to the kept environ of the grave,
              With the horrid mental scars this war makes.
              And we haven't time to complete this place!
              Excuse it, York, that I sensibly rage!
              I must never let pain appear on my face!

Maj. York: This war breeds degrees of a real lunacy
And graver dangers of gathering mutiny,
Such as the French armies withstood last spring![112]

Gen. Gough: It is understandable, given their suffering!

Maj. York: I wonder what keeps all these men so brave?

Gen. Gough: A steadfast faith I hope is not misplaced.
This trench is the only safety we all share?
And for its repair, we've not a moment to spare!
I'll want to talk to our company of engineers.
Drive now, Henry! Go ahead to headquarters,
Alert, through command, our Fifth Army raiders.[113]
At sunset, we need to probe our forward sectors!
We need a last count of our German foes
Before time is up, and we need come to blows!
Outrun the thousand ways this war afflicts
Frail human sense in this inhuman gauntlet!

End of Act One Scene One

---

112 Last spring: As the war wore on, the French Army was experiencing widespread mutinies by early 1917.
113 Fifth Army raiders: British soldiers famed for their bold raids through No Man's Land, the desolate area separating the German and British troops.

ACT ONE
SCENE TWO

ARRIVAL TO AMIENS

Place: British Fifth Army Headquarters on the Brown Line defensive trenches before Amiens.

Present: Gen. Hubert Gough, Col. Byron Blunt, Mr. David Kupfer, Maj. Richard York, Maj. Henry Lancaster, Capt. Geoffrey Reilly, RFC[114] Capts. John Hawkins, Dylan Connor and Blair Devlin, Lts. Chandrahas Rana and Dumisa Zulu

Scene: *Maj. Lancaster and Capt. Reilly, RFC, are speaking to one another in the foreground. Col. Byron Blunt, who has come to confer with General Gough, arrives at the British Empire's Fifth Army headquarters located at the center of the British forward position near Amiens, France. The headquarters is a modest clapboard cabin structure whose exterior is surrounded by bustling men, who carry munitions of all kinds and sizes. The weather is clear and bright. Three immense Vickers cannons loom beside the headquarters, dwarfing the men and the clapboard edifice. To the west of the position and emerging above the distant horizon are the elegant and timeless Gothic windows and steeples of Amiens Cathedral.*

Maj. Lancaster: How can you fly that winged crate above the sphere:
Through the unanchored, unbound suspense of air?

Capt. Reilly: I can take novelty, the suspenseful fear,
But, you know, the sky we see is a veneer,
Shallow indeed is Earth's breathing atmosphere,
One loses one's breath not a mile up from here!

---

114 RFC: Royal Flying Corps, predecessor of the British Royal Air Force.

Maj. Lancaster: Look smart! Our good General now appears.

Gen. Gough: Henry, did orders get to the raider's contingent?

Maj. Lancaster: They are preparing now for their new mission.

Gen. Gough moves to greet Col. Byron Blunt.

Gen. Gough: Byron, thanks for coming around:
Germany is bringing the hammer down!
You'll understand when you hear what we face,
And with war, it's an accelerating race!

I've just met Haig and Sir Winston[115] up the line,
They've noted our supplies are cut rather fine,
And averred I'm the sole man under such plight
That I might lose the whole war overnight!

Col. Blunt: Pressure never ends, it grips all continents!
To himself

I've come with Kupfer of Vickers, for inspections,
To fill what we can of your requisitions.

Kupfer: The start of spring emptied all our magazines -
Seventy-eight thousand men on machines -
At it twenty-four hours a day, laboring!
Yet there are more necessities to perform
There's nothing that eats machinery like war!

Viewing the cannon

I see you've Vicker's answer to Krupp's[116] Bertha!
They say she can raise Hell out of Earth, ah?
That's a trade joke...

---

115 Sir Winston: Lt. Col. Sir Winston Churchill left government after supporting the disastrous Gallipoli campaign, returning to the military and visiting the Amiens area just before the bombardment.
116 Krupp's: Friedrich Krupp AG was the largest arms producer in Europe at the beginning of the 20th century; competitor of England's Vickers.

Gen. Gough: *To Blunt*

                                      When I heard of you last
                'Twas from the dismal, lost coast of Hellas,[117]
                Where victory escaped our flailing grasp.
                No man should bear the whole brunt of such loss,
                We all fail together, my friend, and pay the cost!

Kupfer: I've heard just beyond here's the worlds largest gun!
                She can hit Paris! Now that's a rare cannon!

Gen. Gough: We'll soon invent a gun that will cleave the sun!
                It's sure, the days of human valor are done!
                War has been wrested from knights by mechanics:
                It's all hills of shells and cannons and tactics,
                While we provide men for bloody saturations!

                You know, I thought we had them with our tanks,
                When Sir Hugh[118] broke through the German ranks
                And for five open miles Germany hurdled back:
                For we'd discovered a new mode of attack!
                But the Germans fitted lorries with cannons
                And made new shells to pierce armored canvas,
                Routing us back to original positions!
                Thousands perished for that advance of inches.

                Aye! Don't we all have cause to curse the hour
                We became heirs to this hell-born power?
                Our virtues prop these tools of our vices,
                Until human flesh and bone are grinded!

Kupfer: You will find columns of your necessities,
                Attended by new recruits now arriving.

Gen. Gough: Good! Byron, why not join us as we confer;
                Later, rejoin the mission of Mr. Kupfer.

---

117 Hellas: Principal landing point in the Dardanelles during the battle of Gallipoli.
118 Sir Hugh Elles: (1880-1945 C.E.) First commander of a British tank battalion, 1916.

Gough, Blunt, Reilly, and Lancaster enter the clapboard headquarters where the parties to be introduced have convened.

Gen. Gough: Gentlemen, we have one more visitor:
Colonel Blunt is here on a needs tour.
Byron! This is Major York of Devonshire,
And from Ireland, this Captain Dylan Connor;
From Welland, Canada, John Hawkins;
From Brisbane, Australia, Blair Devlin;
From Delhi, India, Chandrahas Rana;
And this, Dumisa Zulu from South Africa;
And from Lancashire, here's Lancaster,
Who will now relate to us our orders.

Maj. Lancaster: Good day, gentlemen, I've come from London
To acquaint you with recent goings-on.
A few know, some rare cataclysmic events
Have struck a keystone of our alliance.
Russia has fallen by, she's become a casualty
Of her own inner faults and of German intrigues
Which used a radical, Lenin, to procure peace
By means of revolution and general uprisings!
Lenin's Bolsheviks have brought down the Czar
With a force like that of an exploding star!
One man, exploiting violence and fears,
Toppled an empire of three hundred years!
Setting all Russia's peoples at opposition,
Her earth is now a red sea of convulsion,
Of murder, pillage and persecution!
The Romanov Empire's life has ended!
'Twere like the German inserted a poison,
In Russia's weak, colossal abdomen
And exploded her vitals with corrosive ruin!
The worst, we may imagine, is apprehended,
While her thousand-mile front lies undefended!

Gen. Gough: Is it not the elements of vice that work so:
The Czar's regime dividing before their foe
Shows how corrupt the monarchy had grown!

Maj. Lancaster: Russia has broken covenants that bound us,
Before our foe, she has abandoned her guns,
By so doing, she has abandoned us!
Our compounded alliance being split,
Our armies and arms are now at deficit:
Russia's front has been stripped of defense,
So Germany has wheeled her forces west,
With the means necessary to our conquest!
A half-million men in two score divisions
Fill the roads and rails from here to Munich!
Included is our ariel foe Von Richthofen,[119]
On a special train, with his entire squadron!

Maj. York: They say all our knighthood has been removed
To the contested clouds of the altitudes.

Maj. Lancaster: The point is, they are bringing everything to bear
To finish our Empire off right now! Right here!

Col. Blunt *to himself:*   *No!*

Maj. Lancaster: We have beaten the Germans 'round the world -
From the Falklands to China, we're the victor.
We have dashed designs in Africa and India,
And her allies, the Ottomans, have lost Mecca;
At the Suez were they also decisively defeated!
We've defeated Germany's bid for dominion
'Round the Earth, even to Jerusalem!
Yet, they come upon us again in full breath:
They come upon us with powers fully wrenched!
Whereas we have pulled all the concerted strengths
We may, from forces of the air, the earth and sea,
Yet we are pushed to this last extremity!
Therefore are you here, kinsmen of Empire,
Come to aid us, as sons to a needful sire!

The will of our foe is to gain the channel ports,

---

119 Von Richthofen: Manfred, "The Red Baron," notoriously daring fighter pilot.

Wherein our safety navigates its last resort!
For, if they possess French ports on the channel,
Our empire will be summarily dismantled.
They also seek to drive a consequent wedge
Between ourselves and our allies, the French,
Who themselves, on our flank, are under stress,
As we are about to live this war's next test!

Col. Blunt *to himself:*   *No!*

Capt. Devlin: Pardon, sir, to help morale of rank and file,
                May my men know what began the great trial -
                Which launched our journey of ten thousand miles?

Maj. Lancaster: Aye, but how to put it to you simply?

Gen. Gough: If I may, Major, I'll try to do so swiftly.
                This continent of Europe had known peace,
                One which lasted for a full century,
                Since the last coming of a world thunderer,
                Since the last weaponed soul of a conqueror
                Careered across all of Europe's frontiers -
                Till that genius of war was chained by his peers!
                It took together all the European nations
                To bind that manic will in sequestration,
                And since Napoleon sailed for far St. Helen,
                Peace in Europe had been a piece of heaven!

                Europe's peace had been propped, pillared by empires,
                Which were tranquil, without territorial desires:
                The Spanish, the French and the Russian
                Along side the British and the Ottoman!
                But in midst of the continent was weakness
                In the form of a tyrannical governance
                Wielded by the Austro-Hungarians,
                Who ruled her peoples by the weak suggestion
                Of a hollow crown and brutal oppression
                Till her name became "The Prisoner of Nations."
                And till she had but one friend: the Germans.

Among her prisoned peoples, the Serbians,
Came to loathe the Austro-Hungarians,
And pursued avenues to their liberty
Including the killing of Austrian kings!
The environ was ripe for dark invention,
For weakness in the wind breeds revolution!
And violence inhabits in such air,
Seeking monstrous birth in a prone atmosphere!

 In that cauldron lived Gavril Princep,
A Serb student of no particular merit,
Who harbored none other than one ambition:
To kill a prince and free his prisoned nation!
But he was a very poor shot with a gun -
They say he never hit his mark but once!
Whenever he missed his aim, 'tis said he wept;
The world has wept since that day he found it!

The whole day surrounding the fatal event
Is framed and famed as one of accident.
Death's harvest from that fateful day grew by chance!
It was the Serbian National Day
It was stately celebration, without a state!
'Twas a stateless environment filled with rage!

Through Sarajevo drove Prince Ferdinand,
Heir to the crown of Austro-Hungarians,
With his beloved wife, in an open sedan!
They were part of a regal procession,
But his driver turned in a wrong direction,
Steering straight into the eye of an assassin!
Who himself had lost his directions that day,
But ended up before - foes he'd sworn to slay!

Princeps let fly! And the worst shot of an empire,
Set the globe aflame with his unerring fire!
The Austro-Hungarians swore death to the Serbian;
The Serbians turned to their friend, the Russian,

Who turned to allies of France and England,
While the Austro-Hungarian turned to the German
And to their southern neighbor, the Ottoman!
Thus, Europe formed into camps of opposites
Based on a series of common alliances!
Alliances made to secure peace for the world -
But these agreements turned the world insecure!
For any offense given to one - all offended -
Therefore, one offense alighted all defenses!
To secure that the common defense was defended,
All Europe's defenses were turned offensive!
Fueling a general flame: a chain reaction,
Which overwhelmed Europe to the last nation!
When Prince Ferdinand's driver made that wrong turn
His blunder effectively ripped apart the world!

Then it was that men no longer wound the clock
But time's motion wound men to paths that were locked!
For Germany knew the Russians would attack
And she'd be exposed to fighting on two flanks
Thus, before time, she had to strike for France!

Maj. York: The German may be arrogant, rude, unkind…
But he has a virtue - he's always on time!

Gen. Gough: Thence declarations of war crossed the board,
And the peace of a century was overborne!
Ten million men in a day were set in motion;
No power of Earth could halt the progression.
All this had, I must say, the magnificent feature
Of wheels moving smoothly in a chronometer!

Ours was the last nation toward war to verge;
As Lloyd George said, pulling the fatal lever:
"Millions of lives were doomed, as we ourselves hurled,
Into the depthless gulf of a war encircled world!"

Thus one shot from an insignificant knave
Blasted the feeble props of a golden age!

Thus we, who sought to bring law to the world's poor,
Have brought the poor world to this lawless war!
For if ever England is with war concerned,
The war concerns and wakes the whole world!
Thus the world is come to see the tragedy we play
On this blood-soaked, barren and unbearable stage!
But here we are to battle and here it is we'll stay,
For of opposed combatants - we must win this day!

Col. Blunt *to himself:*   *No!*

Maj. Lancaster: It is a grave thing the loss of Russia to consider;
                She was a needed plank in our ship's timber!
                But though our vessel is shattered and torn,
                With what remains of a hull, we must drive on!
                We have called in all the manhood we can free
                From our forces of the air, the earth and sea,
                Still we form fifty-seven divisions in readiness
                While we've yet to finish protective trenches!
                While beyond the trench, where our men are curled,
                Broods Ludendorff,[120] the new thunderer of worlds,
                With one hundred divisions and six thousand guns,
                While our arms do not achieve half the sum!

Col. Blunt *to himself:*   *No!*

Gen Gough: An attack of great import is now expected,
              While the Empire needs to be defended,
              Or we may see the end of our civilization!
              We must be as whole, obdurate and sound
              As posts of pure diamond drilled into the ground!
              Ludendorff is not far off; his artillery he forms,
              Soon he'll pour on us with his thundering force.
              You may be sure this fight, this pivotal time,
              Will bring our glory or end our common life!

---

120 Ludendorff: Erich Ludendorff, Germany's Quartermaster general. He was the strategist of the German offensive of 1918.

All Attending: Very good, sir,
                        Very good, sir!
                                      For England!
             On our honor, sir
                        We will handle them!

Gen Gough: Captain Reilly! Get your flyers off the ground:
             You have just time to do your last recon;
             We must know all we can of what's going on!

Exit all save Gen Gough, Col. Blunt, and Maj. Lancaster and York.

Maj. Lancaster: How in hell have the Germans accomplished this?
               They attack more boldly, the more they perish!
               I hear they dismantle church bells for smelting
               Which had rung to congregants for centuries!
               Yet they keep on molding new armories,
               And they keep coming, forming new armies!

Gen Gough: We are where man's genius wrenches highest,
             As we will do all things, for our own defenses!
             Our genius is not to suffer disorder or fear;
             For with war and Ludendorff in full career –
             It will never be permitted us twice to err!

Maj. Lancaster: Yet, do they not keep coming, the strong devils?

Maj. York: Pity we cannot send them all to St. Helen's!

Gen. Gough: They'd have bridged the impassable oceans,
             Just to advance their colossal ambitions.

Col. Blunt: Damn this war! Is there no other decision?

Gen. Gough: It is never easy, is it, my dear Blunt?
             To know the gravity of our situation,
             To enclose our too-human hearts in flint,
             Our too-expressive faces in forms of granite,

And send this generation to the face of death
And feel its grip through every foot of trench!

Never mind, Byron, if the Germans were not our foes
Lancaster and York might be at each other's throats!

Maj. York: No more of that, we lost![121]

Maj. Lancaster: *laughing nervously*   Your women survived!

Blunt gazes hard at a passing soldier's guise.

Col. Blunt: My God! Is that not John Swinford, alive!
He drowned at Hellas! I saw him go under!

Gen. Gough: You're confused, Blunt; that is Sir John's brother.

Col. Blunt: Then is he not his family's... sole survivor?

End of Act One Scene Two

---

121 We lost: Refers to the War of the Roses, 1455 - 1487, the civil wars between the Houses of York and Lancaster. The Yorkists lost at the Battle of Bosworth, August 22, 1485.

ACT ONE
SCENE THREE

IN THE TRENCHES

Place: The Red Line defensive trenches before the city of Amiens

Present: Col. Byron Blunt, Maj. York, Dr. Henry Meacham, Capt. Blair Devlin, Capt. Dylan Connor, Capt. John Hawkins, David Kupfer, Lt. Chandrahas Rana, Lt. Reiss, Lt. Dumisa Zulu, and assorted soldiers: Pvt.s Gaines, Potter, Weller, Shelley, Mahaffey, Lemley, and Gunner O'Rourke

Scene: *Elements of the British Fifth Army populate the middle of the Red Line defensive trenches; the surroundings resemble the Brown Line defensive trenches, though there are more signs of being a proper habitation; some of the walls are shelved and filled with personal belongings, along with photos and postings of articles and letters. There are places to sit which look as though regularly and permanently in use. On the level ground overlooking the trench is a standing piano which Captain Hawkins is playing, while comrades stand nearby gathered in song. Other soldiers are in groups talking, and still others are in the trenches cleaning and arranging their kits, their weapons or other possessions. Captain Connor is staring knowingly at Col. Blunt, as Blunt works on his figures with Kupfer.*

Capt. Connor: Now I remember where I have seen him!
              It's him. Look up, to view a walking ruin!

Capt. Devlin: Who do you mean?

Capt. Connor: Aye, 'twas Blunt was his name,
              He was second under Hamilton.[122]

Capt. Devlin: The same?

---

122 Hamilton: Sir Ian Standish Monteith Hamilton, commander of the Mediterranean Expeditionary Force, Battle of Gallipoli.

Capt. Connor: It was he at the battle of Gully Ravine[123]
                 But he was a general at the Helles landing!

Capt. Devlin: Oh yes, that's where we've met!

Capt. Connor: Can you forget?
                 I with Dublin's Fusiliers, you with ANZACs.[124]
                 At the heart of that damned, bloody attack!

Capt. Devlin: I dread thoughts of that world-dividing strait:
                 The cold swim ashore, through blood-red waves.
                 What was the loss that day, forty-eight hundred?

Capt. Connor: Aye, for bits of ground we later surrendered.
                 Of my mates, we landed there a thousand strong,
                 Then…eight hundred eighty-nine of us were gone!

Capt. Devlin: On him lies the greater weight of Gallipoli,[125]
                 The burden of a quarter million casualties,
                 All of whom died for a Turkish victory!

Capt. Connor: He looks pale and mad as old Greek Ajax![126]

Capt. Devlin: Was that the hero who thought brawn over craft
                 Would win the heaven-forged shield of Achilles?[127]

Capt. Connor: Aye, but his loss ended with his insanity.

Capt. Devlin: Songs of Homer, are they not still inviting?
                 I think Helen's strange, eternal powers
                 Yet linger where stood Troy's topless towers;
                 That her voice still wanders the earth's waters,
                 Beckoning forth nations of would-be lovers:
                 Not to find the warm fire of her enchanting eye,
                 But her cold shadow, for which all heroes die!

---

123 Gully Ravine: Battle fought at Helles, Gallipoli June 28 - July 5, 1915. Helles is across the Dardenelles from the site of ancient Troy, it faces the plains where the Trojan War was fought.
124 ANZACs: Nickname for the Australian and New Zealand Army Corps in World War I.
125 Gallipoli: Fought on the Gallipoli Peninsula, April 1915 - January 1916; 220,000 British and French troups died.
126 Ajax: A Greek hero of the Trojan War who sought the award of Achilles' armor, which was instead bestowed on Odysseus.
127 Shield of Achilles: Famed as having been formed by Vulcan, god of metallurgy, in his divine forge.

Capt. Connor: Blunt did not find the gilt shield of Achilles
Only its shadow and our mortality!
He did not find glowing turrets of Ilios,
Only Turks, defending their barren coasts!
He did not find the crown of Agamemnon,
Only wire and thorn on a bleak horizon!
He did not find any heaven-forged armor,
Only wounded soldiers and shred cadavers!
He sought a conqueror's glorious fight,
Only to fill hills with senseless sacrifice!

Capt. Devlin: Well, they've knocked him down, haven't they in rank?
They've got him counting bullets, mortars and tanks.

Capt. Connor: I'd have him count hosts in hell a thousand years.
That, for all our loss, might provoke his tears!

Capt. Devlin: Aye, but we still defend England, while she's here.

The scene continues with Kupfer and Blunt.

Kupfer: The air smells of metal, sulfer, chemistry:
Things new conceived in Krupp's laboratory!

Col. Blunt: Smells to me more like stuff of alchemy![128]

Kupfer: If Vickers had such profitability!
Krupp's ever planning some new device of death:
Torpedoes, bombs, cannons, bullets and gases,
All we do is attempt an equivalence!
The amounts of metals required in war -
It's metals and new munitions by the score!

The scene shifts to Maj. York and Pvt. Shelley, who is painting a figure of Amiens cathedral, which dominates the distant horizon.

Maj. York: Can you paint the artistry of an entire age
Into the compass of that confined frame?

---

128 Alchemy: A form of chemistry and speculative philosophy practiced in the Middle Ages and the Renaissance.

That has a four-hundred-seventy-foot nave!
The length of her latitudinal transept
Is two hundred and twenty-nine feet in width!
And that says nothing of her tower's height,
Which reaches fourteen stories into the sky!
Everywhere she is fitted with rare artistry,
From massive rose windows to statuaries,
Comprising the labors of three centuries!

Pvt. Shelley: Sir, how do you know the details of these things?
Artist

Maj. York: One should know what is worthy defending!

Col. Blunt and Kupfer make their way over to Maj. York.

I loathe to bid you, Blunt, but it's time we turn
To this new architecture of an underworld!
Yes, here we are, Blunt. Welcome to the trenches.
They wind five hundred miles in that direction,
Miles of mud, all the way to Switzerland!
The Germans have dug their trench with precision:
It winds just as ours, a perfect reflection!
Like the mighty sea's tides, her ebb and flow,
Are reflected in a line along the sand shore,
Or like a burnt forest and its living remains
Mirror the impress of a career of flame!

Zero point four miles to the east and ahead,
You'll find our mirror in dress, diet and stench!

York, Blunt, and Kupfer come to a large group of men who are taking a rest from their normal duties. Capt. Hawkins plays a favorite tune on the piano atop the trench.

Capt. Hawkins: Can you believe we hear them sing like us,
Oft times on still nights, when in a chorus.

Maj. York: Pardon, men! Are there any carpenters here?
We need some to work with our engineers.

Capt. Hawkins: Most of England's tradesmen were volunteers
We are those that were left, the conscripts,
A batch of uncalloused teachers and artists!

Major York moves on to the next soldier, as he sadly grimaces.

Maj. York: Here's Liuetenant Rana, let's have a word with him.
Pardon, Liuetenant?

Lt. Rana, Clerk: Yes, sir…

Maj. York: As no doubt you heard,
Mr. Kupfer and Colonel Blunt are on a needs tour?
To assess what we may want along the front
Say what you will of your needs now to Blunt!

Lt. Rana: Well, blankets for a start, for my men at night;
It's far colder here than in our native climbs.
Otherwise, I am precise in flash sightings[129]
To determine where enemy guns are firing,
And I diligently work on the trigonometry
And scope and arc our guns accordingly,
But find thirty percent of your bombs are duds!
To kill a German, I have oft to impale one!
The two of you did say you're from Vickers?
We hear the French bombs are much superior,
As to Germany's, we are far inferior:
The time it takes me to hit them with a live bomb
They can hit us with two, usually dead on!

Kupfer: We'll find what is malfunctioning.

Lt. Rana: For Vickers it's a question of capacity,
For us, sir, it's a question of surviving.
Clear?

---

129 Flash sightings: The trigonometry used for determing enemy gun emplacements during World War I.

Kupfer: Yes! Thanks, sergeant, who then is next?

Capt. Hawkins *Plays: "If You Were The Only Boche[130] In The Trench"*

> "If you were the only Boche in the trench,
> And I had the only bomb,
> Nothing else would matter in the world today,
> I would blow you in to eternity.
> Chamber of Horrors, just made for two,
> With nothing to spoil our fun;
> There would be such a heap of things to do,
> I should get your rifle and bayonet too,
> If you were the only Boche in the trench,
> And I had the only gun."

A soldier among a lateral group, reading a magazine, begins to speak animatedly.

Lt. Reiss: I tell you that the whole world has turned on its head!
Writer   Have you seen this work of 'the great new artist?[131]'
               Primitivist images of whores in brothels!
               This, the new "educated" call brave and modern?
               It took man a million years to learn how to paint
               With perspectives and dimensions well-ranged
               And all man's advance is deformed by a rake!

               Or what of the other modern theorist, Freud,
               Saying all human motives grow from the groin!
               As though man were a beast: a slave of instinct!
               As though we've learned nothing of civility!
               Or that we are not the heirs of divinity!

               And, oh yes, there's the last of the unholy three
               Darwin, who claims we're apes by ancestry!
               Oh, what a fall's been wrought on humanity!
               Artists once vied, who could apprehend the divine

---

130 Boche: A derogatory term for a German soldier in World War I; the song was a popular one during the war.
131 The great new artist: Picasso, the painting referred to is "Les Demoiselles d'Avignon."

And mimic His beauty, casting the human eye?
Philosophers once delved in God's designs
To waken man by discovery of his device!
We once believed the promise, the prophecy,
That we were the heirs of a divinity!

But all that divine conception's overturned:
We're told we've the parentage of a worm!
We've overcome a thousand moral obstacles
To fit ourselves in new primitive manacles!
If we sack God, remove him from our family,
We'll loose all hell's fiends on our humanity!

Pvt. Potter: It appears there has been the passing of an age,
Salesman   Things assumed in shelters of youth have changed.

Pvt. Gaines: Sophocles? Can I recall what he said?
Actor   "The gods know neither age nor death alone
                All else almighty time confounds in one,
                Earth's strength decays, decays the strength of man;
                Faith dies and falsehood burgeons in its place
                The same wind never lasts twixt friend and friend,
                City and city; but for some forthwith,
                And for some later, what was sweet turns sour
                And what was hateful pleases in its stead."

Pvt. Weller: Then there is Aesop, when asked what kept Jove busy:
Teacher: "Bringing down high things and exalting things of low degree."

Pvt. Potter: So it's been written, things are always changing!

Lt. Reiss: What never changes? Someone's always opposed to us!
                It was the Spanish, then the French, now the Germans.
                Of our empire, someone's ever envious.
                Always being opposed - that's impervious!

Lt. Zulu   There is a land exists north of us called Somalia,
Chief   A fruitful land of central Africa,
                Her people are of one color, one religion,
                One language, one history binds the nation.

You'd think there's no basis for confrontation,
But absent any other reason for opposition,
They base their anger and adverse aims on clans -
Cousin wars with cousin in the divide of man...
Don't you call these enemies 'Cousins German'?

Dr. Meacham: Opposition will always be with us,
While contrary poles themselves surround us.

Pvt. Gaines: What do you say, Doc?

Dr. Meacham: It's one of the constants.

Pvt. Weller: What?

Dr. Meacham: It's better to begin with beginnings.
If you wish to discourse of things changing?
Einstein's the most avant-garde with theories.
He makes Picasso and Freud seem pygmies!

Dr. Meacham picks up a large stone at random.

Firstly, he averred that there is nothing at rest,
Not even this stone, which appears to be fixed,
But its materials are even now becoming sand,
Altering in her qualities even while in my hand,
Till in the end, she passes into being nothing
Till like air, her contrary, she's disembodied!
Meantime this stone sits on a revolving planet,
Which moves round the sun in an oval orbit,
While our Sun's system circles a galaxy
Which whirls through the universe unendingly...
There is no material existing that is at rest -
Any sense of place we have is relative!
Second, Einstein stated this stone we see,
Is not mere matter, it's an energy,
Energy moving and changing, if slowly,
Round the inseparable atom's constancy.

Pvt. Weller: Damn, Prof, it's our very souls you unhouse
                 When we are soon to stand on shaking ground!

Dr. Meacham: The point is what has changed is our perception,
                 It's now thought that all we see is in motion!
                 The only things of true permanency
                 Are constancies of energies relating -
                 Such the speed of light[132] and force of gravity;[133]
                 Or like a vacuum's permeability;[134]
                 Or the laws of definite proportion,[135]
                 Or the inseparable bonds of the atom,[136]
                 Or the forces of action and reaction
                 Of equal magnitudes in opposition![137]
                 All matter is infinitely changeable!
                 Permanency has no material corpus:
                 All that's permanent is relative forces!

Pvt. Shelley: Such as between ourselves and the Germans,
                 These damnable Huns, who wish to scourge us!

Dr. Meacham: Actually, in them exists the same contention
                 Of the negative and positive in relation,
                 Vying for supremacy in their proportion –
                 Like ourselves, a mix of vice or virtue
                 Depending on your conscious point of view,
                 But we'll have an opposite, that's perpetual!

Capt. Hawkins: Eternal? Like harmony's interval?

---

132 Speed of light: The speed of light in a vacuum is 2.998×10^8 meters per second and is deemed to be constant.
133 Force of gravity: According to Newton's law of universal gravitation, the attractive force, F, between two point masses m_1 and m_2 along the line intersecting both points, is proportional to the product of the masses times the gravitational constant G and is inversely proportional to the square of the distance (r) between them, i.e., $F = G \frac{m_1 m_2}{r^2}$. The gravitational constant is empirically determined, i.e., via observation and experiment.
134 The permeability of a vacuum: The magnetic constant is the constant force, F, resulting from a current of 1 ampere in magnitude, flowing in two parallel conductors placed one meter apart in a vacuum.
135 The law of definite proportion states that a chemical compound always contains exactly the same proportion of elements by mass.
136 The atom: Considered indivisible since it was hypothesized by Democritus, until the beginning of the 20th century, when its ability to be split was theoretically foreseen and practically realized in 1938 by a practice called nuclear fission.
137 Newton's Third Law of Motion: To every action there is always the equal and opposite reaction. The magnitude of the forces of two bodies on each other is always equal and opposite in direction.

Dr. Meacham: That's not chance, note harmony's consonance:
              It's enforced and bound within dissonance.

Pvt. Weller   Doc, you describe war without armistice.

Dr. Meacham: No! Opposites are necessary elements:
              It's not war, but one of life's conditions,
              That we are edified by oppositions.
              It's long been a philosophical thesis
              That if you remove from life her opposites
              You end strife and with it… all existence!
              And that if you put an end to rivalry,
              There'd come to be the end of everything:
              Life, in the agreement of things, would cease!
              Whereas opposition keeps things refreshing:
              Like a river kept pure through her flowing,
              Life never stagnates, it's always becoming,
              And like seasons and ages, ever revolving!

              Then there's a matter of one's perspective.
              Look at the galaxies which fill the skies
              And planets and stars viewable to the human eye.
              All of these spheres which we see possess spin:
              They have axes, poles and gravitation,
              When viewed from one pole they've one rotation
              From the other, it's the opposed direction!
              The perception differs with the perspective,
              The German views us from the opposed direction!
              But our strengths depend on relative morality,
              For what is just is prone to surviving!

Lt. Reiss: You have taken us too far to contemplate!
              Are we not here because of Germany's hate?
              Yet you say they are more or less like us?
              Professor! Where's the moral compass?

Dr. Meacham: If they are less virtuous than England,
              It means our opponent has a weakness,

But she's not all evil, nor we all goodness;
But this war is a test of relative fitness,
A test of our virtues and of our motives.

Pvt. Weller: This perception, everything is energy,
Edifying opposites by conditioning,
Strengthening each other through interacting,
What is the motive, where is the sanity?

Pvt. Shelley: I thought I was fighting for my home and kin?

Lt. Reiss: I thought we fought for the House of Commons?

Pvt. Gaines: I thought we fought for the old Union Jack?

Dr. Meacham: Aye, the central trust thread through the flag
Is what holds together our common ranks!
What upholds the House of Commons walls?
The glory of justice: our common law!
What upholds a home from roof to cellar?
Its central hearth and love of its dwellers!
We fight for all of these many things withal,
But all these wondrous things are relational!
But surely, as we all may also know,
In one's family we are sometimes opposed,
As in our nation, is it not always so?
Conservatives and liberals stand as foes,
But by the law of the land, we are composed.
We are joined by our laws and testaments,
As our alliance is by treaties and covenants,
Whereby man reconciles with his opposite,
In a manner which strives to be harmonic.
A means whereby man overcomes his disputes,
In the communion of his common virtues!

The better a nation is woven with justice
With governance reconciling its opposites,
The more a nation is liable to flourish,

For its strengths are peacefully replenished!
Note, the contrary of Earth's basic elements,
Their reconcilement keeps life youthful and fresh!
And reconcilement of the world's opposed poles,
Is what balances Earth's motion as a globe!

Pvt. Weller: *Looking around at the barren desolation*
Is England worthy of all this sacrifice?

Dr. Meacham: We must discern: in what cause do we unify?
In the cause of virtue or the causes of vice,
And which, by our gathering, do we sacrifice?
Is there a greater cause than our filial life?
Or the justice and freedom whereby England thrives?

Capt. Reiss: We fight also to save yon cathedral's stone!

Dr. Meacham: *Observing the stone he holds his hand*
Aye, look you! This stone is illusion entire
For here in my hand, I hold prisoned fire!
As in yon stone – behold! So in yon spires!
We defend that energy, that fiery faith
Whereby walls of that cathedral were raised!
It was that loving bond, the faith of man,
Which raised yon monument from the sand!

Capt. Reiss: Doctor! *That's* a constant which you should refer!
'All flesh is grass, so does glory the flower
The flower will wilt, and the grass wither,
But the Word of God will stand forever![138]'

Dr. Meacham: Only such a relation may be maintained
Even as every material thing does change!
And here is another point that is pivotal,
Such a force of relation is unassailable:
Not given to age or like matter to wither,
As long as we hold to it, it holds forever!

---

138 The word of God… will stand forever: Isaiah 40: 6-11.

Even against such a material menace
As the German army faces us with,
If we hold together in our faith and spirit,
We form bonds that can never be defeated!
We can only suffer defeat if we turn renegade,
Only if we first abandon our essential faith!

Pvt. Shelley: It's a far way, Prof, that your mind does wander.

Dr. Meacham: Don't lament opposition, we'll face it forever,
Revel in the relation that holds us together!
By that relation we will prove superior.

Kupfer: How to address the practical in this environ?
This constant: iron always sharpens iron!

Kupfer and Blunt walk into the shadow of a massive gun, surrounded by her gunners. The area is disorganized and ill-kept.

Col. Blunt: If you leave these bombs diffused on the ground,
You'll sometime hear their accidental sound!
I want munitions stacked appropriately
Housed safely until they're ready for firing!

Gr. O'Rourke: All due respect, sir, in the heat of battle,
There is not a bomb here that doesn't rattle!

Kupfer: Let's see, you've equal fifty tons of TNT;
What square area can that serve as blanketing?

Kupfer is seen computing the area to which he is referring.

Your load's within limits of our rationing.

Gr. O'Rourke: Thank you, sir!

Kupfer: Let's move on, Blunt - over there!
Who'd have thought studying volume a career?
Yet, the more I study and work at war

The more I and our shareholders prosper!
I noted, sir, you're among our investors.

Col. Blunt: Doubtless I have some holdings in the venture.

Kupfer and Blunt move along the line to a part which stands out as being the most meticulously defensible, organized and clean, even when carved out of and embedded in a bed of mud.

Col. Blunt: Well! I say, soldier, you've made quite a habitat!

Pvt. Mahaffey: Well, sir, the trick of it, sir, is to adapt.
                Nothing motivates as when in such a crunch,
                That next day your flesh might make a horse's lunch!

                The trouble is, one errant bomb's fallout
                Can blast all preparations in this redoubt!
                War! Here is nature's pruning machine,
                Made to advance the strong and devour the weak?
                Yet here war devours indiscriminately!
                Such is the force of this war's machinery
                It makes useless our God-given gallantry,
                Not to mention our genius for adapting!

Kupfer: That's why we're here - societal capacity!
                You seem well supplied by our inventory...

The men move further along the line to encounter a lone soldier who is downcast in the shadow of his trench.

                Soldier, we're making survey; need anything?

Pvt. Lemley: Might you have a supply of humanity?
Poet   If we all had our lot, we would need nothing!
                What's the bother? What's the value of this toil?
                We're food for the clutching abyss of the soil!
                This is my horrid den, my cavernous trench,
                While without there rives a universe of death.

Blunt casually picks up a handful of soil, holds it, and studies it.

Col. Blunt: The mud of your trench is redder than the rest.

Pvt. Lemley: It contains the remains of dearest friends,
                Here it was I witnessed their blood-soaked deaths!
                For what is it we make these sacrifices?

Col. Blunt: *to himself as he lets the soil fall:*   *No!*
                I half listened, Prof, to your contention
                On the constant nature of opposition.
                Its workings here bring annihilation!

Pvt. Lemley: No chivalrous knight was ever so pure
                Whose virtue would prevail on this field of honor!
                For no virtues have forged such adamant armor
                To blunt the weapons of this war of horrors!

End of Act One Scene Three

ACT ONE
SCENE FOUR

IN THE SHADOW OF CATHEDRALS

Place: Another part of the Red Line defensive trench system before Amiens Cathedral

Present: Col. Byron Blunt, a messenger, Maj. Gavin Blunt, his group of raiders and, subsequently, Fr. Condorcet, a priest of the cathedral

Scene: *Col. Blunt is temporarily separated from Vickers' representative, Kupfer, and is meandering along the trench line where he is overtaken by a messenger. He is later surrounded by a group of No Man's Land Raiders*

Messenger: Sir! I was sent this direction by Mr. Kupfer!
                  Are you Blunt? He said that you had wandered,
                  I've a dispatch for you, sir, from London.

Blunt puts the dispatch envelope in his jacket pocket, while he signs for it and then looks up in a shocked amazement.

Byron Blunt: Is it true? Gavin!

Gavin Blunt: Shall we never be done?

Byron Blunt: I thought you had been confined to your home,
                  To nurse your lingering wounds from the Somme.[139]

Gavin Blunt: The Empire is demanding all of her sons!
                  They take the weak, the lame, the old, the young;
                  I had thought you to be on permanent leave?

---

139 Somme: The first battle of the Somme occurred between July 1 and November 18, 1916.

Byron Blunt: They've got me here taking inventories.

Gavin Blunt: I would quickly dry that ink on those sheets,
All the signs are things will soon get bloody.
Seriously! You need leave immediately!

Byron Blunt: At your age, they have made you a raider?

Gavin Blunt: No one knows how to assess strengths better.

Byron Blunt: What's it like out there?

Gavin Blunt: Deathly sporting, really,
We each send through desolate fields these teams,
Probing lines thoroughly, for points that are weak,
So to engulf a prone area with strength,
Then find to a rare victory, some new means.
We seek weakness evident in our opponent,
We seize their armor's chink and scourge them for it!

Byron Blunt: I am as loath to ask, is there any word of your son,
Of our Adrian, any word from Babylon?

Gavin Blunt: There you lay hold of a chink in my armor,
When I think of my poor son, I stammer.
I thought it hell itself when I heard the Turk
Had invested the city of Kut's suburbs;[140]
I found Hell had a deeper, darker cavity,
When I was told the city was under siege;
That her defenders were starving and dying!
Yet my passage down Hell's steep was not over:
Adrian was among Kut's survivors,
Taken by the Turk, among their prisoners,
Marched across the barrenness of those deserts,
Over sands of the world's merciless furnace!

---

140 The city of Kut: The Siege of Kut was a major battle in World War I occuring at Kut-Hal-Amara, where Ottoman forces surrounded the city on December 7, 1915. Several relief efforts failed at the cost of 23,000 allied killed and wounded, and the British Army surrendered April 29, 1916.

To wherever he is now, chained and tormented,
Against such thoughts…my soul has no defenses!
Lord! That this war demands such sacrifices!
'Twined with him, my soul has been led away
To gulfs in Hell… while he crawls a prison cave!

I pray for this war's end every day,
Only by war's end, can Adrian be saved!
You know what it is to lose a beloved son:
I've not forgot that your Henry is gone.
Killed by a U boat moving 'neath the water
Furtively, noiselessly, bent upon slaughter!

Byron Blunt: There is nothing to do, for what we've undergone;
We must serve our England and remain strong!

Gavin Blunt: Must we eat this thorn, to behold the flower?

Byron Blunt: Glories and miseries come with the seat of power.
We serve our imperfect England with our metal,
The good and the bad, the thorn and the petal…
But we must protect her both root and stem
Even if it means our corporeal death!

A Raider: Major Blunt, sir, we had best be moving on.

Gavin Blunt: Right! Space yourselves! Move forward in a cordon!
I'll move left and venture to that horizon!

By the by, I am glad to know Pierce is at home.

Byron Blunt: Thank God for the just laws of our good home,
Our family's sole survivor is left alone!
May God go with you on your mission, Gavin!

Gavin Blunt: God won't suffer himself to breathe this poison.
Remember what I've said! Leave here, Byron!

The men under Maj. Gavin Blunt's command move silently forward with signaled farewells to Col. Byron Blunt, who continues his walk along the line until he comes upon a young priest from Amiens Cathedral, Fr. Condorcet, who is alone in a section of trench, seemingly blessing the emptiness.

Col. Blunt: It's a nice place you have there, Father, to work.

Condorcet: This Hell on Earth! Are you well? Are you absurd?

Col. Blunt: I was speaking of the Cathedral. It is yours?

Condorcet: It is no man's, though it is there that I serve.

Col. Blunt: I didn't mean to take you from your duty;
                It was just a greeting.

Condorcet: This is a blessing.

Col. Blunt: I don't understand; are you blessing the mud?

Condorcet: These bits of flesh and bone used to be someone.
                I beg you, leave me finish!

Col Blunt: I feel foolish.

Condorcet finishes his blessing...and holds up one bone fragment and then another.

Condorcet: This bone, the carpal of an opposable thumb,
                It is only part of a sum: the rest is gone!
                This other, a hip joint, if I am not mistaken,
                The soldier this was, was blasted to atoms.
                The government has found an answer for this:
                They're collecting bodiless bone fragments,
                While constructing at Verdun, a vast edifice,
                A huge magazine they say, in shape of a dome,
                Where they'll warehouse these relics in a home,
                With a stone carved: 'Tomb of the Unknown.'

Before the official harvesters are gathered
I'm blessing souls of those that were slaughtered
And do so on the behalf of their Father.

Col. Blunt: My God, someone's father has to come see this?

Condorcet: Father of Heaven, not their native parents!

Man wasn't meant for this disintegration!
Man ought rise above God's other creations.
In nature's realms, in paths of her wilderness,
Where one ever risks to meet one's opposite:
The creatures of God are suited with weapons,
Fit to defend them in animal kingdoms:
Such as with the lion's claws or the bull's horns
Or the boar's tusks or the porcupine's thorns
Or the crocodile's ridged and plated skin
Or with the triple hide of the elephant!
Each is armed to be wary the predator.
But these armors oppress the possessors,
For they are harsh in their accoutrements
And make harsher still their bearer's sentiments:
For the inborn enmity that comes of instinct
Makes even the bees too ready with their stings!

How different are humans in our origins!
We begin not in the shell or in a nest,
But in a warm womb, a living chrysalis,
From which we emerge soft and delicate,
And needful, how more so, man is dependent!
We are needful of a mother's love and favor
And of a father's nurture, through his labors,
Forming lasting bonds beyond the scope of nature.
And witness a babe's soft and smooth skin,
Are we not formed for love by adornment?

Col. Blunt: I suppose this a suggestive argument?

Condorcet: Oh yes, now look deep into this difference.
How humanity's unique in appearance:
We have not brute claws, but fine hands of grace;
Not thorny limbs, but arms made for the embrace;
Nor fangs, nor coarsened faces, but soft lips
Which beckon the sexes to unite with a kiss!
And unlike the animals which roar out their breath,
We've voice whose soft use is an instrument!
And look you, how so deeply dyed are our eyes,
That our inmost souls are viewable to the sight.
Inventory the wonders of human faculties:
For speech, for discernment, for reasoning;
These gifts point to a divine origin,
But have not all these gifts been misgiven!

We have overcome obstacles of nature's realms,
But not our opposite: the vice within ourselves!
We've climbed the highest mountain heights,
We've conquered the unapproachable skies,
We have conquered the pole's frozen ice shelves,
But we are not able to conquer ourselves!
We have overcome the pole's frozen glaciers -
But not the clamorous pride of our natures!
We've breached obstacles of extremity,
But never obstacles of our human envy!
Such are our divine gifts for invention,
Our strength to overcome other oppositions:
'Tis as though we'd stole sacred fire of heaven![141]
But these virtues now so armor our vices
That our frail humanity may not survive it!

Our speech, our reasoning, our discernment,
Our judgment, should lead us to greater justice!
While our emotions, our feelings, our sentiments,
Our conscience, should lead us to be piteous!

---

141 Sacred fire of heavens: In Greek mythology, the god Prometheus angered Zeus by stealing his fire and sharing it with humans; as punishment, Prometheus was chained to a boulder and his liver was consumed by a giant eagle daily, regenerating itself overnight.

But even to ourselves, are we not merciless?
We sacrifice sons for our vices' lust,
Rather than shun lustful vice for our sons -
Our strengths defend the weaknesses in us!
This war is the prideful versus the envious
And the gluttonous profit in the midst -
While our virtuous sons are sacrifices!
We have overcome nature's every challenge
But our own faults, we've no power to manage!
We've climbed adverse ladders of evolution -
To slay ourselves on points of ambition!

Fr. Condorcet raises the hip bone and gazes on the Cathedral.

With help of this once-useful axial hip[142]
This man may have braved that spire's ascent...
To form sculptures there, nearest the heavens!
Instead this soldier's vaporized in trenches!
You see the bone of this disembodied thumb?[143]
It might have formed yon rare cathedral dome.
He might have been like to those generations
Who were humble and serving in their stations,
Who labored tirelessly for many a century
To create cathedral glass of such artistry:
The colors are unexampled in nature,
Of novel beauty and immortal order!
But the soldier practiced instead to use a weapon;
Such was not assigned us by the will of Heaven!

Look you! The thumb that may clasp in friendship
Or mold statues of yon church of worship,
Is disintegrated here, and useless!
Man! The perpetually self-opposed one,
Fitted adroitly with an opposable thumb!
Look you! Here is another: a shattered coccyx![144]

---

142 Axial hip: The axial hip is that part of the human anatomy that allows humans to stand upright, unlike all the other animals in nature.
143 The opposable thumb: That part of the human hand which renders the hand unique in nature and capable of composition.
144 Coccyx: Refers to the human tailbone which the tribes of the Levant consider the bone from which our immortal forms grow in heaven.

The Tribes of Levant believe in this coccyx,
They believe our heavenly frames form round it!
Thumb, hip and coccyx ship with countless remains
Of those blasted to atoms, in this war of the vain!

Col Blunt: There's reason we're come to this.

Condorcet: Oh?

Col. Blunt: Justice!

Condorcet: Justice! A fine name pinned to your native flag,
darkly But the name is no inference of the act!
Are all babes born in Devonshire[145] angelic?
Are all babes born Bavarian[146] demonic?
Have they not all a portion of goodness?
Isn't the goodness of each worthy uniting,
Rather than over a roared syllable, dividing?
We need defeat the evil in each opposite host
By the virtues inherent in each opposite soul!
Stop this war of names, English or German!
And unite the virtues of being human!
For Justice is not a name owned by a faction,
But a most human gift - housed in a relation!

Col. Blunt: That's fine, I understand, you are a priest.
What does one do when such evil's unleashed?

Condorcet: Humanity must use its gift for discerning,
And behind the good in all, be uniting!
We need recognize conditions of evil,
In our opponents and more so in ourselves.
Pity the damned evil, but kill it in the shell,
Before unleashing some other fury of Hell!
When poles collide with vice and virtues forged,
They shatter even the air of this frail orb!

---

145 Devonshire: A county in southern England.
146 Bavarian: A state of southeast Germany.

We must clasp, embrace, kiss, love our opponents!
As God bore us, did he not demand reconcilement?

How otherwise have we used our human gifts?
How do we pay him by whom we've been honored?
We use God's gifts to make ourselves monsters!
We use our speech, if it serves, for lying,
We use our graceful hands for bloodletting,
We use reason to devise these plots of war,
We use arts to sow amidst brother's discord!

The soldiers say this trench is half way to hell,
That's true! I'd say we've been digging damn well,
This have we done with our human free will!
Pardon - my soul's bleeding, I get that incensed
To see divine vessels, shredded in a trench!

Fr. Condorcet kneels and prays.

To be our best in how we relate, I pray,
That one just law may differences arbitrate,
And such law save us from this horrid fate!
May we overcome sin and our human tears
And embrace in our joy for a thousand years!

*Fr. Condorcet feels the human relics in his hands and begins his
passage back to the Cathedral of Amiens*

Good day to you, stranger!
Turning back to view Blunt
I meant soldier.
I pray you are not lost, like all these others!

*Condorcet turns back again to go. Blunt hits himself on the head
and yells to himself.*

Col. Blunt: Stop beating! It is for England! For England!
The empire needs all her sons to build upon!

Blunt puts his hands on his hips and his thumb touches the correspondence in his pocket, which this while he had forgotten.

Col. Blunt: This should be my recall! Damn this war to hell!

In his rage, Blunt tears at the envelope, almost ripping the enclosure, which flips out and lands on the ground. He picks the correspondence up and reads:

Patricia Blunt: "Byron,
          The unimaginable has happened!
          Pierce has been called up. He has left Britain.
          I have here his hurried note, with his terse goodbye!
          He is gone, Byron, without awaiting my reply!
          I would have stopped him, chained him to the ground
          Rather than see my last son's life hewn down!

          The law is supposed to provide a closed door
          For Pierce, our family's sole survivor!
          What's become of government's covenant?
          Have we no right to save our love's last remnant!
          Was not our Henry enough for England?
          Our first son, whose eyes mine no longer spy,
          For the sea's moving face is his eternal sky!
          Where is our oldest son? Entombed in ocean!
          He's still on his ship's deck, still at his station!
          In suffocating depths, drowning for the nation!
          I still feel Henry's cherub hand on my face,
          His haunting hand reaches from his ocean grave!
          How much more, Byron, must we sacrifice?
          How can we lose our remaining son's life!

          I feel the dread, as our ancient Mother Sarah,
          When Abram and Isaac left for Moriah![147]
          She must have seen the wood borne on Isaac's back,
          She must have heard innocent Isaac ask:
          'Father, we've wood but where's the fatted calf

---

147 Moriah: The holy mountain in central Jerusalem.

Whose sacrifice will earn God's blessing thanks'?
She knew that God had demanded his life!
Sarah knew Isaac was the promised sacrifice!
God forbore to take the knife from Abram's hand,
Vowing never to ask such sacrifice of man!
God sent Abram an intervening angel,
Sparing Isaac, the fatal knife's arrival!
God told Abram he himself would provide the sheep,
To be sacrificed for man... as an offering!

Will you save Pierce? Not from God, but England?
She demands more sons of God than God himself!
Will England not allow us to save ourselves!
God never asked of man as much as Lloyd George.[148]
Since when does England house a divine lord?
What unknown heaven's worth this grieving?
Such a new Eden is beyond our achieving!
What is the pay for this requested sacrifice?
Where hides England the sufficient paradise?

Byron, please be mindful of our covenant
Remember you must honor me your promise,
It is I, whom you swore forever to cherish!
Cherish my will and send our boy to his home;
Forbear not to see him dissolve in the Somme!
Pierce is that radiant frame of our love:
He is all that we have left, he's our only one!
Intervene with the powers you know that be:
Demand Pierce be allowed to live life's lease!
What shall we know, if we lose Pierce's light?
The lingering, empty and lifeless life
Of the fruitless tree that has been petrified,
That lives unrenewed by water or light,
That stands a ghost, in a perpetual night!

Let England find another pawn for her war,
Another sacrifice to die in this storm!

---

148 Lloyd George: David Lloyd George, Prime Minister of the United Kingdom, 1916-1922.

Listen to the soul of your steadfast wife,
Save our Son, if you would save our life,
Listen. Love. Attend!

Your Bride, Patricia"

Col. Blunt: God! Let it not be, Pierce is bound for the Somme!
Henry! Pierce! And Patricia!   Are we all gone?

End of Act One Scene Four

ACT ONE
SCENE FIVE

REPORTS TO GENERAL GOUGH

Place: The Brown Line defensive trench of the British Fifth Army before Amiens, France, on March 21, 1918 at 1:30a.m.

Present: Gen. Hubert Gough, Col. Byron Blunt, Maj. Henry Lancaster, Maj. Richard York, Capt. Geoffrey Reilly, RFC; later: David Kupfer, Dr. Meacham, Capt's John Hawkins, Blair Devlin, Dylan Connor and Lts. Chandrahas Rana, Dumisa Zulu

Scene: *A closed meeting is convened at the British Fifth Army HQ to assess present and comparative strengths between the British Army and German forces under Ludendorff. The scene is the same as formerly, but the deep of night has fallen. The room has a single lamp, hanging over a work table filled with maps and miscellaneous information. The first participants surround the table, when Col. Blunt abruptly enters and interrupts the discussion.*

Col. Blunt: Pardon, men! I need a word with Sir Hubert!

Gen. Gough: Colonel! Captain Reilly's giving report.

Col. Blunt: This is urgent!

Gen. Gough: At this time, sir, what isn't?
                 I beg your pardon, Blunt, what on earth is it?

Col. Blunt: There has been a mistake in army records,
                 My last son's not filed as a sole survivor,
                 He has been called from Home Reserve to action
                 Against the laws of our Army's convention!
                 We lost Henry at sea, and have nobody
                 But our Pierce, who's in Home Guard infantry!

Gen. Gough: Byron! We all know well how you must feel,
                But the sole survivor law has been repealed.
                Everyone who can raise a weapon,
                Is on ship or train bound here from England!
                You may ask York, here…

Maj. York: I have your son's name.
                He's just arrived. He was on my son's train.

Maj. Lancaster: Blunt, you must know how grave this matter stands.
                You suffered such want of troops on Hellas' sands.

Maj. York: I know this comes as small consolation, Blunt,
                Many of us now risk our only son.
                Look, I will send for Pierce, you may talk to him,
                He's assigned with my son, to my division.

Col. Blunt: Damn…   Damn…

Gen. Gough: Blunt, what information did you bring?

Col. Blunt: Yes, sir, Kupfer and I are ready with inventories.

Gen. Gough: Very good, bring Kupfer and our Red Liners.

*Dr. Meacham, David Kupfer and Capts. Robertson Hawkins, Blair
Devlin, Chandrahas Rana, Dylan Connor, Blair Devlin and Dumisa
Zulu enter.*

Gen. Gough: Good evening, gentlemen, we've had news
                That must be shared. I want no one confused.
                Proceed, Reilly!

Capt. Reilly: Our last light recon is done
                And we've estimates of numbers on our front.
                Total German troop strength in this sector
                Rounds to one hundred divisions or better!
                Of which forty divisions face the Fifth Army,

Thirty more are in reserve and secondary,
While we've counted six thousand gun emplacements
Ranged along their second line entrenchments!

Gen. Gough: Blunt?

Col. Blunt: *Reading somberly; the inventory sheet begins quaking.*

Our arms comprise seventeen divisions;
We have in reserve five further divisions,
With twenty-five hundred gun emplacements!

Blunt crumpling the page, then to himself.   *No...*

Maj. Lancaster: Let's see, that puts their numbers at four to one?

Maj. York: A division for each... thousand yards of ground!

Gen. Gough: We have one more report from Captain Meacham?

Dr. Meacham: Yes, sir! I've come from the infirmary.
A strident new influenza[149] is raging,
Affecting fifteen percent of our able troops.
Numbers are rising of those subject to flu.

Gen. Gough: Damn the chance! One flu bacillus radicalized
And lays flat a portion of our able lines!

Dr. Meacham: What is strange, it is seizing the young and strong,
Moving quite swiftly, illness is not prolonged.
Subjects become well in a week or are gone!
We think the real culprit is Cytokine Storm,
When flu immune reaction over performs!

Capt. Reilly: We can see Germany's infirmary tents,
And note them during our reconnaissance,
Rising behind their lines, filed in masses!

---

149 Influenza: The 1918 flu pandemic known as the Spanish Flu, which lasted from March 1918 to June 1920.

Gen. Gough: If we are as sick, it's to no advantage.
Anything to consider, Mister Kupfer?

Kupfer: You have countless needs we can't deliver!
We can fill no inventories for ten days,
That's laboring without stint at double pay!
Our warehouse's empty, there's nothing else to say.
But there is a warning I would deliver,
There are Krupp guns near here of such power,
They can launch shells and crush the Eiffel Tower!

Maj. Lancaster: France may surrender with Paris imperiled!

Gen. Gough: Such a thing, I think, would make France more feral!

Maj. York: But it would please the Germans you know:
Divide our half strength before our double foe.

Maj. Lancaster: France could flake, like outer shells of cesium[150]
If we haven't gravity to hold her in union.

Gen. Gough: Let me digest all of this information,
Await orders…for changes of formation!

Enter Lt. Pierce Blunt.

Pierce Blunt: Hello sir!

Byron Blunt: Good God Pierce!   You oughtn't be here!
Your sudden departure fills your mother with fear.

Pierce Blunt: I'm aware. My duty called, could I forebear?
Have not the lands of England always fed me;
Have not waters of England always bathed me;
Has not England's justice always sheltered me?

Greater praise there is not than reverence,

---

150 Cesium: An alkali metal, extremely reactive and changeable at low degrees of temperature. Its electrons easily peel away.

Greater love there is not than obedience.
Here shall I praise England, here I serve our home,
For she's the greatest good the world's ever known!

Byron Blunt: Pierce, you do not know, the odds here won't hold!

Pierce Blunt: No more so, sir, than they were at Agincourt.[151]

Byron Blunt: My good son - this is not that kind of a war!

Pierce Blunt: We Blunts have served England for centuries;
In that service, there shall be no changing!
Then 'tis I whose faith bids me to sacrifice,
And I will prove conqueror of greatest kind,
For the weak vices of the mind I subdue:
With all the invulnerable armor of virtue!

Byron Blunt: Son, know you not, Henry's loss was enough?
Mother and I've lost enough of what we love!

Pierce Blunt: Forgive me, sir, to you both I will return
Only when war ends on this convulsing world!
Besides sir, not a car, train, boat or lorry
Could you find before the battle starts storming,
We're both stuck on this front by necessity!
And you know 'Necessity takes no holiday.'[152]

Byron Blunt: God of Heaven!

Pierce Blunt: Sir, do not be bothered,
All will be well, when once the war is over.

Byron Blunt: Good God...

---

151 Agincourt: The Battle of Agincourt occured October 25, 1415, when 6,000 English troops were surrounded by 36,000 French. English losses were 112 dead or wounded. French losses were 7,000 - 10,000, with 1,500 taken prisoners.
152 'Necessity takes no holiday': A quote of Rutilius Palladius, a Roman writer of the 4th century C.E.

Pierce Blunt:	Can I tell you what a time I had At a party given last fortnight, a dance? You know the air itself is of brilliance On occasions of military cotillions: Everyone shines, ladies and officers, In fairest jewels, dresses and uniforms, By music and light, the whole night was adorned, And the dancing, how harmonically formed!
Byron Blunt:	I remember occasions, with your mother, I've not noted before how you look like her…
Pierce Blunt:	It was a grand time, but an awkward arena, For Andrea was there and so was Elena! Can you imagine?
Byron Blunt:	You've mentioned them.
Pierce Blunt:	Andrea's the sort whose happy being domestic, She's quiet, reserved, needs to be protected, As a rare, frail bird, who needs to be nested! Then there's Elena, all life round her glitters, Like light shimmers on the moving face of waters, As though the rarest, brightest gems of the world Were hung like a thousand suns round her shoulders[153] And she beckons all the gallants of our age, Like Helen commanded war on Troy's stage.
Byron Blunt:	Remember the cost of conquering Ilios: The victorious were soon all slain or lost![154]
Pierce Blunt:	It was a bind, sharing my time between them, Each was blushing to say that I was handsome!

---

153 Round her shoulders: Refers to the jewels of Helen of Troy.
154 All slain or lost: The Trojan War is renowned for the victors having suffered grave misfortunes after the victory at Troy; they either died on the way home or did so on their arrival.

Well, let's face it, sir, appearance rules the day:
In some matters, nature still holds her sway!

One of the English raiding party that was led by Maj. Gavin Blunt breathlessly enters into the room.

Raider: Pardon, sir, I have come here speedily,
                  From what we learn at the front, all is ready:
                  The fields have gone silent with idleness,
                  The guns have gone mute, the troops are motionless.
                  But they're a fearful party from Germany
                  With their raiding parties and close infantry,
                  Their gun batteries and massive cannons
                  Their brand new tanks and Ariel squadrons!

Gen. Gough: Don't worry, soldier, and be of good heart,
                  They are all just Germans, differently armed.
                  And something of us you should distinguish!
                  We are to valor born. We are the English!

Col. Blunt: Is Major Blunt back?

Raider: Was ever such a man?
                  He took one of their officers by his own hand!
                  But a sniper has wounded him on his return
                  He is on the Red Line now, with his prisoner.

Gen. Gough: I want you to go there, Blunt, learn what you may,
                  Anything you can of how they'll attack today!

Col. Blunt: Aye, sir!

Gen. Gough: This feast of battle will soon display
                  Camps of opposites moving to be engaged.
                  When this massive hammer swings for the anvil,
                  We will witness unexampled upheaval!

Something will give and it will not be us,
Though we're tried like pure gold in a furnace;[155]
Make ready, men, hence comes the invasion -
Through every pore between here and heaven!
Prepare everywhere troops are arranged
To fight at close quarters and at long range!

Let the veterans of the Red Line entrenchments
With reservists advance to Blue Line positions
While Red Line will man with raw conscriptions.

Maj. York: Come, Lieutenant Blunt, that's our reservists,
We're a long way from blue line entrenchments!

Byron Blunt: For God's sake, Pierce, take a minute and stay!

Pierce Blunt: I'm sorry sir, but duty bears me away.
I'll be fine, though it wouldn't hurt if you pray.
Wish Major Gavin well for me, if you may!

Maj. York: You can see by the light of his gallant eyes,
He's prepared, Byron, for this destined fight!

Byron Blunt: England! Are you truly worthy of his life?

To Pierce   Farewell son, God be with you and be strong!

Pierce Blunt: Don't worry, Father, we won't be parted for long.

Mr. Kupfer: General, I think that completes my mission.
I could use some method of transportation.

Gen. Gough: There you have a need, Kupfer, I can't handle!
There is no transport from here to the channel!
Every wheel sweeps east now, to join our arms,

---

155 Pure gold in the furnace: "because God tried them and found them worthy of himself as gold in the furnace he proved them and as sacrificial offerings he took them to himself." Book of Wisdom 2:23-39.

For we are bound for a feast, a feast for Mars,[156]
Where, in sacrifice, we will be ripped to shards
Or survive to live, with our undying scars!

End of Act One

---

156 The mythological god of war.

ACT TWO
SCENE ONE

THE PRISONER

Place: The Red Line defensive trench, Amiens, March 21st at 4:00 a.m.

Present: Maj. Gavin Blunt, Dr. Meacham, Pvt. Gaines, and Maj. Gerule Bergman of the German 17th Division. Arriving, Col. Byron Blunt

Scene: *A makeshift shack stands as an outpost above the second line British trench network. The shed resembles the British Brown Line headquarters but smaller. Having the aspect of being built without any foresight as to a prolonged use, it is a barely serviceable shelter. A lamp hanging by a wire from the center peak of the structure illuminates a simple, square table. Maj. Blunt is lying on a cot against the wall; sitting next to him, Doctor Meacham treats his wound. Standing at attention is Pvt. Gaines who trains his rifle on the newly captured German prisoner, Maj. Bergman. Bergman is seated quietly in a corner of the shed as Col. Blunt arrives.*

Col. Blunt: I've never known thousands of troops to be so quiet....
          A whole army is on the move, yet they are silent!
          How are you, Gavin? Doctor, how's this patient?

Dr. Meacham: He's suffered a bullet to the abdomen,
          I cannot tell if it has struck an organ.
          We'll have to get him back to the field tents,
          Where I've the proper means and medicines.

Col. Blunt: Can he wait out the present surge of traffic?
          If you go now, you will go against the current.

Dr. Meacham: I can sense the tension: it hangs in the night,
          And will so, till the first onset of light,
          When the bitter edge of this battle breaks,

In the chaotic clash of an enfilade,
Which upon us and around us will cascade!

He bleeds slowly, it bodes well for waiting.

Col. Blunt: Troop movements should wane before the dawning.

Maj. Blunt: Byron! I told you that you have to go!
                     What is this?

Col. Blunt: You caught the German alone!
You're punctured a bit but still the hero.

Maj. Blunt: Byron, I cannot speak strongly enough,
You must go! No matter how, now move off!

Col. Blunt: Stop the struggle, I'm here to question the prisoner.
There's more, Pierce has come with the Home Reserve;
In few hours, everything has overturned!

Maj. Blunt: There is no time, find Pierce and get out of here!

Col. Blunt: There's not time enough, nor a transport near:
All the force of Empire is in full career,
Moving at a crest and like a tidal wave,
At this very time, to this very place!
Nothing moves averse this gathering motion:
I'd be swimming against a tidal ocean.
Besides, Pierce is here and what's the remedy?
I can't stop him, so I'll stay here dutifully.

Maj. Blunt: *to himself*   *No!*

Pvt. Gaines: You'll find the German's effects on the table.

Col. Blunt: *picking up a paper*
This refers to an offensive, "Saint Michael,"
What are the preparations of Germany?

Maj. Bergman: Do your worst! You will get nothing from me.
Other than a strong suggestion that you leave!
I can say in all annals of history,
"Michael" has no match for its intensity.
Nor for scale or quantity of weaponry!
To win, sir, in the gathering crucible,
You must just survive the invincible!

Col. Blunt: When will it begin?

Maj. Bergman: Is anything so certain?
The days of your empire, friend, near their end.
Days we leave the world's land to one neighbor
And Earth's navigable seas to another
While we dream of owning clouds - are over!
We're emerging from shadows of your power!
The sun does not shine for the British alone,
You'll find sunlight is not a thing you can own!

Maj. Blunt: It never ends. The prideful breed of England
Against some striving one, the envious German!

Col. Blunt picks up the standard army issue German belt buckle.

Col. Blunt: What's this engraved, 'God is with Us'
You think you own God! What arrogance!

Maj. Bergman: Like an Empire on which the sun never sets?
We are the chosen to rule this continent!

Col. Blunt motions to a clump of field bags and jackets heaped on the floor.

Col. Blunt: Throw me that black field bag, would you Private?

Pvt. Gaines does so.

Dr. Meacham: If you've no objection Blunt, I'll take Private Gaines,
We'll need a gurney, to bring Gavin on his way.

Col. Blunt: Right.

Dr. Meacham: Don't allow him to move while I'm away!

The Doctor and the Private go out the door.

Col. Blunt: Let's see, 'GB', and name, Gerule Bergman,'
The normal expeditionary bag of a German.
This can't be right, writing on these documents;
How can this be, this handwriting's… Gavin's?
They must have confused the satchel's contents.
How can your work be in a German's purse?
Perhaps things got confused, bags overturned?

Col. Blunt reads the documents.

This, 'British Fifth Army troop concentrations,
Strength proportion by point of trench defenses:'
This map is of British… not German systems?

You were with him alone, then up came your men,
After you were met, the sniper's bullet?
Sure! How else… keep a traitorous dog quiet!

My God, Gavin! Did you do this for profit!
How much did you ask for the sale of England?
Of my estate are you so envious
You would stoop to something this treacherous?

Gavin Blunt: I did it that there be an end to this holocaust!
Yes, Brother! Even if it means England's loss!
What more can stop our nation of the valorous,
Than if, in this battle, Germany's victorious!
Having so few sons of England to venture,
We will cease to bleed forth our nation's treasure.

All this must end, all this misplaced ambition,
Before it rips our posterity to ruins!

Byron Blunt: Are you mad! We stand against a falling world,
And you! Our secrets to the Germans unfurl!

Gavin Blunt: Aye, it's we, who fall beneath a dying age,
Passages of history are so always!
There is always a rise and a fall, a change,
No prop of mortal making can survive the fate!
Some illness deep in relations of men festers,
Where a weakness breeds, like to a cancer's,
Which manifests cracks in societal structures:
Like in a tempest sea, a storm or a volcano!
But we suffer it where most we need a hold:
In relations among men, who are most prone!

Witness the fissure that cleft the Austrians:
That shattering event, the gath'ring consequences,
When out of a nation's agony and death throes
Two alliances formed, equal and opposed!
Witness the dark tragedy of what occurred:
Strong nations ravaged the weak like predators!
Going for throats of the weakest of the herd,
So went the bloody hands of we conquerors!
Witness Belgium who, naked of any defenses,
Was first ground beneath Germany's ravages!
Witness the far-flung empire of the Ottoman,
Whom Europe deemed "the dying Imperium,"
When we saw her prostate - we flew for that strait[157]
Whose possession might secure the Turk's last days!
Witness the bloodied, beaten and bankrupt Russian,
Whose corruption gave way to revolution,
Which cost and will cost the deaths of millions -
All this deviltry done, for points of ambitions!
We scourged the naked, beaten, and abandoned
When we ought have been... a Good Samaritan!

---

157 That strait: The Bosphorus Strait, the Dardanelles.

All this, for no man or empire is satisfied,
No matter to what heights we may arise!
Nor boundless oceans, nor endless continents
Satiates the will of man's wrong ambitions!

Byron Blunt: Stop it, Gavin! It is England's law that binds all
Within a covenant of justice that's imperial!
We rescued the world from a thousand jealous gods,
Her diff'ring lands, from a thousand rival chieftains,
To make common peace and common Empire
And make harmless man's ill-concieved desires!
We reconciled a thousand opposed camps
In world-circling sanctuaries of justice!
Think you that England's glory and her ascent
From the habitation of our brief islet
To world-circling dominion was an accident?
Gavin! We bestow superior justice!
Our empire's upheld on pillars that are virtuous!
Gavin! You've broken your word to our fathers
Even as you have to our ancient monarchs!

Gavin Blunt: Half of England fights for justice nonpareil,
The other covets Earth's precious mineral!
We are each by vice and virtue imbued,
While we breathe in this quaking world!
As there is no place in all of nature known
Which hasn't some poison lurking in shadows,
So it is in councils of men, in his relations,
There will always be some evil in every good
As there's some good in every evil brood!
There will always be a foe to overcome
While the moon moves, changing 'neath the Sun,
There is a foe, even in breasts of England!

Just so, we brought the world laws of state
Only to lead the world to this lawless place!
Where vice of our pride and luxuriance
Fights Germany's vice of being envious!

While common virtue dies in these assaults,
At the awful cost of our innocent sons!
We are ever naturally at war,
Each seeking advantage of the other,
Using terms of bloody war or blissful peace
As occasion serves, for expediency;
Perhaps it's better so: openly fighting!
Rather than contending as hypocrites
And misusing the names of peace and justice!

The highest of England's mortal laws is flawed:
For no mortal law may ever compose us all!
Conquerors can never reconcile the world,
For their virtues are the first thing conquered!
And when we reach the fell passes of an age,
And conquerors overwhelm the passing stage,
They ravage and feed on the weak of the race
As we've done since days of Abel and Cain!
But our crimes do not end in a garden profaned,
But cross mountains and seas with global range;
And we're not confined by a knife in our harms
But wield tools of Vulcan's[158] Olympian arts
To launch fires on the killing fields of Mars!
Where their effects collide and combine,
And chance to kill, even more than designed!
By virtuous study we have learned so well
We've built this living anatomy of Hell!

At what justice, Byron, do we excel,
Who show no merciful justice to ourselves?

Byron Blunt: This is madness! Father would stand none of it!

Gavin Blunt: I think he would prefer that a grandson live:
               That from our self-made hell, one were shepherded!

---

158 Vulcan: The Greek mythological god of metallurgical arts.

You must find Pierce and leave here together.
Some semblance of us needs be remembered!

Byron Blunt: You kill our father in this! Gavin, it's traitorous!

Gavin Blunt: England's loss is her future's only defense!
I have lived for four years beside this trench
And viewed the deaths of its passing tenants.
Nothing changes the steady procession,
While the maw of death consumes millions!
We strive like the eagle with the night hawk,
Predators that unto death, are interlocked.
I had to find any means to make it stop!
I'll do anything to again see my son,
His torment and this war must both be done!

Maj. Bergman: Such weak knees, your brother's are trembling!
Your England will prove easy dismembering.

Col. Blunt: One more word from your mouth makes transit,
And I'll blast your guts right back to Munich!

Gavin Blunt: "The gods, when they divided out 'twixt three,
This massive universe, heaven, hell, and sea,
Each one sat down contented on his throne,
And undisturbed - each god enjoyed his own,[159]"

Unlike those dim gods, content on narrow thrones,
We half-gods make war - for empty hollows!

Dr. Meacham and Pvt. Gaines enter with a gurney.

Dr. Meacham: Every eye's fixed, every jaw's clenched,
A million men flex, awaiting the onset!
We are all prisoners now, the stage is set,

---

159 'Each god enjoyed his own': Homer.

	We bide like we are mice, nervous in a trap,
	Waiting the pull of a lever, the final act!
Col. Blunt:	How could you give England's life away?
Gavin Blunt:	How can one give something of value away
	Between two entities that are the same?
	The only difference between us is a name.
	What difference is there between conquerors?
	Traitor? Look between you, view your mirrors!
Col. Blunt:	Can it be, Doc? How can these events trespass?
	That Russia should break our allied covenants,
	That faith of France should stand at the precipice,
	And here, that my brother's turned traitorous!
Dr. Meacham:	What!
Col. Blunt:	Keep me, Doc, from access to your bag,
	I cannot be trusted with a scalpel in hand!
	Private! On my brother, train your steady gun,
	We've another here who is bound for prison.
Gavin Blunt:	We are all prisoners here, of our ill ambition!
Col. Blunt:	And Pierce! You kill my son in your suicide!
Gavin Blunt:	Pierce with some other millions is sacrificed!
	What matters it if they're British or German?
	We each devour our own, like bloody Saturn![160]
	We've gone back in time to a barbarous age
	When Saturn, king of gods, his own children slayed!
	We've the might and dim judgment of Titans,[161]
	Not the justice or mercy of a God enlightened!

---

160 Saturn: Roman parallel of the Greek god Chronus (Time), who devours his children in Hesiod's Theogony.
161 Titans: The older order of Greek gods who were powerful but deemed less enlightened than the later Olympian gods, who overthrew the Titans.

Are we the heirs of Giants or Typhoons?[162]
Look how by our vicious selves, we're consumed!

England has dethroned jealous gods by thousands,
For some peoples' committed human sacrifices?
And we unhoused a thousand warring chieftains?
You think we're better than these "barbarians!"
Look around you, Byron, view this vast altar,
For a thousand lesser gods, we commit this slaughter!
When will we dethrone gods of our wrong ambitions
And raise not just God's name but his real justice?
When shall we stop this war's obscene slaughter?
Cease bearing our sons to a flooded altar?
For behold! We are all spiritual cripples:
Blind even to our own sins and evils!
How laughably are we self-mocked:
We proselytized for God, whose law we've forgot!
The first of all laws human or divine,
Was the first we betrayed, the first left behind…
Byron, we must adapt or we'll not survive,
For this war's weapons leave no one alive!
We'd best adapt, and a new manner of life accept,
Or beside God himself, there'll be nothing left!

'Twas for us, the beast in Nature to subdue,
But look you! We have only amplified her!
'Twas for us the beast in Nature to subdue,
But it's the beast in us that engulfs the World!

A sound beyond expression of exploding thunder cracks the atmosphere, as the Earth shakes beneath the effects of 6,000 heavy Krupp guns, in a cannonade, firing at once.

Col. Blunt *screaming:*   *No!*

Dr. Meacham: What percussive power! Oh God of the Heavens!

---

162 Typhoons: Typhoeus, the final son of Gaia, was fathered by Tartarus and was the most deadly monster of Greek mythology.

Man's collective hate, herewith, meets in contest!
Thank God for the atom, matter's eternal base,
Whose durable frontier, no power can penetrate!

Gavin Blunt: Why do the nations rage
And the people utter folly?
The kings of the earth rise up,
And the princes conspire together
Against the Lord and against his anointed:
Let us break their fetters
And cast their bonds from us!

End of Act Two Scene One

ACT TWO
SCENE TWO

UNIVERSE OF BATTLE

Place: March 21st, 7:30 a.m., the Blue Line defensive trenches before Amiens

Present: Maj. Richard York, Maj. Henry Lancaster, Capt. Blair Devlin, Capt. Dylan Connor, Lt. Marcus York, Lt. Pierce Blunt and troops. Later Lt. Chandrahas Rana

Scene: *The scene quakes with the near-constant shellfire landing on and reverberating through the trenches. A miasma hangs in the narrow seam inhabited by the troops. The air is a fume, barely breathable. The atmosphere is rent by appalling sounds so cacophonous some of the men's ears puncture and bleed. This largest continuous bombardment ever launched in the history of mankind has lasted over three hours.*

Capt. Devlin: Has not the Sun come up and gone again?
                      Does she not rise again, after having set?

Capt. Connor: Has not the moon arisen and filled her sphere
                      Silvering a week of nights and disappeared?
                      These moments pass as though 'twere ages staled,
                      While unending bombs have our ears impaled!
                      Time treads like worms while these mortars wail!

Maj. R. York: It is both height of day and deep of night.
                      The Sun's overclouded, eclipsed is her light,
                      While we linger, paralyzed by this plight!
                      But hold, men! What comes to be, passes away again,
                      Whether clashes of furies or smiles of friends.

Capt. Devlin: I thought only God could so shake the Earth,
                      But Germany shakes her, like some new Lucifer!

Capt. Connor: They're like that angelic rebel, empowered!

Capt. Devlin: God spare us to survive this rabid hour!
From earth and through sky bombs are downward hurled
Shaking deepest holds of a fractured world!
Here are we transfixed in a daemon's whirlwinds,
With no way out of hell's abysmal trenches!

Capt. Connor: Thank God we have yet these frail defenses!

Maj R. York: They cannot keep this up, this firing of cannons,
While more torpedoes fall from ariel squadrons,
And a thousand sorts of bullets are shed from nests
Where machine guns and rifles are firing abreast!

Capt. Connor: Soon they'll storm on us with sword and bayonets
To complete the horrors of this universe of death!

Maj. R. York: It's for us to brave it, men. Be brave, man!
We fight for our home, for the life of England!

The cannonade lessens in intensity as the machine guns heighten in their firing, relaying a different sounding. One now hears the biplanes of the sky, howling.

Capt. Devlin: I hear aloft the German ariel squadron:
Their engines sound like a groaning titan
Whose hundred weaponed and fiery arms arise
To infest the clouds, for conquest of the skies!

Capt. Connor: As though the ancient titans had risen at once
From the barbarous depths of Tartarus,[163]
Emerging from their hell with obscene arms:
Killing mechanisms that are half-divine,
While we have only shields of a mortal kind!

Lt. Blunt: Free my valor from this imprisoning trench!
Allow I fight our foes, though it means my death!

---

163 Tartarus: In mythology, a deep, gloomy pit or abyss used as the dungeon of the underworld.

Maj. R. York:	Pierce! Don't seek to move too prematurely,
	Not when such forces are a-field and flaring!
	It's not like when a tempest through a forest moves
	Whose winds force old or weak trees to remove.
	This attack resembles the all-sheering typhoon,
	Whose storm downs all: the fit, the strong, the youth.

Lt. Chandrahas Rana hurls himself into the trench.

Lt. Rana:	Damn! There is not an inch of air out there,
	But bullets and bombs infest it everywhere!
Capt. Connor:	Where is Hawkins? Where's your twin brother?
	I've seldom seen one of you without the other,
	He's well? Whose voice was of so fine a timber?
Lt. Rana:	His voice's beauty you'll have to remember,
	A bomb hit, and burst his larynx to vapor!
To Maj. York	Communications down! So I was sent 'round:
	In ten minutes there will be a single whistle sound -
	We're to move to the rear, every man and rank:
	An hundred thousand men of us will fall back,
	In hopes too swift an advance will make them divide:
	We've the mission to thus break up the German line!
Maj. R. York:	Very good. Men! This is it, we are against it!
Lt. Blunt:	Major! How many Germans are out there?
Maj. R. York:	Spartans never asked the enemies' number,
	Only where best they might be encountered!
Lt. Blunt:	Aye, sir!
Maj. R. York:	Right men! Ready to move rearward!
	We are not quite knights emerging from the lists,
	But victory's still won by acts of courage!

It depends on more now than individual merits -
Victory depends on our relative coherence!

Over a thousand years our Britain has grown,
Through which our fathers overcame all foes.
Over a thousand obstacles we've been thrown
And we survive, as the best union ever known,
That now our powers span the various globe,
For ours are the fairest laws this world holds!
Should the sacred union of our island break,
Chaos would ensue, in a reactive wave,
That over distant oceans would radiate,
Bringing barbaric darkness in its wake.
We must sacrifice all to avoid that fate!

It is England's word that orders the world,
It is our word we most solemnly serve;
A just principle than which nothing is higher,
For it is the hold that binds our empire!
We must keep our word to the ordered world
Lest the order of the world become unfurled!
We must move back, for that is what best serves...
We will persevere, for we will hold to our order!
Hold, men! Against this adversity we engage!
Let our forces be one that none can penetrate!
A thousand years we've endured every chance,
Let's fight with our lives, that this be the last!

Capt. Connor: Sir! There's gas, a luminous phosphorescence,
Descending, like the Memphian pestilence![164]
Sure, nothing of nature has ever devised this.

Maj. R. York: What poison ventures aimless in that cloud,
Bourne on the winds to bear us to a shroud?
Sure there's devils in this storm, they've let all loose -
Everything they have, from every ambush!

---

164 Memphian pestilence: The tenth pestilence brought by Jehovah on the Egyptians.

384

Capt. Connor: Do you see the occult, phosphorescent death,
              An unknown cloud of plague devised by men!

Maj. R. York: Put on your masks, boys, for your own defense,
              Our cousin German poisons God's gift of breath!

Lt. Blunt: *In prayer and while putting on his mask*
              I'm of the age of the faithful and the brave
              Britons never, never, never shall be slaves!
              Is it in Percival's[165] path that we now make trail?
              Is this the sacred quest for a Holy Grail?[166]

A blaring whistle sounds above the din, while the men move rearward, over the trench in unison.

End of Act Two Scene Two

---

165 Percival's: One of King Arthur's legendary Knights of the Round Table; principal knight related to the story of the Holy Grail.
166 Holy Grail: A sacred object figuring in literature and certain religious traditions, most often identified with the cup used by Christ at the Last Supper.

ACT TWO
SCENE THREE

THE RETREAT ON THE SOMME

Place: 10:30 a.m., The Red Line defensive trenches before the city of Amiens

Present: Maj. Gavin Blunt, Col. Byron Blunt, Maj. Gerule Bergman, Dr. Meacham and Pvt. Gaines, Capt. Blair Devlin, Capt. Dylan Connor and Pvt. Reiss, entering: Maj. Richard York, Lt. Marcus York; later entering: Maj. Henry Lancaster

Scene: *Having been impressed there by the commencement of the German bombardment and held there by its duration, The Blunts, Dr. Meacham, Gerule Bergman and Pvt. Gaines are now in the Red Line Trench. Diving back into the trench, the British Fifth Army Blue Liners temporarily escape the German offensive. A low lying fog intermixes with poisonous gases. The men don gas masks, giving them the appearance of inhuman beings, characters of a surreal, grotesque dream.*

Col. Blunt: Who are you then, behind the gruesome mask?

Maj. R. York: Still York! Surviving by the seat of his pants!
    From forward trenches, through ravines pursued,
    We ran barbed fields, then through the blasted wood!

Capt. Devlin: Get down! Another bomb has been hurled.
    She'll hit! Blasting a canyon through the world!

A bomb hits, quaking the ground and moving a wave of earth through the air.

Pvt. Gaines: A new cavern is rived and the Earth's appalled
    By rapacious gnashing of the thunder ball!

How many are there? How many hollows!
All alike – flesh-strewn, blood-drenched grottos!

Dr. Meacham: Such explosions rape mass of its energy,
Creating dead mass of a dead society!

Capt. Devlin: Men fly like clouds across the sky's blue main,
Before the consuming front of a hurricane!

Dr. Meacham: Flayed like electrons from an alkali metal,
By heat, shorn from their shields electrical!

Pvt. Gaines: Who can stop the killing range of this cascade?
What force on Earth will it not penetrate?
The heart of the empire will be severed,
The empire from its heart will be dismembered!

It's the death of an age! We may never return
To the familiar bosom of our lost world!
Luxuriant growth of thousand years
Here falls and dissolves like a summer's tear!

Maj. R. York: Have faith, men, and rely on the gift of time,
Time will allow us to reform, to reunite.

This angry storm, this living fury, needs fuel -
As the violence grows, it also consumes,
Until, by the march of time, her fury's subdued,
Therein lies the opportunity: the interlude!
Violence of this offensive will soon lessen,
In the interval, we'll regain our defenses,
And do so while we recuperate our reason,
While we regain the sense of a quiet season!

Pvt. Reiss: Gaines is right! It is the passing of an epoch.
Our flag is down, she's done: the knell's struck!
Nothing can stop the effects of this avalanche -
What can we do? With no means to combat!

The Germans will pour over what's left of our host,
From there, she will overwhelm the French coast!
All we've known, with this day is overthrown,
Even an empire for three centuries composed!
Then what will make us fight? What's to die over?
But our cracked altars and ransacked sepulchers!

Maj. R. York: Calm down! Think on our channel sea, so well-wrought,
She's a shield that saves our home from assault.
Our hearth, our kingdom, our heart remains a state
No power on Earth will ever penetrate!

Maj. Lancaster jumps into the trench from the stream of retreating soldiery.

Maj. Lancaster: Catching your breath?

Maj. R. York: Aye, while there's the moment.

Col. Blunt: Well, we have to move or we stay for death!
We've orders from Gough to retreat on the Somme -
Our flanks are exposed, they're already blown!
We fall back to our inmost trench round Amiens;
There we'll gather and concentrate a defense!

Maj. R. York: How hold the French?

Maj. Lancaster: Stalwart and standing yet!
They bring up arms to the south, some reinforcement.

Maj. Bergman: We won't be stopped by Amiens, nor by the coast,
Nor by nature's barrier, your English moat!
We'll not stop till we have London by its throat!
And your isle's prostate beneath the death stroke!

Maj. Lancaster: Who behind the mask is that?

Dr. Meacham: A prisoner.

Maj. Lancaster: Your silence is our mercy's minister, sir!
Speak and you'll breathe this poison vapor!
Mercy to a German? Given him who has none!

You are welcome, German! Back to the Somme!
Back to the fields your first offenses won![167]
I wish you joy of this pillaged province,
Joy in ruins of mutilated villages,
Joy among these graveyards and skeletons,
Joy in these lands that grow nor grain nor herb -
Joy in an earth without fruit or flower!
You've attained German aims, the utmost known:
The paradise of Somme, again overthrown!
With equal measure of mercy and justice:
Welcome to your hell, you are triumphant!
Take this German to some other scope of trench,
He does not belong here among our men!

Capt's Devlin and Connor take control of Bergman and remove him from the trench.

Pvt. Gaines: We are again to swim the swelling Somme,
She's again to fill with our kindred blood?
The boundless ocean will rise with the flood!
Never did Kidron's[168] brook rise with such sacrifice
When a million lambs were wringed by the knife,
In Passover hope that it would please God's eyes!
How much improved will be our future world
For all this dying blood pouring into her?

Col. Blunt: Damn it, York! Where is my Pierce, where's my son?
I'd hoped in this parade to see my beloved!
But it is only masks I see, not my Pierce's face!
I'm become crazed, gazing on faceless trains!

---

167 First offenses won: German early advances in World War I over ran the Somme Valley, but the Germans were turned away at the Battle of the Marne; this turning back of the German forces is thought to have determined the war.
168 Kidron Valley: Location near Jerusalem of a stream, that is prone to flash flooding, that was notable during Passover, when the blood of sacrificial lambs ran through its banks.

| Lt. M. York: | He was beside me for the retreat, all the time! |
| | He was fighting as we marched – he held the line! |

| Pvt. Reiss: | Aye, sir! He was a champion, if ever there was! |
| | He was unflinching, facing these assaults! |

| Maj. R. York: | He stood a valorous soldier, his faith never lost. |

| Col. Blunt: | Where is he! |

| Lt. M. York: | Last seen, sir, he was due east. |

Blunt moves menacingly to where Gavin and Meacham are taking cover, out of earshot.

Byron Blunt:	By God, Gavin! If Pierce suffers or is dead,
	I'll set upon you with murderous revenge.
	I'll end what the Germans began! Damn it, man!

Gavin Blunt:	Brother, forgive! I labored to spare you this,
	I've lost my honors trying to prevent it!
	I don't want Pierce, like Henry, condemned,
	Or to suffer as I do, or as my dear Adrian:
	I can feel the torture of his prison day,
	His ravaging hunger, the sun's merciless blaze.
	From our vice, as from this cage - we need escape!

Byron Blunt:	This weakness of yours, this blind cowardice,
	Allows wrongs of our opposites their triumphs!
	As one opposite gives its contrary strengths,
	The sins of one opposite on the other's feasts!
	The strengths supported by virtue cannot survive
	By misplaced, cowardly surrender to vice -
	For your cowardice fortifies their avarice,
	When we should forgo all vice, for justice!
	And you shield your wrongful, injurious sin
	With what some term noble "name"of pacifist!

Gavin Blunt: Sacrifice all for justice? Then all would be well?
Then what were you doing in the Dardanelles,
When you wrought on that peninsula all hell,
And senselessly, such number of thousands fell?
Just? As when the German over ran Belgium,
Or just as you landed on the foothills of Ilium?
Germany maneuvered to be the Turks' defender,
Much as we did to be Belgium's protector -
Gaze in a mirror. Darkly you'll see a specter
It is both our foe and our self - conqueror!

Byron Blunt: You know as I do the laws of nature's edicts!
The necessities of military tactics!
Need I commend Darwin's work on selection?
Survival devolves to the fittest nation!
You must grapple with your wary opponent,
Probe for weakness every niche and crevice,
When you find it, you define it and resolve:
Defeat of your opponent is the only law!
The enemy has to be defeated, you idiot!
Don't you understand the world we live in?
You want it different? Can you change it?

Gavin Blunt: You see! Since the first sword forged the first aegis,
Or since the first invader inspired a fortress,
Or since human fear employed the first engineer,
We and our foes have engaged in long career:
A death struggle to find the superior!
We have done so by discovery of every edge
Which prevails in a struggle to the death!
We've done so discovering God's engines,
Hidden in nature's deepest elements!
We've read nature's secret, layered writs
Through the chemists' deep experiments
As through the physicists' far-sightedness
And the diligence of a thousand scientists,
Whose vast knowledge we've given our armorists!
Who've built new munitions for our own defense

Until we've devices there's no defense against!

Thus, when we've come to a dying age's impasse,
When the world's weaknesses awaken wrath -
We foes grope into each other's national souls
To violently probe weakness that's also our own!
While with the growing knowledge of God's device
All our gathering powers are amplified,
Till in this frame of hell itself we collide!
Yet are we blind to God's true design:
That within ourselves is the foe we should fight!

Byron Blunt: What! Are you become some sort of prophet?
If God, in his omnipotence, wants things different
He might suggest it! He should pay a visit!

Gavin Blunt: That he did and we crucified him for it!
Know this, to know power of God's devices
But not what ought to be our proper sacrifices,
Makes us like those powerful, deformed Titans:
Dangerously equipped! Blind! Unenlightened!
We are still spiritual cripples, Neanderthals
Who cannot sacrifice vice from within ourselves!
We prefer the sacrifice of our children:
We bleed them to death for man's common sins:
Pride, gluttony, envy, and wrong ambitions!

Are we not still backward as was old Rome
Who scourged and sacrificed God's holy ones!
You take comfort to fight for the name: England,
But our justice, Brother, is a bloody fragment!

Byron Blunt: Madness, Gavin, madness, you're misguided!

May I ask you two - Doctor Meacham! Private!
Don't relate the late actions of my brother!
How can he do further harm to another?
He's crippled…

Dr. Meacham:	If we can help, Blunt, we will.

Col. Blunt: Can you care for him?

Dr. Meacham: We'll try for a hospital.

Byron Blunt: Fool! I hope to find Pierce and to overtake you!
To Gavin   Meacham is going to do for you what he can do...
            Goodbye, Gavin!

Gavin Blunt: I pray you find him, Byron!
           Let us lose no more sons, no more loved ones.
           God never asked for such burning holocausts,[169]
           He asked we know him and act with obedience!

Col. Blunt moves back to the section of the trench with York and Lancaster.

Maj. Lancaster: The air! The atmosphere begins to clear.

Maj. R. York: They've stopped the poison!

Lt. M. York: German troops are near...

Col. Blunt: Once again, lad! Where did you see Pierce last?

Lt. M. York: Due east sir, in the new-made "No Man's Land."

Maj. R. York: If you venture blindly, Blunt, you won't come back!
           There's nothing left there, but the wake of wrath!

Byron Blunt: I would scour hell itself to find my lost one![170]

Maj. Lancaster: Well, Blunt, you know best what you will confront.

Blunt climbs over the lip of the trench and labors eastward into the miasma.

---

169 Holocausts: Burnt offerings refer to Hosea 6:1-6, Psalm 40:7 and Hebrews 10:1.
170 I would scour Hell itself to find my lost one: Psalm 2 and Matthew 18:1.

Maj. R. York:	Men, we must prepare to leave. Get your gear!
	We move again, to the trenches to our rear!
Pvt. Reiss:	We move from trenches to caves to craters!
Pvt. Gaines:	Wait! Where's Shelley, Lemley, Rana, and Weller?
	Of our martial brothers, where's the remainder?
Maj. Lancaster:	If they have not returned, they have not lived to.
	Pick up your gear, men, we must get on the move!

End of Act Two Scene Three

ACT TWO
SCENE FOUR

WOUND IN WIRES

Place: The new No Man's Land between the British Red and Blue lines

Present: Col. Byron Blunt, alone within a field of wounded warriors, later Lt. Pierce Blunt

Scene: *The area between the British Red Line trench and what was the Blue Line has suffered the most withering cannonade in the history of warfare. Churned up generally and punctuated with craters, and in places afire, the ground is interspersed with unexploded shells and mines and razor-studded barbed wire. Fumes, poison vapor, embers and ash fill the atmosphere, so much so that a constant cloud eclipses the sun. Blasted trees forming grotesque figures and the remains of newly wounded soldiers are strewn over the landscape. Throughout one hears sounds of scattered bombs exploding, intermittent gunfire, and the groaning engines of bi-planes over head in the low skies, and intermittent evidence of balloons firing their helium jets. Bombs whistle in their descent.*

Wounded Soldiers: God!   Ah!
                               Medic!   My legs!
                          I need water!   Amanda! My wife…
                            Captain!   Are you there?
                    Oh… these fires! Where are my children?
                    Can I not die!   Ever burning!
            I can't breathe this ash, this dread poison!
       Is there no hope for us? Help us dear Father!
         Can you free me breathing this sulfur?

Col. Blunt: I thought what I had just left had been hell!
            I'd not seen suffering, nor in the Dardanelles,

> Not this scale! Only devils can compass it!
> Who could dream it? Who could imagine this?
> Has man ever witnessed such desolation?
> As though hell laid waste to all creation!
> It is an execrable scene, a hideous dream,
> Promised in Pandemonium's[171] depravity.
> It looks, as must have, the Valley of Hinnom,[172]
> Where Ahaz[173] sacrificed in fires his damned son!
> What name had the god who demanded such stock?
> What 'god' did Ahaz worship? Yes - Moloch!
> Which way I go there are treacherous pits
> If I don't stumble in death, it's accident!
> How to be nimble, how differentiate?
> Everywhere I step, there I desecrate!
> Son! Pierce! Lieutenant Blunt! Are you out there?

A Soldier: Oh sir! Save me! I can't move. I am here!

Blunt sees a mangled soldier, takes off his mask, and realizes it is not Pierce.

Col. Blunt: I am sorry. I must go, I must find my son!

A Soldier: We are all of us sons, everyone!

Col. Blunt: I must go on! Son! Lieutenant Pierce Blunt!

Pierce Blunt: Father! Good father, I knew you would come!
                 I knew you would brave death to save your son!

Col. Blunt runs to Pierce, who is wounded and bound in barbed wire which extends from his legs to around his head. The razors of the barbed wire have cut Pierce about the face and body. Col. Blunt notices Pierce's mask is off; he tries to put it back on.

---

171 Pandemonium: The capital of Hell in Milton's Paradise Lost.
172 Valley of Hinnom: One of the two principal valleys surrounding the old city of Jerusalem. This valley is associated with the site of Gehenna. See Map, Part Four, "Moriah"
173 Ahaz: A Judean king renowned for his wickedness, whose worst deed was sacrificing Rimmon, his own son, to the pagan god Moloch.

	Don't put that thing back on me! I could not breathe!
	I followed orders, sir, I did my duty!
Byron Blunt:	Thank God I have found you, my dear Pierce,
	I knew you'd be here, where fighting was most fierce!

Pierce Blunt: I can't move, Father, which way I go is pain,
                 The razors of the wires have me encaged.
                 My legs have been shot, I know not how often,
                 It's kept me impounded, by wires inwoven!

Col. Blunt begins the hard task of disentangling his son from the prison of wires.

                 Ah! The least motion against them; my skin rips,
                 Father, it pierces like thorns of the sharpest.
                 My lungs choke, with chemical fumes they tire;
                 My eyes are blurred, burned with molecular fire!

                 I fought in fields as though I were Achilles
                 But we're all heel,[174] before the killing machines,
                 No armor is sufficient to shield our humanity!
                 The only shield is a peaceful path to trod:
                 There's no shield for this but that of the true God!

                 I saw her figure before me, through the war,
                 Will Elena still love me - now I am deformed?

Byron Blunt: She'll see only your glory.

Pierce Blunt: That's insanity!
                 It is the eye, not the soul, that's the judge of things!

Byron Blunt: I have water for your eyes, and to drink.

Col. Blunt sets Pierce free.   Pierce collapses, bleeding from many wounds.   Col. Blunt sits him up, puts his hand on his head in

---

174 All heel: As in being vulnerable. After the Greek hero Achilles was dipped into the River Styx as a baby, he was made invulnerable other than in his left heel, by which he was held.

paternal blessing, and softly applies water to his eyes and pours a
bit in his mouth.

Pierce Blunt: Father, please, would you take off the grotesque mask!
                That I may see your beloved face, at the last?

Byron takes off his mask

Byron Blunt: Germans attack in strength to north and south,
                Not here, where this cloud has left the air in doubt.
                But I note - there! Gathering gunfire occurs!
                As the Germans come, they shoot the injured.

Pierce Blunt: How merciful!

Byron Blunt: We'll flee their guns and blades,
                Through this hell and fire, we will make our way!

Col. Blunt picks Pierce up in his arms, setting off to go.

Pierce Blunt: You expect to carry me so many miles?

Byron Blunt: We'll make it through, the stronger for our trials!
                I would carry you, son, as far as needs must,
                Such is the cause, our bond of filial love!

                I remember when you were a newborn babe,
                While you were of a soft and vulnerable state,
                What an angel you were, buoyant and beautiful,
                How you sat with your Mother was wonderful:
                I would sit quietly and gaze upon your silhouette,
                Marveling at love. My heart burst with content!

                Then of course came the days of your curious age,
                When there was nothing kept sacred from your play:
                Objects of danger were better hid away!
                Your active hands oft found some perilous store,
                That the youth of your mind wasn't ready for!
                When you and Henry made homemade sling shots,

When half the house windows were knocked out!
You had to be scolded, you so seldom listened,
Your cheek glistened with tears of admonition.
But juvenile harms and hurts taught their lessons
By the depth and scope of your abrasions:
Remember when you deeply gashed your knee?
Sure you learned not to leap the yard's wide stream!

Then came your youthful rebellious days,
When surely no word from me held any sway.
You knew best, and despite my entreaties,
You would do as your youth beckoned, blindly!
And then the havoc of you and your brother,
You and Henry, ever fighting, ever together,
You so loved and so rivaled each other!

Pierce Blunt: I remember. I miss our Henry! Father!
I have always loved you, Dad, more than I've shown.

Byron Blunt: Do not worry, son. I won't leave you alone!
Come on then, rest and we'll soon get you home,
That you should have grown to so beautiful an age,
To have your beauty scarred and such strength maimed!

*Pierce has passed into shock and a wounded state of sleep. Byron
Blunt labors, with Pierce in his arms, up and down ravines, hills,
and through craters, surrounded by wounded soldiers, by pit fires
and their acrid smoke. The air is filled with ash and the thinning
density of a poisonous gas.*

What a scene is this! Nonpareil misery,
As though my men have risen hauntingly
From still and distant tombs of Gallipoli,
To range in this field, crippled and crawling!

My eyes, for Pierce's single pain, weep and burn -
How must you feel, God? Man's common Father?
He who has begged us to behave in manner divine

Must gaze on these hecatombs with bleeding eyes!
I do not envy you, Lord, your life's eternity,
You sense death's agony, You feel this passing,
In a sorrowing soul that's everlasting!
It was not your will, nor that of Heaven's host,
That one of these, your little ones be lost,[175]
That man should rise to such height and grace
Overcoming obstacles age after age,
To have his beauties scarred and strengths maimed!

Gavin, you were right! The law that allows this
Is insufficient. It is a useless fragment!
For if justice breaks and allows mighty opposites
To assume the mount of war in blood-soaked conflicts -
Through the fissure pours hell's dreaded mien!
Like lava finds way through earth's vulnerable vein
And unleashes fire in rivers to consume the plain,
Until all in its path dies and earth closes again!

What did Doc say? All is relational:
It composes men to arise above all,
Like the sky-kissing spires of yon cathedral?
Or in the constructs of our nations and laws;
But at some age, stone itself does crumble,
Just as every age of man ends up in rubble!
The only survivor is the relational:
That relation here's - apocalyptical!

What relation would allow peaceful dissolution
And hold the virtues of man in universal union?
One law between men that would arbitrate
When the earth from her prone basis shakes
And she opens her bosom to the death of an age!
When opposites are trooped together and go,
Converging for war 'round their opposite poles!
Sure that law ought lay in unassailable state -
Which nor base vice, nor desire can penetrate!

---

175 Little ones is lost: Psalm 2.

If only vice and desire were sacrificed,
Not hecatombs of these mutilated lives!
What law has the chance? Will man adapt through this?
Gaze on this murder! The first act God forbid -
Since the first sacred list of justice was writ!
And what was it taught us through the prophets?
That we are unmindful of the Rock that formed us?[176]
We forget the God who through love begot us!
That sacrifice or oblation God wished not
But ears open to obedience! Have we forgot?
These burnt offerings,[177] sin offerings - God sought not -
But souls open to wisdom and the Word of God!
We must learn the Word He gave to Mankind:
That God desires mercy, not sacrifice!
Or if sacrifice – then the sacrifice of vice!

How in the end are we alike to Rome!
Murdering God's sons for temporal kingdoms!
An unwarranted sacrifice that is damned:
One which God never asked of Abraham!
It is I, I who for so much am to blame!
What's worse - all men may sing my sad refrain!

Byron sits down to rest and weep, with Pierce still in his arms, awakening.

Pierce Blunt: Dad, I cannot breathe, it's so hard to speak…Ah!

Byron rises again to go.

Byron Blunt: Come, Son, I can see our moving line, they move on!
                Hang on, Pierce! Hang on for dear sakes, for your Mom!

Pierce Blunt: Tell Mother… I faithful… love her…remember!

Byron Blunt: God! In conspiring this death, I am a member,
                I myself have doomed my life's dearest treasure!

---

176 The Rock that formed us: Deuteronomy 32.
177 Burnt offerings: Hosea 6:1-6, Psalm 40:7, and Hebrews 10:1.

End of Act Two Scene Four

ACT TWO
SCENE FIVE

THE END OF EMPIRES

Place: The British Fifth Army Headquarters, Amiens

Present: Maj. Richard York, Lt. Marcus York, Maj. Henry Lancaster, Dr. Meacham, Maj. Gavin Blunt, Fr. Condorcet, Capt's Blair Devlin and Dylan Connor.
Later entering Gen. Hubert Gough, then Col. Byron Blunt with Lt. Pierce Blunt.

Scene: *It is the morning of March 26. Arriving breathlessly from their long and embattled retreat, the surviving troops of the four day rearguard movement are exhausted and in a state of shock. The scene occurs in the new Fifth Army Headquarters, on the immediate outskirts of Amiens. Bombs drop sporadically, mainly from the Royal Flying Corps, aimed on the dispersed German forces. The planes' engines emit a continuous chilling groan.*

Maj. R. York: The world has never witnessed such courage!
We've held, through the crucible of a furnace!
They've pounded every molecule of ground,
They've crushed the dust to the deepest sound -
But we have come through the din unshattered,
Though they've tried the deepest bonds of matter!
Our virtues have held, we've been fierce in defense,
Like immoveable swallows, before the prone nest!
You men! Through the worst hell men can make,
Held this ground when England's life was at stake!
If with all the Huns have thrown, we've held through this,
Gentlemen, we will rise to be victorious!

Maj. Lancaster: While we moved our forces in retrograde,

The strength of Germany's assault did abate.
Time has been our best ally and our friend;
She's allowed us to mount a moving defense!

Maj. R. York: And our French allies! Let us never forget,
They've kept their word and proved intrepid.
They held the south flank against the offensive!

Maj. Lancaster: They stand unbroken and magnificent
While we stand in an alliance united!

Entering Gen. Gough.

Gen. Gough: We have held! The Germans failed in their design,
While before Amiens, we have held the line!
The ground we've given has made them disperse:
They've not men left to hold what they've conquered!
Our stream of reinforcements now bear the fight
They and our brave fliers who attack from the sky!
But you men! You have done all England required!
You answered Germany's fire with greater fire!
Our England is held fast by two great anchors,
In both of which we have proved superior:
For we have faith and courage to the last man
And nature provided our impenetrable island!

Maj. Lancaster: May I ask sir, our loss - have we a number?

Gen. Gough: An hundred thousand: dead, wounded, surrendered.

An exhausted Byron Blunt enters with Pierce Blunt in his arms.
The gathered company is shocked into silence as Blunt stumbles to
and collapses into a chair.

Col. Blunt: If you bear my family some measure of love,
Protect what remains of my slaughtered son!

Dr. Meacham moves to attend Pierce.

Gavin Blunt: Oh God! The war scythes us again with its wrath:
Gaze on our Pierce! Our best, our bravest, our last!
Oh Byron! Once gone, we never have them back!
No more shall we hear his laughter or his sigh,
Nor more see the beautiful glint of his eye.

Capt. Connor: I take back what I said of this walking ruin.
All the sorrow of the war is come home in him.
I take back what I said, he's so pathetic -
True it is!   Who digs the pit[178] falls into it!

Capt. Devlin: Nor the glory of Ilios, nor her treasures,
Nor Helen's beauty, that the world remembers,
Are worth the sacrifice which Blunt endures,
He fought for a nation and has lost his world!

Capt. Connor: Vulcan never made such divine armor
As could shield Pierce from Germany's hammer!

Capt. Devlin: Blunt undergoes more than loss of his Achilles;
He feels Ajax's lunatic agonies
For of his son there was no protecting!

Maj. Lancaster: When we've subdued the German and their Kaiser,
We'll have subdued the last of Earth's monsters!

Gavin speaks but he is unheard by those who confer.

Gavin Blunt: Oh! There will be room for chaos to come again!
If we rule but a whole half of Earth, what is left
Of a world will never come to rest,
But it will rise in the eternal quest,
Ranged in opposites, in wars for conquest!
Then will ensue another conflagration
When some marauder carves up a weak nation!
When a daemon fully armed and hateful moves

---

178 Who digs the pit: Psalm 7:15

At the head of massed armies - in a cult of doom!
For man always suffers from his native weakness:
He can never unify in a single justice
But ever thinks in his own self-interest!

As elements and vacuum have their existence,
As long as they are in conflict, harrowing weakness,
As long as there are eathquakes, torrents and storms,
Man will be a child of everlasting war!
There will always be some tyranny to overcome;
While the moon moves, man chafes beneath the Sun,
For there is no end of man's false ambitions -
And man, in law, will never form a union!

They will come to batter, batter, batter,
At all the bonds of matter, matter, matter,
Until man's hope scatters, scatters, scatters...

Shouting It gnaws in the deepest reaches of my soul,
      Adrian! You are in whereabouts unknown!

Capt. Devlin: There's a Blunt whose reason has blown a bolt.

Capt. Connor: This bleeding scene, what man's soul does not revolt?

Lt. York has moved over to Pierce, who is being attended by Dr. Meacham.

Lt. M. York: Pierce, lad! Come to! Can you hear me, old boy?

Dr. Meacham: He does not hear you. His life is destroyed.
      Through these three days, he carried his dead boy.
      Pierce is beyond all the arts man can employ.

Col. Blunt: Oh Patricia! What immeasurable loss is this
      Which no power of the earth can interdict?
      Breathe, my son! Breathe by the grace of God,
      That's it! I see your eye glimmer, your head nod...

Pierce! You are the foremost blossom of our love!
Patricia! How proud we are of our dearest son!
So composed are you, son, of so many gifts,
The very seat of heaven I thought you might lift!
I thought for you, Pierce, life's chief adversity
Would be a blank canvas that needed painting!
Or a bountiful thought that needed relating,
Some obstacle to the advance of the beautiful,
Which you might surmount on behalf of the world.

Yours was the princely power at your birth,
Your fragile form surrounded in splendor.
Before the day star, like the dew, we begot you,[179]
Oh Patricia! Henry! Pierce! What did I do!

Gavin Blunt: We are so conceived and in pain we writhe:
For we are born companions to the wind.
Salvation we have not achieved of the earth:
Ours the dew, 'tis a dew of light and sacred worth
But it is the land of shades that gives birth![180]

What blood's lost for the names "English" and "German"
When it had all been saved, if just "human"!
We die here for nations of Earth - material,
When we should live by one light - relational!

We had best not be cast in the bounds of stone.
We'd best listen, best learn, must not cease to grow:
This last obstacle of Man must be overthrown!

Col. Blunt: He has burst the inner sanctuary of our love,
My Patricia, by this war we're undone.
All the love we sought to save is overcome!
War has fissured us to love's last atom!
Look how in the trial and chance of war,
By metal and poison, our son was swarmed!

---

179 Like the dew: Psalm 110.
180 But it is the land of shades that gives birth: Isaiah 26.

409

Maj.s Lancaster and York and Gen. Gough are conferring at the central table. While they talk together, Gavin Blunt again speaks to himself.

Maj. Lancaster: What number is our war dead and wounded?

Gen. Gough: With this battle, we are over a million.

Gavin Blunt: Died so many? So died we one and all,
               For a fragment of life's veritable law!

Maj. R. York: What an account!

Maj. Lancaster: Are we come to so many?
               I've another number here that's heartbreaking:
               Given initial numbers of this war's infantry,
               We've suffered one hundred percent casualties!

Gen. Gough: By this war, our former world will be gone:
               The Empires of the Russian, the Ottoman,
               The Austro-Hungarian and the German,
               And we, dear God, have lost a generation!

Gavin Blunt: The rain's come, the river swells, the winds blown -
               The Earth has shaken, the houses have come down![181]

Gen. Gough: This battle should secure at least a truce.

Gavin Blunt: An interlude, soon found disagreeable!

Maj. R. York: The Germans must revel in this event,
               By our victory, our generation is dead.

Gavin Blunt: Don't worry, your opponent will come again!

Maj. Lancaster: I'm unsure, in administration of our Empire,

---

181 The house has come down: Luke 6:43.

	What is the physical number? What is required?
Gen. Gough:	A million of arms and administrators.

Maj. R. York:	Are we come to our empire's period, then?

Gen. Gough:	Who is to say? But I recall the great legend:
	After the Greek heroes overcame Ilios,
	The conquerors on their way home were lost
	Or were destroyed, arriving to their native coast!

A sonic boom is heard of a bomb striking the cathedral.

	What? The Hun wants his visceral strength displayed!

Maj. R. York:	A bomb has burst through the Cathedral's nave!
	Have you heard anything that sounded such wrath?

Maj. Lancaster:	Look! The thing's shattered the Cathedral's glass!

Dr. Meacham:	Major Gavin Blunt has joined with Pierce at the last.

Capt. Devlin:	Sir Byron too loses his living aura.
	He and Pierce look like that statue, the Pieta;[182]
	They look just like Christ and Mary were framed!

Condorcet:	Pierce died honorably and in military brocade,
	While Christ died whipped, beaten and in chains.
	Christ sacrificed for the law of God himself,
	While we die here for laws that serve ourselves!

Fr. Condorcet moves to give the Unction of Consecrated Oil to Pierce's body, while Meacham checks on Byron Blunt.

	Through this holy anointing, may the Lord,
	In his love and mercy, help you with the grace
	Of the Holy Spirit.
	May the Lord, who frees you from sin, save you

---

182 The Pieta: Famous statue by Michelangelo, depicting the Virgin Mary cradling the dead body of Jesus.

And raise you up.
Dr. Meacham: Byron Blunt's senses by shock have been seized,
The Blunt family leaves nothing in relief!

Condorcet: Gavin Blunt's fire has left his eyes' encasement,
Perhaps with Pierce's, they arise in spirit.
God set them out and blew breath in them to be dyed:
That like cathedral glass, they might bear his light!

End of Part Three

"Your leaders have turned turtle in their shells."

BUT BY THE CHANCE OF WAR

PART FOUR
"MORIAH"

CONTENTS
PART FOUR
"MORIAH"

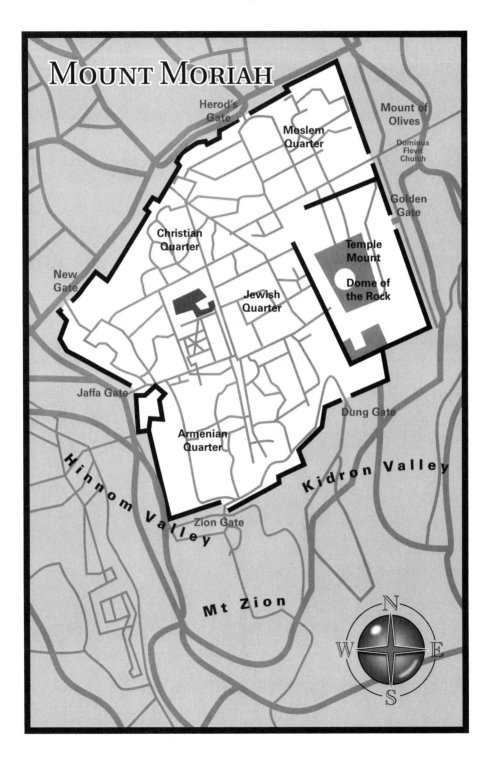

CHARACTERS
PART FOUR
"MORIAH"

FROM THE UNITED STATES:

John Hawkins	Secretary of State
Elena Hawkins	Secretary's Wife
Caleb and Aaron	The Hawkins sons
General Jim Reiss	Military Liason
Major Patrick Killean	Communication Officer

FROM ISRAEL:

Ariel Ben David	Defense Minister
Colonel Ethan Rosen	Mossad Officer
Dr. Lars Bethe	Physicist
Rabbi Gamliel	Archeologist

FROM THE SURROUNDING REGIONS:

Arif Abdul Nur Hasan	Minister in Exile
Dayyan Abdul Baith Hasan	Premier
Ecebay Aslan	Head of State
Akbar Nasser	Head of State
Faiz Abdallah	Head of State
Laghari Jafari	President, Pakistan
Chandra Sengupta	Prime Minister, India

FRANCISCAN FRIARS:

Brother Elias	Friar, Dominus Flevit
Brother Masseo	Friar, Dominus Flevit

Miscellaneous:

Tourists
Technicians
Military Personnel

ACT ONE
SCENE ONE

DESCENDING JERUSALEM

Place: Twenty thousand feet over Jerusalem and descending on Tel-Aviv

Present: Secretary of State John Hawkins, Elena Hawkins, their sons Caleb and Aaron Hawkins

Scene: *The Secretary of State, his wife and their two sons, ages 5 and 6, sit in a Boeing 737 jetliner dedicated to the office of the Secretary of State, United States. All other personnel aboard are confined to the cockpit or the rear of the aircraft. As their sons play, John and Elena Hawkins are involved in an intense discussion.*

Sec. Hawkins: Why must it always be an emergency?

E. Hawkins: Man only moves for urgent adversity,
        And here's where three adversaries meet:
        Peoples divided by a common deity!
        It is also where three continents combine,
        Where Africa, Asia, and Europe collide:
        If there's a change, any tectonic shift,
        It affects the roots of three continents!

Sec. Hawkins: Well, you would know, with your poli-history:
        I've always said, you should be secretary!

E. Hawkins: I told you not to take this job long ago:
        You took the world's most unforgiving post,
        The one that assaults one's health and ego most.
        It is a modern type of Gordian knot:[184]

---

184 The Gordian Knot: In legend, an intricate knot that cannot be untied, but eventually was cut by Alexander the Great; today, a metaphor for an insoluble problem.

How to unite those divided by one God?
Each proud of his inheritance,
Each with assumed title to dominion,
Each claiming the private post of chosen:
God's own exclusive heirs, his own assigns,
Peoples for whom all vibrant life was designed,
Who are either all-seeing or all-blind?

Anyway, why the need to meet Ben David?

Sec. Hawkins: He claims he holds someone with a state secret,
Who, if we wait, may not live to share it!
He says it bears out many of his recent claims:
Knowing the secret, our attitude might change!
Anyway, he claims this matter is so urgent,
That it is worth my cutting short our trip.
If it's something small, Ben David pays for it!

The children engage in a wrestling match over a certain seat and begin yelling in the struggle.

Caleb Hawkins: This is my chair!

Aaron Hawkins: No, it is not! I was here!

Caleb Hawkins: No, you weren't! Besides, I was the first there!

Sec. Hawkins: I really don't need this, boys. Now stop it!
Aaron had that seat! Now back off, Caleb!

Aaron takes the seat in triumph, as Caleb, dejected and sulking, moves to another chair.

E. Hawkins: John! You favor Aaron and Caleb feels it!

Sec. Hawkins: I don't favor one! I favor peace and quiet!
What I favor most is they act with kindness!
I've done with their constantly being jealous.

E. Hawkins: Children are jealous of a parent's affections
And covetous of each other's possessions.

Sec. Hawkins: Well, let me tell you, they'd best get over it!

E. Hawkins: With some time, they ought to grow out of it.

Sec. Hawkins: With regard to time, I do not have ample;
It's time these two stop playing the rebel:
It's time they start listening to their father!

E. Hawkins: The abrupt end of the trip's got you bothered.

Sec. Hawkins: I just want some peace - is that too much to ask?
Just give me some peace, boys, and can the thanks!
I'm sorry, boys…your Dad's under some strain.
Why must this place always make such claims?

E. Hawkins: Each of us thinks that we think perfectly,
What demands more perfect thought than divinity?
With belief in perfection, there is no moving,
We all begin with defense of our thinking.

Sec. Hawkins: Like Sisyphus of Greek mythology[185]
I push a rock up an unrelenting steep,
Only to be cast down the mount again,
Without aid or the comfort of a friend!
Even Sisyphus had one glorious day,
When Orpheus' descent made all of Hell sway,
If for a moment, to his harmonic lay!

E. Hawkins: For a hundred years it has been the same:
The West negotiates to keep pleasures gained,
While Muslims fight in order to lose their pain;
How is it to suffer desert's ceaseless blaze,
Or be a brother other brothers disclaim?

---

185 Sisyphus: Mythological figure condemned for eternity to roll a massive stone up a hill, only to watch it roll back, until relieved for a day when Orpheus invaded the underworld with harmony.

Sec. Hawkins: Each of the three is orphaned by the others.
                It's never easy, is it, to be brothers?

E. Hawkins: Were it not among the three and centered here,
                It would be others and occurring elsewhere:
                If half the earth were allied, the half left
                Of the world would never come to rest,
                But would rise in the eternal quest,
                To face its opposite in a war of conquest!

Sec. Hawkins: Our days at Harvard and Yale seem a dream,
                We were sheltered there from reality:
                Those airy days seem like a fantasy to me now,
                Such time we spent in soft unordered clouds.

E. Hawkins: The sun is brighter here than any I have known;
                It suffuses the clouds with its echoes:
                Grasping their fringes, creating rainbows.

Pilot: We have begun our initial descent.
                If you look left, you can see Jerusalem.

End of Act One Scene One

ACT ONE
SCENE TWO

DRIVING OVER MORIAH

Place: Jerusalem on December 2, a sunny afternoon

Present: U.S. Secretary of State John Hawkins and his wife Elena Hawkins, Israeli Defense Minister, Ariel Ben David and Arif Abdul Nur Hasan. There is also the driver and plain clothes security officers.

Scene: *A group of three black SUVs pull up on a crowded city street in the middle of west Jerusalem to pick up two men standing among a group beside the road. They seem out of place amidst the mass of tourists, as they are dressed similarly in immaculate suits and sunglasses. The area is otherwise one of normal tourist bustle. The middle SUV picks up the men and whisks them down the road.*

Sec. Hawkins: I don't like to be taken by surprise
While on holiday, my wife, my kids and I!
I don't understand this emergency?
It had better be worth our leaving Greece,
Or you may yet earn my animosity!
Besides, this is outside normal protocol
And will be viewed by some as hostile.
So, Ben David, what brings me to this land?

Ben David: Not what, who: Arif Abdul Nur Hasan,
Brother to the mercurial Hasan: Dayyan.

Sec. Hawkins: Yes, I know the name. You were once a player.
You fell off, didn't you, not quite top layer.

E. Hawkins: I don't recall you from social occasions.
Did you play a part in any legations?

Sec. Hawkins: Driver! Where are we going, what direction?

Ben David: We're moving east over Moriah mountain -
        The juncture, they say, between Earth and Heaven.
        The mount where Abraham offered Isaac,
        Where man's sacrifice to God was deemed perfect:
        Hence, the source of Israel's first covenant.

Arif Hasan: I was the Minister of Interior.
        Dayyan, for a time, was my sole superior.
        I was just and our people I ably served!
        Till occasion of my brother's second purge,
        When I was asked to inform on friends, neighbors.

        Thereafter I resigned and kept myself low,
        As the nearer one is to tyranny's throne,
        The sooner that one may be next to go!
        I returned to my studies of the Quran,
        To regain what I could, of my hope for Man.

E. Hawkins: We noted that purge, a commonplace event,
        When tyrants decide their enemies or friends.
        But this willingness to befriend Israel -
        For a Muslim, it's a bit apocryphal?

Arif Hasan: "A people of the Book were the Hebrews made
        We're bid to argue with them in a kind way!"[186]

E. Hawkins: A sentiment of the Quran not often displayed.

Arif Hasan: "Well, Allah has no mercy for the merciless."[187]
        Knowing my brother's plans wrought my distress:
        Knowing what he is able and ready to attempt!
        And something must be done for Jerusalem:
        The holy city of Muhammad's ascension,
        Lest we all lose our own paths to Heaven!

---

186 Surat al Ankabut 29:46
187 Sahih Al-Bukhari 9-473

Sec. Hawkins: Let's confine ourselves to bounds of reason;
What made you move to an act of treason?

Arif Hasan: First, my brother and I are polar opposites
How we view the Quran, how we interpret.
And then there is the menace of things unsaid:
About the nature of Dayyan's dread ambition,
He's left me no course but to this sedition!

He has set his gaze on the three holy cities
Claiming to fulfill an ancient prophecy:
That a conqueror of Islam will arise
To master the holiest sights in God's eyes!
That conqueror, with his initial mission done,
Will serve Allah by making the world one:
The start of his venture begins in Jerusalem!

Ben David: You Muslims rule a third of the vast globe
And our mouse's portion, you can't leave alone!
You rule Arabia, half Asia, the Middle East,
Save this sliver off a Mediterranean beach -
But you want it still! To the last morsel!
And clothe your will within a would-be moral!

E. Hawkins: It never ends, this undying crucible:
The claims of Isaac and Ishmael made audible!

Ben David: It goes back further: back to Cain and Abel!
They've a thousand capitals and we have one,
Yet our grain of sand stirs envy in the Muslim.
So many capitals; yet they want Jerusalem!

Arif Hasan: I'm come to save the place of Israel,
Rather than witness its pending burial!

Sec. Hawkins: What acts of Dayyan's roused this reaction?

Arif Hasan: My wife and I attended a state function

427

Where we heard persons speak of likelihoods
If Dayyan strikes outside his neighborhood!
There are those you think on the U.S. side
Whose words are worthless: they are Dayyan's allies.
Some want war, nations with vast oil reserves,
For whom the spike in pricing is a worthy capture.
While by bribes, Dayyan has others coerced,
That a great war will serve their greater commerce!
Those Dayyan cannot sway to himself with gifts,
He'll subdue with threats of promised violence.
Don't you see! There is no concern for justice!
Dayyan feeds each a meal of self-interest:
You may fill with the corruption fed to you
Or have your seeming security removed!

And I heard Dayyan laugh and loudly taunt -
He yelled: "What of the Jews does anyone want?
They've nothing to feed man's loin or stomach!
Israel before the world will be condemned
For not having right food to enslave a friend!"
The conversation betrays his present readiness.

You see, when my brother ventures the world,
Israel will have, other than you, no protector.
She'll be abandoned before this predator!

E. Hawkins: Hold! Your brother's shown some prior lunacy,
But does he believe an obscure prophecy?

Arif Hasan: I think he uses prophecy to feed his vain glory,
And the benevolence of Allah's blest name
To court more followers to a quest profane!
It is not the Islamic faith that is the problem,
But Dayyan's lack of it - his faithless rebellion!
I believe his only gods are the twin fires
Of his overwhelming pride and his desires.

Ben David: What say you? Will you take this seriously?
While you waver, Dayyan is making ready.

Sec. Hawkins: We're negotiating with Dayyan's emissaries
We must do what we can to work for peace!
We will do what is in our best interest.
That's served, at present, by negotiations.

Ben David: You think to wear him out with concessions?
As you feed him, this monster strengthens!

Arif Hasan: Your "peace" is my brother's idea of cowardice!
He counts every inch you give a triumph.
The will for peace at any price is a weakness
Which feeds my brother's growing avarice:
He laughs as you bless his every progress!
Feebleness compels my brother's hostilities:
For you beg for peace, while on your knees!

Sec. Hawkins: Enough! Dayyan is someone who is trivial:
We will control him using proper channels!

Ben David: It is sad to see how little the world has gained.
It's learned nothing from Jewry's harvest of pain!
'Twas not long ago, a very few days,
Since the Czechs by the world were betrayed[188]
And "peace" by Chamberlain[189] was loudly proclaimed!
Europe looked on Hitler, the corporal, with a sneer
'Til beholding his power in paralyzed fear,
When Europe's weakness launched his fatal career!
Then, too, the whole Earth was circled by Hell,
For everyone sought to spare themselves!
To the monster Hitler, the people then prayed
For a delusive peace that never came,
Until six million of the Jews were slain!

Must we part to preserve your self-interest?
In parting, we invite the like deathly harvest!

---

188 Since the Czechs were …betrayed: In 1938, the British attempted to appease Hitler by abandoning a commitment to protect Czechoslovakia against invasion; Hitler then invaded.
189 Chamberlain: Neville Chamberlain, British Prime Minister who signed the Munich Agreement in 1938 (supra), ceding a region of Czechoslovakia to Nazi Germany and opening the way to invasion.

Are we to be betrayed, abandoned again,
Or will you uphold terms of our alliance?

Sec. Hawkins: Stop moralizing, tell me something concrete:
Do you know what your brother is planning?

Arif Hasan: Yes! That he plans to attack Jerusalem!
Any propitious chance may ignite the event,
And once on mission, there will be no end,
His allies and he, their ambitions will launch
On that first objective like a pack of wild dogs!
With coordinated land and air assaults,
Using weaponry never before unleashed,
That will fill Israel with untold suffering!
He will use every means in his domain
The order of the Middle East to derange,
Until Jerusalem is conquered or razed!

Sec. Hawkins: He hasn't the power to begin what you suggest.

Arif Hasan: He has the necessary power; he masters it!
The more you interdicted nuclear weapons,
The more you excited his envy for possession -
And the more other powers ably fed him!
He now has a complete array of bombs,
Capable of bursting matter's deepest bonds!

E. Hawkins: You know, there is always one slips the net,
Always one who acts unlike you expect!

Sec. Hawkins: For this information, what do you expect?
You want asylum for family and friends?
I cannot make promises as to that.
You know, we do not want to offend Dayyan.

Ben David: Then there are those who act as you expect
And do what's easiest, what's in their interests.
It seems Dayyan knows well his opponents

He bribes half the East, while half fear his threats,
And you don't want him to feel any offense!
His lands are a magazine of nuclear missiles,
He arms cadres in European capitals,
And you think negotiations are ample?
You would have made a great biologist:
What a culture you raise to breed a pestilence!

Arif Hasan: All my family, all that I hold most dear,
                  I left within the threat of my brother's sphere
                  To tell you this perilous future is near!

E. Hawkins: You left them in the place most dangerous,
                  While against Dayyan's rule making trespass!
                  You betrayed them! How can you be so callous?

Arif Hasan: You understand my brother? What weapons he has?
                  Nothing in a thousand miles will escape his wrath!
                  My family is as safe, at their slight remove,
                  As we are here or as monks of Timbuktu!
                  This tyrant holds a knife to the world's throat -
                  Not just to mine, my wife's or to your own -
                  Dayyan threatens us all, no matter how remote!
                  I am as safe among Dayyan's enemies
                  As I was when living among his family!
                  My wife, my children will better survive
                  If some part of our world is left alive!
                  Hence I've come to you, to beg you to rise!

E. Hawkins: Can this be true?   Or is this histrionics?

Arif Hasan: You were right, Ben David, no one listens.
                  What need I say to make you awaken!
                  You think you can, but you cannot contain him
                  While he brings the Middle East to ruin!

Sec. Hawkins: One more outburst and I'll abandon this!
                  What more have you about these alliances?

Arif Hasan: Just this: those whose word has been given you
               Pretend a support for what the U.S. would do;
               But just at the time that you need these allies,
               You will find your desperate pleading denied!
               They are allies of yours only in name;
               In the moment of your need, you'll be betrayed:
               In the midst of the fray, they will change sides.
               Unknown to you, with Dayyan they've aligned!

               And there are nations Dayyan has at his side,
               That you are unaware of through your spies.
               He has access to technologies of covert friends.
               With up-to-date satellites, with ready tie-ins,
               He can see us! Even now he can track us!

Ben David: You score one, Arif! He does look aghast!

Sec. Hawkins: What will he do to capture Jerusalem?

Ben David: You mean as he destroys this Holy Mountain?

Arif Hasan: To see his mission done, this soldier of God,
               Will fall on these lands like an all-biting dog!
               Your American interests in the Mideast
               Will come under coincident attack and siege.
               Your allies will turn on you, and your armies!
               While through Europe, Russia and Asia,
               Where Dayyan has placed active militias,
               There will be staged riots and rebellions
               Until chaos rages like a contagion,
               Spreading with threatening conflagration!
               With that and Dayyan's nuclear power
               He'll threaten the world with the works of an hour!
               Then Dayyan will make to you his offer:
               That Jerusalem must be delivered
               And all U.S. forces must surrender
               That garrison in or near Arab sectors!

E. Hawkins:	My God! Your brother's afflicted with madness!
Arif Hasan:	Yes, and I fear his madness will have no end While his eye perceives an unowned sunset: He deems all the earth to be his opponent!
Driver:	I have an incoming, sir, marked urgent!

The Secretary grabs an offered cell phone.

| Sec. Hawkins: | I'll need quiet. Leave me undisturbed!
On whose soil? What's being done to confirm?
We want all we can get. Do a fly-over!
Are we picking up aircraft on the radar?
Check everything, the whole perimeter!
What did the different satellite feeds pick up?
Are there heat traces, any radiation?
Where's the President? How soon can he be?
Where's the VP?   In Iowa, fundraising!
Where is the nearest secure intel area?
I'm not sure, somewhere on Mount Moriah.
Get a GPS fix on this audible file!
Dominus Flevit, got it! That's two miles. |

The Secretary throws back the phone, taps the driver, who goes to maximum speed. Hawkins then turns to Ben David in anger.

	Have you launched anything at Dayyan?
Ben David:	Has he already? You don't mean? Oh damn!
Sec. Hawkins:	Is he so mad as to bomb his own nation? We've report of a seismic detonation!
Arif Hasan:	What has happened may be a chance event, But if it is, he'll use it to his advantage. So my brother, the predator, ascends, Even with a roar from within his own den!

Sec. Hawkins: So help me! If this has all been an act!
                Do you know this church: Dominus Flevit?

Ben David: We have a shared intel center beneath it
                That has access through an archeology pit.
                It is easier than going 'round the full circuit,
                And we can bypass an hour's worth of security,
                As the access was made for emergencies!

E. Hawkins: My God John! Has it really just happened!
                We're moving so fast, where are the children?

Sec. Hawkins: Nothing has happened that we can't manage.
                The kids are behind us, following our passage.
                What is this steep descent we are come upon?

Ben David: To achieve the site Flevit Church stands on,
                We must pass over the Vale of Kidron.[190]

End Act One Scene Two

---

[190] Vale of Kidron: Location of a stream historically prone to flash flooding; during Passover, its banks were said to be red with the blood of sacrificial lambs.

ACT ONE
S C E N E   T H R E E

BENEATH DOMINUS FLEVIT

Place: The Franciscan Church of Dominus Flevit, on the Mount of Olives, overlooking the city of Jerusalem

Present: Franciscan Brothers Elias and Masseo, assorted tourists singly and in groups. Arriving later: John and Elena Hawkins, Ariel Ben David and Arif Hasan, and the Hawkins children. Later yet, Rabbi Gamliel

Scene: *Typical of popular tourist sites, the Franciscan Church of Dominus Flevit swarms with tourists, sightseeing groups and guides in its courtyard and garden. A few tour buses have parked nearby. The surroundings are autumnal, with gardens surrounding the Church's principal structure, notable for its design - built to mimic the shape of a teardrop. A simple building of the Israel Antiquities Authority stands next to the church. In the immediate distance is Jerusalem, whose skyline is filled with jutting spires and domes of temples, synagogues, churches and mosques. Two friars field questions from the assembled sightseers. The mood is buoyant as a tourist asks a question of Br. Elias.*

Br. Elias: You must understand the circumscribing age:
'Twas of conquerors and captives of the state.
Conquerors ruled with fists, chains and whips,
The normal assortment preferred by tyrants.
It was an age of the rule of the mightiest,
When rule was of the sword, moved by hatred.
The poor, the hobbled, the weak, and the lame
Were killed, enslaved or put out of the way:
Physical weakness was accounted a sign of sin,
A weakness that the Roman would not forgive!

Christ came, in all ways the Roman's opposite.
With his hands he healed the blind and the deaf;
He did not shun lepers or keep them removed;
He embraced them, as he bathed their wounds!
But don't be enthralled by his supernal works;
The oddity was not so much in his miracles,
But he cared for those that Rome manacled,
And aided them, to overcome their obstacles!
Christ showed his strength in caring for the weak.
The Romans showed theirs, being predatory!

In another area of the courtyard, a traveler poses a question to Fr. Masseo.

1st Tourist: Where was Issa[191] tempted by the devil?

Br. Masseo points to a part of the city.

Br. Masseo: Above the highest wall of the Second Temple,
Where Moriah stretches down yon mountain cliffs:
The Devil placed pleasures there, in the precipice!
And bid Christ view the world's kingdoms beneath him
To be ruled, if he would, through subjugation!
But Christ on that dark daemon strongly turned,
To say it was God and God alone he would serve!

He chose to be God's humble, contrite servant
Than over Earth's vast demesne to be tyrant!
He came to serve the weak, not to enslave them;
He came to love mankind, not to destroy him!
Thus did he overcome the Prince of Hell,
As he sacrificed the weakness from himself!
In truth, he proved conqueror of the greatest kind,
For in himself, he subdued the vice of mankind.
Thus he showed to God his loving reverence,
In a way love's shown best, through obedience!
Thus did he prove worthy of God's service:
For he proved himself pure in his motives!

---

191 Issa: The Arabic name for Jesus.

Another tourist asks Br. Elias

2nd Tourist: Why did the world so misunderstand him?

Br. Elias: He was not at all the Messiah they expected!
There was the thought the Messiah would come
As a raging Lion, from the House of Judah,[192]
Who would battle and crush Rome before him.
In style of a conqueror, a king, a David!
They did not expect this peaceful civilian,
Who came not on a horse, as a crusher of cities,
But astride a donkey, voicing God's mercy?
Mankind expected one who'd serve the wants of men.
One was delivered who served Heaven instead,
With the consonance of a constellation:
Unswerving in peaceful, loving relation.
Mankind could not understand his mission!
Who could, given surrounding conditions?
It is enough, is it not, to say this:
Where Christ strode he brought mercy and justice,
Whereas conquerors, most oft, do the opposite!

Another tourist questions Br. Elias.

3rd Tourist: Why's the Church shaped so? Who's the architect?

Br. Elias: It's shaped like a human tear, for here Christ wept,
For he knew Rome would remain the tyrant
While through the world, there was growing defiance,
And that amidst, Jerusalem would perish!
Christ foresaw the devastation, the tragedy,
And felt it so deeply, his mortal eyes did bleed!
The sorrow that Christ felt was the true architect,
For here it was that for all, the Christ wept.

---

192 House of Judah: Descendants of one of the tribes of Israel; the House of Judah was also the House of King David.

Sirens that were distantly heard are now dominant and dust clouds
rise from the line of SUVs rapidly approaching; they careen into the
courtyard to the astonishment of the friars and the tourists.

Ben David: These sacred places! Always full of tourists!
                  Well, man's always a tourist in God's houses!
                  We come and remark on God's truth and glory,
                  But then we leave the holy house empty,
                  And we - emptied of what makes the house holy!

Arif Hasan: This is the last we may see of the sun:
                  I think what was threatened may have begun!

Sec. Hawkins: We are here, Elena, get ready to run.
                  Here is the car with Caleb and Aaron!

E. Hawkins: Come boys, come! Run! You have to follow us!

With anger, John Hawkins grabs Br. Elias forcefully. The drivers and
security agents move in an organized scrambling.

Br. Masseo: What's the meaning of this startling intrusion?
                  You fill our church grounds with such confusion!

Sec. Hawkins: We have no time, Friar! Where are the diggings?
                  We haven't much time, we've an emergency!

Ben David: The luxury of ample time was ours once;
                  Now the iron grip of time owns us!

Sec. Hawkins: We need know where the archeology site was!

Ben David: It's just over there!

Br. Elias: It's here to the left!

Sec. Hawkins: You, Friar! Guide us down through the entrance!

Br. Elias: Very well! With apologies to our guests!

The Secretary, his wife, their sons, Ariel Ben David, Arif Hasan and the drivers and security guards move swiftly together, behind the friar, to the small building beside the church next to which is a covered aperture, marking the rim of a deep cavern. At the side of the building, Br. Elias picks up a pair of electric lanterns and hands one to Elena Hawkins. As they are moving down the shaft, Br. Elias explains:

Br. Elias: When Flevit church was under construction
                  And they dug the sanctuary's foundation,
                  Underneath they found various cemeteries
                  Which had lain undisturbed for centuries:
                  This is a passageway by which we link
                  To all the ages past, that lay beneath!

                  What can be the nature of your emergency,
                  That finds us winding through a site of history?

Sec. Hawkins: I'll explain later on; let's keep on moving!

Br. Elias: We can't move fast without proving disturbing!

                  This is the first site found, that of the Ottomans,[193]
                  It can be gauged, for you see: the cerements!
                  At this next stage they found Byzantine[194] graves,
                  You can see apocrypha, which is quite ornate.

                  Next we step in time of the second temple,
                  The age of Roman rule over Israel:
                  The time of king Herod, of John and Jesus,
                  You can see by the style of sarcophagus.

                  Further beneath, a kokh-style necropolis,

---

193 Ottoman: The Ottoman Empire ruled Jerusalem from 1517 to 1917 C.E.
194 Byzantine: Jerusalem was under direct Roman/Byzantine rule from 73 C.E. to 638 C.E.

Likely built in the time of Maccabeus,[195]
During his wars with the Seleucids.

*The group comes upon a lone figure in the halo of a lamp, alone in
the surrounding darkness, working at the dig.*

Good morning, Gamliel, I have a group here.

Rabbi Gamliel: Ben David! Is it you? Can you come near?

Ben David: It is I, Rabbi, as you have long feared.
               Go on, Father! As you would do with tourists!

Rabbi Gamliel joins the group as they venture deeper in the labyrinth.

Br. Elias: Here are the tombs from the Age of David,
               When Solomon's first temple was erected!

E. Hawkins: If we go deeper, we'll find that dismal path
               Homer,[196] Ovid and Dante carved with their craft.

Br. Elias: Now, we descend to a time, here the remnants,
               Approaching Abraham, Ishmael and Isaac!

               Beneath this descent is the earth's oldest sand:
               It was the face of Earth at the birth of Man!
               Beneath us is part of that primary dust,
               God sculpted as he breathed in Adam's lungs!

E. Hawkins: Friar, you are worth the price of admission;
               You give a great lesson for the children!

Sec. Hawkins: We are at bottom now, where to, Ben David?

Ben David: Gamliel! Where did we stow the mechanism?

---

195 Maccabeus: Judas Maccabeus, Judah the Hammer, led a revolt against the Seleucid Empire, 167-160 B.C.E.
196 Homer, Ovid and Dante: Each author wrote of a hero's descent into Hell.

Rabbi Gamliel turns an unseen handle, which emits a clang, then a groan, then a hiss as a large formation of rock opens, revealing an illuminated inner chamber full of technicians, men and women, at their computers and instruments. Soldiers wearing uniforms of various styles ring the perimeter. The room has a dark blue, luminescent hue, emitting from a long series of different-sized plasma screens which convey live images and scrolling information. The group enters, and Br. Elias stares in awestruck wonder.

Br. Elias: Oh Constancy!   As old and as new as the graves!
               You have come here, for war is to be waged!

End Act One Scene Three

ACT ONE
Scene Four

BROTHERS IN ARMS

Place: The joint Israeli and U.S. intel center beneath Dominus Flevit Church, Mount of Olives, adjacent to Mount Moriah.

Present: John Hawkins, Elena Hawkins, Caleb and Aaron Hawkins, Ariel Ben David, Rabbi Gamliel, Arif Hasan, U.S. Gen. Jim Reiss, Israeli Col. Ethan Rosen, Dr. Lars Bethe, Br. Elias, Maj. Patrick Killean, and various technicians and military personnel. Later appearing: Dayyan Abdul Baith Hasan

Scene: *Dedicated to Middle Eastern intelligence and communication, the chamber is a study of motion. The center connects Israeli and U.S. forces stationed in the Middle East, Arab and Persian sectors. Outside of Moscow, Peking, London and Washington, it is the most proficient technology center in the world. Hawkins angrily addresses Ariel Ben David before Elena and he speak privately with Brig. Gen. Reiss and Dr. Lars Bethe.*

Sec. Hawkins: Ben David! I want time for an assessment,
My anger toward you need not be mentioned!

Ben David: Nor mine, Secretary, at the moment!

Sec. Hawkins: Do we know any more of what's happened?

Gen. Reiss: Some mischance, is my interpretation.
We have detected no single launches,
Nor any evidence of Israeli offensives.
The area is of no strategic importance;
It is lightly populated and desolate.
It might have come from Dayyan or his friends,
In order to found a rationale for conquest!

Or it may have been launched by his enemies,
Knowing with whom we'd side eventually!
It's certain this event won't have fingerprints,
And its likely cause will remain one of chance.

Dr. Bethe: The blast was of nuclear generation;
You can see infra-red of radiation!

Sec. Hawkins: Could it have been a nuclear accident?

Gen. Reiss: Given their inventory of weapons, hell yes!

The scene shifts to Ariel Ben David, who is speaking with Col. Rosen.

Ben David: Ethan! Present disposition on our borders?

Col. Rosen: Status quo, we have issued no orders.

Sec. Hawkins moves to Ben David.

Sec. Hawkins: Now speak frankly! Is this Israel's doing?
Was Arif's warning a matter for setting?

Ben David: Secretary, you know our preparations,
With what great care we maintain defenses,
Our very existence depends on strictness;
Would we stumble in attacking that nation?
Would we hand to Dayyan this provocation?

Sec. Hawkins: You'd best be very sure of it, Ben David -
If we find meanwhile you had a hand in this -

Elena Hawkins interrupts and whispers to her husband.

E. Hawkins: John, remember, keep temperate control.
Defense of Jerusalem, Ben–David's home,
Is the guiding principle of his soul!

Ben David:	Secretary! You know that a single flame
	Can burst its way, can grow and radiate,
	Moving where blown, by wind and current,
	Gathering in strength, to raze a whole forest!
	With discretion, I need alert our forces!

Sec. Hawkins: Inevitable, isn't it!

Ben David: And the alternative?
Who can foreknow a fire's uncontrolled path?
Or interdict all passages from hatred's wrath?
We are as we've ever been: surrounded.
It is, as it's ever been, through millenniums:
We're the uniquely marked and colored hen,
That opposed colored hens savage to death!

Ethan! Begin stratagem two-three-seven!

Gen. Reiss: Sir, I have live wire from Premier Dayyan,
He wants to talk, he says he can tie in.
He says he seeks to view the traitor Muslim?

Sec. Hawkins: You say he can? Has he the capacity?

Gen. Reiss: He confirms that he has the technology.

Sec. Hawkins: Give him the data link. Get him distracted!
We have to know his successive actions
To counter them all with like reactions!

Hasan! Can you provide us with some time?
Can you keep your brother busy on that line?

Arif Hasan: I'll do what I must to avoid a doomed fight.
But I would like the conversation private!

Sec. Hawkins: It can be private, as far as that makes sense,
If you'll do what you can to help us in this!

Though, if one word imperils security here,
This soldier will put a bullet in your ear!

Arif Hasan nods assent as a soldier and a technician show him to
an enclosed glass room within the general chamber. It is a formally
secured communications portal with a desk and chair, a microphone,
a camera, and a dual-feed viewing screen. As they are beginning setup
in this section of the center, Rabbi Gamliel confronts Ariel Ben David.

Rabbi Gamliel: This is why I took up the labor to dwell
              A guard, at guard post, to this portal of Hell.

Ben David: You are here, Gamliel, for I trusted best
              You would keep that dim passage's secrets.

Rabbi Gamliel: Something has happened, or we wouldn't be here.
              Something has happened: the seed of our fear?
              I am here in hopes to calm your warlike temper,
              To be your counsel and to bid you remember
              The abiding wisdom of our sage Hillel:
              "What is hateful to you, do not yourself!"
              Hillel taught this to be man's legal pinnacle,
              The sum of all prophets bound in a little -
              Yet for humanity, it's the obstacle!

Ben David: My friend, I will do as reason would have me do;
              Now, I must attend to what the day will prove.
              Remember Hillel's other saying, which succeeds,
              "If I'm not for myself, who will be for me?"
              In the chaos of war – I trust nobody!

Rabbi Gamliel: Please, Ben David, don't act precipitously!

Ben David: We are faced with an imminent attack.
              We have a knife to our throat, to be exact.
              Know this! I'll not lamely and quietly lament
              While asked to crawl in some new oven of death!
              But I will make them pay for the attempt!

Rabbi Gamliel: Just make sure that in the Temple's defense,
You don't destroy the temple within yourself!
For if you go too far, there is no way back,
What would be launched from here, won't allow that!
Be careful, thoughtful, about what you would do
With these weapons no one has ever used!

Ben David: I really love you, Gamliel, but enough!
I am very busy. I've war to conduct!

Col. Rosen: Ben David! We're coming under bombardment
From surrounding terrorist embankments:
From West Bank, Gaza, and Sinai positions,
And sites within Syria and Lebanon!

Ben David: Secretary! We must move now to correspond
To where we can link strengths: that's Hebron!

Gen. Reiss: That action will be deemed provocative!

Sec. Hawkins: Take Hebron! Otherwise, maintain the defensive!

Gen. Reiss: Dayyan's armies are moving across his borders
In two directions and in perfect order!

Sec. Hawkins: Where are allied defenses? No oppositions?
There should be furious armed resistance!

Gen. Reiss: No counter movements. His lines are all equal,
If there were fighting, there would be upheaval.
We can confirm, Dayyan is launching aircraft;
There's no counter-launch, no counterattack!

Sec. Hawkins: Damn it! Get Akbar Nasser on the line!
Has his army no ears, his air force no eyes?
His forces were all dutifully arranged
Opposite to Dayyan's aims - what is the game?

447

> Alert our garrisons and the carrier fleet,
> Raise the nuclear subs: it's an emergency!
>
> Then get on scrambler for Ecebay Aslan.
> If we count on anyone, he's the man.

The scene shifts to Arif Hasan as he prepares to speak with Premier Dayyan Abdul Baith Hasan via satellite.

Technician: You can listen and be able to see him here,
               But for security, this camera will not veer!

               Initiating satellite access, all clear!

The technician leaves the inner room and closes the door behind him. The soldier remains inside, with his firearm pointing to within an inch of Arif's ear.

Dayyan Hasan: How this would disgust our mother and father.
               There's my brother, the traitor, the scholar!
               Their favored son, who turns his cowardly back,
               At the onset of history's greatest jihad!
               How came you to this: to be my enemy?
               To betray Islam, country and family!

Arif Hasan: Dayyan! You left me to this necessity
               When I witnessed your acts of savagery,
               Confronting laws of Allah and humanity!
               The law, not a name, demands my loyalty!
               Islam, country and family are blessed names,
               But it is right action that demands our faith!

               We learned of "the best jihad" in *our* school -
               It's "speaking truth before a tyrannical rule!"[197]

Dayyan Hasan: Your betrayal breaks not just my heart in this...
               Your actions have wrought real consequences,
               The countryside is flaring with rebellions!

---

[197] Riyadh us-Saleheen Vol 1:195

I have five minutes! Why have you done this?
Who listens to us?

Arif Hasan: One soldier with a gun.

Dayyan Hasan: And it's from me you thought it well to run?
It matters not to me, what they hear from us!

Arif Hasan: I left, brother, for in truth, your recent acts
Are in no harmony with the good of man!

Dayyan Hasan: I did what I discovered necessary
To defend my capacity for governing!
At the onset, you were of help to me,
In discovering this growing treachery;
I had to move with expediency.

Arif Hasan: I found, at a stage too late, who would be slain,
Their crime was in how they deem right to pray,
Or in how their pilgrimage is made,
Or in something as simple as their name!
Or because they were weak and you thought you may
Butcher them quietly, for the sake of the state!

Dayyan Hasan: There is no place in all of nature known
That hasn't some poison lurking in shadows,
And I find it here, even among my own!

Arif Hasan: You abandon our own when you kill them so!
You abandoned them before a predator,
The one that in your own soul finds harbor!
You moved predictably in your manner,
As when the lamb is prone before the panther:
You act not for the law, but as destroyer!
You sent your aggressive minions
To kidnap the innocent to your prisons,
Or worse, sent in stealthy, senseless assassins
To silence those opposed to your ambitions!

Dayyan Hasan: With ungrateful stings, I am in agony,
And yes, my pain breeds this extremity:
These enemies still threaten me continually!
I had little time and had to act swiftly!

Arif Hasan: "The best leader is mistaken in forgiving
Rather than be mistaken in punishing!"[198]
Do they not follow like dietary rites?
Are not their prayers sung at the same times?
Do they not plead for the same justice in life?
Is it not this justice your acts have denied!
You sacrificed our own for your sinful pride -
For, before Allah, they committed no crime!

You cling to an index citing our differences,
Rather than the sole law which should unite us:
The fundamental law of Allah's justice!
What difference is there in how we pray,
If acts don't follow empty chants of praise?
Cast away these lesser customs you've indexed!
Cease empty praise of Allah. Act with justice!

Look on Allah's creation, in its multitude!
Allah shows a loathing for similitude,
Note that no two stones of Allah are the same,
Yet all stones are made of the same base.
But each has its own imprints and veins,
Not like the common bricks men seek to make:
Why do you demand all people be the same?
Even in sand, though it escapes the sight,
Each differently bears the same sun's light.
How for such differences could you take a life?
Material difference has rendered you blind!

The law is too rigid, if it insists,
For like practices, persons ought not exist!
You use the Quran to sway unwary souls,

---

198 Hadith 1011

But you give its words not the acts you owe!
The law exists as a unifying principle
To bind the beauties of diverse people,
Not to crush those beauties into bricks,
Not to make them pray thus - or die for it!
You claim one God and of Him stand in awe,
But God doth create unity through his law,
The same law you destroy, the same you appall!
Where was your mercy, where your understanding,
When you set your hounds on this bloodletting?
Who are you to decide whom of God's sons
Are those whom he loathes or those whom he loves?
When did you gain entry to councils of God
Or hear judgments from a divine synod?

Dayyan Hasan: You don't see! If I had not moved in such a way,
It is I who would surely have been slain;
I condemned them for rebellious intent!

Arif Hasan: Your finding of such foes will never end.
Who is feared by many, has many to fear:
That is the law your misrule has made clear!
If a power's chief prop is fear and pain,
That power's not worthy of loyalty or faith.
No power is just that is enforced by chains!

Yet, this did not start me on my path of sedition,
But that I heard your damned conversations,
Which threaten the life of so many nations!

Dayyan Hasan: Yes, I thought I saw your eye's glare from afar,
But of that conversation, you heard a part.
It began with the hypothesis "if we were harmed" -
Who could we count on, how could we react!
If we were subject to a foreign attack,
And, as you see, our foresight was exact;
Israel, the puppet of a decadent West,
Will pay in blood for the conquest they attempt!

Arif Hasan: This was an accident or worse, planned by you!
With the intent to delude the multitudes,
To move the world to anger through falsehood!
Even though you know: falsehood can destroy worlds!
Listen while you may! Return to the truth!

Dayyan Hasan: Who is the hound, Arif? Who is the hounded?
It's your own! It's we who are the surrounded!
Their fleets patrol our seas; their jets fill our skies,
While our own country is filled with their spies!
Why do you think I had to launch the purge?
In their very conclaves, the CIA lurks!
And look! Even you, my brother, join them!
You look at this from the wrong direction!
Jews and Christians commit this aggression
With acts of their infernal imperialism!
We are the victim! We are the injured!
It is Israel who is the provocateur!
Turn on the TV news, if yet you may,
Inhumanity of the Jews is on full display:
They say it is the Jews set the world aflame!

Arif Hasan: Nowadays, falsehood travels at speed of light
While truth hobbles and is left behind;
And for discernment of truth, there is no time!
Like the veiled dancer in the old hareem,
You dance well, Dayyan, but surely to deceive!
You find the Jew and Christian your enemy.
Soon you'll find more in Asia and the East;
The world will prove small for your empery!

Dayyan Hasan: If it be Allah's will: I am Allah's servant!
I am come upon Al - Quds[199] in conquest!
The Jews will pay for this cowardly attack,
Their death or surrender is what I demand!

Arif Hasan: Dayyan, the Jew and Christian are our brethren!

---

199 Al-Quds: The Arab name for Jerusalem.

For the love of God, I beg that you listen!
"A people of the Book were the Hebrews made
We're bid to argue with them - in a kind way!"[200]

We are brothers by paternal birth,
Issue of the same belov'd pilgrim of Ur![201]
"Our faiths are founded on common prophets,
Of Ismail, Isaac, Jacob and Moses
And no distinction's to be made between them!"[202]
"The law was revealed to Moses on the heights
Therein was revealed God's guidance and light."
"God sent Issa[203] who taught the law with his life,
Confirming the law, there was guidance and light!"[204]
I beg you, listen to these admonishments
Which I've read from Muhammad's holy writ!

Dayyan Hasan: I am Allah's strength and his forthright sword!
I'll make believers of infidels perforce!

Arif Hasan: No… Like the damned European, you seek conquest;
You will bitterly scourge the world of weakness,
For that is your weakness: you are just like them!
Imperialists who prey on divisions of men,
Whose avarice fed upon our vices,
And who act in manner that is merciless!
Take off the plastic mask, end this pretense.
Do you want to view a godless predator?
Look about you, Dayyan, and find a mirror!

You bear the Book before you of our faith,
But of our faith, your actions bear no trace,
You are just the same, your faith is a prop,
While beneath you've no will to obey God!

---

200 Surat al Ankabut 29:46
201 Pilgrim of Ur: Refers to Abraham, whose calling by God led him out of Ur.
202 Surat Al Imram; 3:84
203 Issa: The Islamic name for Jesus
204 S. Al-i-Imran 3:2-3

Dayyan Hasan: You have favored me by stoking my anger!
Truly, how can we have had the same father?

Arif Hasan: You find the Christian and Jew wanting this time;
Are differing customs worthy we all die?
Or should we abide our common Law of Life?
The easiest law to say, the hardest to conquer:
"If you believe in God, harm not your neighbor!"[205]
The One Law which you must now observe
If you would, the Children of God preserve!
Listen to the One Law by which we may survive
Or these weapons, Dayyan, will leave no one alive!

Dayyan Hasan: I will fall on Israel and see it conquered:
See Al-Quds ours or leave it slaughtered!

Arif Hasan: You do not act in the manner of Abraham,
Nor honor Muhammad's law, so we are damned!
Your finding foes to oppose will never end
While Earth holds yet, the unpossessed sunset!
You have set yourself, like a thing in stone;
You'll not adapt to the laws of God you know!
You're a predator and this a masquerade,
For your acts are acts God must deem profane!
A whore in holy clothes makes the like portrayal:
The profane which hides behind virtue's veil!

Do you think the U. S. will not oppose you?
Do you expect the surrender of the Jew?
If you insist on this mad rush into death,
Like a flaming meteor, you will find it.
Stop now, Dayyan!   While you still have the means,
For what you do will destroy everything -
You can't control the force that you unleash!

Dayyan Hasan: When you oft kick a dog… if past is prologue:
Their appeasement shows that they've no resolve!

---

205 Muhammad's Final Sermon

Arif Hasan:	On the horizon of your predatory glare,
	You'll find some weak prey everywhere.
	Tens of far-flung divergent countries,
	Thousands of varied populous cities,
	A million of mosques, a million temples
	A billion of unaware, sleeping peoples
	Are threatened by unexampled cataclysm,
	Because in One God you perceive a schism,
	And rather than show anyone God's mercy,
	You will prey upon the prone, the weakling!
	Is this, brother, how you wish to relate?
	To rupture our family and our state,
	And threaten lands of Allah with a single fate -
	Because not everyone is made the same?
	Think of the calamity, think of the grave cost,
	And know: God seeks that not one of his be lost.
	Not even you would he mislay! While there's time,
	Brother, consider, before committing this crime!

Dayyan Hasan: There'll be no fight, if they give what I ask.
If there is war, you will have them to thank!

Arif Hasan: You are a conqueror weaker than your prey,
For those you should love are those you would slay!

Dayyan Hasan: But you join prey of the very weakest kind,
Who fall all to pieces when I would strike!

Arif Hasan: I would see you again, if only I can, Dayyan!

Dayyan Hasan: Stay where you are and we'll make it a plan...

The monitor fades to a dull gray. The scene shifts back to the general chamber as Arif emerges from the secure area, followed by the soldier. The people in the room turn and note his entrance.

Arif Hasan: I've lost him. So may we all be lost with him.
His attitude is fixed; he will not change it!

Your weakness and aloofness have combined
With his incapacity to change his mind…

E. Hawkins: Cannot one Muslim leader of some consequence
Interpose himself and put an end to this?

Maj. Killean: I now have Aslan, as per your command.

Sec. Hawkins: Minister! I'm thankful that you've answered.

Min. Aslan: John, I'm just looking at our monitors.

Sec. Hawkins: Our intel concludes this is an accident.

Min. Aslan: Yes, and the world may well blunder into it!

Sec. Hawkins: That is my fear, and one we would like to staunch.
We have to prepare for a concerted launch.
I want the NATO base on alert!

Min. Aslan: John, that can't happen, you know it won't work.
You know well, we first warned you of this menace,
But with all your efforts there's still no consensus
From NATO or its member nations
On a fit regime of suitable sanctions -
And now you want military actions?
None of our member nations is threatened.
At the least, we need convene a vote on this!

Sec. Hawkins: I agree, Ecebay, but this circumstance…

Min. Aslan: I understand, we have no more time for that!
The time when action would have worked is past.

Look, we may alert the NATO bases,
And you may even threaten the use of them,
But a launch from here is a stratagem,
Which would involve internal rebellion.

How can we be first to confront Dayyan
When we've some sympathetic populations,
Who, if but for his name, may rally for him!
How can we be the first ones to use muscle,
If we can't get an agreement in Brussels,
That Dayyan's funding source should be muzzled?
I commiserate; you are in a hard place;
But what you ask is too much, and much too late.
Now, if we can find something to negotiate,
I would be happy if we can arbitrate.

Sec. Hawkins: Thank you for your promised efforts, Minister,

Min. Aslan: I am sorry, John, but I speak with candor.

Sec. Hawkins: We won't assume the alert but the posture.

The linked moniter fades to grey.

Sec. Hawkins: Where's Nasser?!

Maj. Killean: We have the link with Nasser.

Sec. Hawkins: About time, put Nasser's voice on speaker!

To Nasser   I must say I'm struck with disbelief, Akbar!
               You're ordered to stop attacks on your demesne
               By our agreement for reciprocal defense!

Min. Nasser: That was before this illegal bombardment;
               How do we know you're not at the heart of it?
               You must surrender Al-Quds for this,
               Until you do so, we break our alliances.

Sec. Hawkins: Akbar, what occurred was an accident!

Min. Nasser: We don't concede to your version of events!
               Our forces will no longer lend yours cover
               We recommend your base's surrender!

457

Nasser's figure on the screen dissolves to black.

Maj. Killean: Communication at source, severed.

Sec. Hawkins: *Screaming*   NASSER!
                 Alliance as good and as strong as his word!
                 Nasser's broken it, as soon as it served!
                 Vanished like smoke, hopes in human promises -
                 When breathed by men, they end in nothingness!

Gen. Reiss: Sir, the armies of our onetime ally
                 Have turned; with our enemies they combine!
                 They move in unison on our U.S. positions;
                 Worse, they advance, bearing our own weapons,
                 Those sold them through our defense department!

Maj. Killean: Sir! Minister Abdallah is on our set.

Sec. Hawkins: Abdallah! We need you to scramble your jets!
                 Surely, you are keeping track of the day's events.

Min. Abdallah: Really, things are happening far too fast;
                 Should we launch, we will come under attack!
                 Really, you must think about that, Secretary,
                 We cannot jump whenever you make a plea!
                 If you would force us to premature attempts,
                 We must give you over and break alliances!
                 The foot is farther than the hand from the chest;
                 Dayyan's threat is the nearer to our heads
                 Than are the strengths of your vain promises!
                 We really have to think of our own future.

The video monitor goes black.

Maj. Killean: Comm at source, once again has been severed.

Sec. Hawkins: With the given word of our allies broken,
                 The peace of the whole Middle East falls in!

Good God! Look at this chain reaction!
By mischance a bomb falls amiss and explodes
And shatters the vast arc: this half the globe!
The colossal frame of alliance has cracked,
And the time we need for remedy is past!

The extent of the damage? We must reassess!
Damn it!!! Can't we raise the President?!

Maj. Killean: Verified? Sir, the President is in motion
His team's scouting for a secure location.
There are riots, attacks, and explosions
In capitals from Moscow to Washington:
In Belgium, Paris, in Rome and London!
And there are reports from points to the East:
From Delhi and other major Indian cities;
Riots are being reported through Indonesia,
Even to provinces of western China!
They are in protest of the Israeli bombing.
We have Europe now calling for, demanding,
Israel cease hostilities.

Sec. Hawkins: So little time.
How could so much collide and combine?
And convulse the order of the Middle East:
With our endurable alliances breached!

E. Hawkins: The fragile dome of the world, like glass, shatters!

Sec. Hawkins: This shift of armed forces is what matters.
Our forces are halved, Dayyan's have doubled.
His new force moves on us unconfronted.
Ben David, you may fire where fired upon!

Ben David: Thank you! We now have control in Hebron.
Though we are held down by enemy cordon,
They surround us, like our own reflection.

Sec. Hawkins: Tell our jets: to bomb those advancing armies,
Order our destroyers to open their batteries,
Have land-based troops go red alert for hostilities!
Now! Where do we find Dayyan most weak?
Where will crippling him prove his mortality?

Gen. Reiss: Strike his nuclear generation fields.
Any strike there delivers multiple-yield,
Crippling capacity for a hundred years!

Sec. Hawkins: Yes, but even so, there is much to fear,
He purposely placed large populations there!

Gen. Reiss: You know the law of military tactics,
It follows the same law as nature's edicts:
We have to hit him hard where he's weakest!
We must do as the law of war requires:
Answer gathering fire with a greater fire!

Maj. Killean: Incoming! There is fighting in Kashmir,
Along the Indian - Pakistan frontier.

Sec. Hawkins: Damn it, this whole disaster may well spread
Throughout south Asia like a contagion!

Maj. Killean: We have request for immediate tie-in,
Once again, it comes from Premier Dayyan.

Sec. Hawkins: Get it on! Let's hear what he has to say.

The figure of Dayyan Hasan comes on multiple screens and his voice alone resonates over the comm system.

Dayyan Hasan: There you are! So much can happen in a day!
Your leaders have turned turtle in their shells,
Leaving me with your secondary selves.
For this attack on my country, for this murder,
I demand Israel's immediate surrender!

Ben David: What will become of Israeli citizens?

Dayyan Hasan: They will be exiled or sent to prison,
                  And their lands given to Palestinians.
                  With Al-Quds, I must make exception:
                  That will remain my private possession.
                  But the land will go back to the outcasts,
                  So long as they agree with what I exact.

Ben David: Being outcast from home is a horrid thing
                  One we Jews have suffered recurrently:
                  Cast out by Babylonians and by Assyrians,[206]
                  So by the Romans and the Byzantians;
                  With you we were cast from neighboring altars,
                  For a century, by the Christian Crusaders,
                  And later, by gruesome acts of the Tartars!
                  But we knew peace under the Mameluks,
                  And again under the Turk, the Ottomans!
                  Despite upheavals throughout our history,
                  We return to this Mount of Divinity,
                  Where Abraham showed God his affinity!
                  We are always the ones who are cast from home.
                  It's the same in all areas of the globe;
                  And when we can't be exiled enough away,
                  We are burned alive for the sake of our faith!
                  For millennia we have shared the Levant.
                  We would share it now; what more do you want?

Dayyan Hasan: That is easy. Leave our Al-Quds! Get out!

Ben David: Where to go?

Dayyan Hasan: Past my power's furthest bound!

Ben David: How far is that?

---

206 Cast out by Babylonians and by Assyrians: The kingdom of Judah was conquered by the Assyrian ruler Shalmaneser V in the 8th century B.C.E. and by Nebuchadnezzar II of Babylon in the 6th century B.C.E.

Dayyan Hasan: Well, things change, who can say?
                   At least fourth a world, then fourth a world away,
                   Then we'll have to see, how succeeds the day!

Ben David: The world, it's said, is pillared by three things:
                   On truth, on justice and on stable peace.
                   Your falsehoods and actions threaten all three!

Dayyan Hasan: Your presence in Palestine is criminal,
                   So is defiance to Muhammad, your denial!
                   You must bend to the will of the Prophets.

Ben David: Like to Moses?

Dayyan Hasan: Yea, he among the thousands.

Ben David: Half the earth adopts our foremost prophet,
                   But the core of his law, man abandons!
                   And the Moriah, built with more than hand and eye,
                   Built by our faithful, by their prayerful sighs,
                   You condemn to ruin and our people to die?
                   We'll not stand by while you commit this crime!

Sec. Hawkins: What we need here is time, Premier, to think!
                   We need time for calm and negotiating!

Dayyan Hasan: No! We are tired of the endless parley,
                   You have five minutes or I'll crush a city.
                   You have five minutes for deciding!

                   I must observe prayer time now: the ninth hour,
                   I, with the world, turn my back to your power!

Dayyan turns to face Mecca, his opening prayer can be overheard.

                   Blessed, praised, glorified, extolled and exalted,
                   Honored, magnified, in all places lauded,
                   Be your chanted Name, the Most Holy One.

Sec. Hawkins: Close the microphone!   Damn it, Ben David!
How can you expect a negotiation!

Ben David: Is it true then? Are we just your puppets?
The wedge where through thrive imperialists!
We will not stand by here and be butchered,
Like an abandoned lamb led to a slaughter!
No help for Israel? Are we left alone again?
To greet death without an ally or friend!
Secretary, we will not die quietly!

Sec. Hawkins: We're left to crawl narrows of necessity.
If there's to be peace, something must be done!

Ben David: What?   Will we beg for another sanction?
Look how Dayyan's warlike will is dampened!
Oh yes, he does appear to be frightened!
Or shall we urge stealthier spy missions,
Or attempt plots to raise more seditions,
Or shall we attempt another cyber war?
Those delays only enraged him the more!
Everything we did to hold him back
Only lent fuel to his resolve for attack!
Should we go before the world to commiserate?
Convince the United Nations what's at stake?
While half the world with half the world debates,
Our actions have proved too little and too late!

This is the fruit of vice, and our weakness:
As we watch, they all act with expedience,
To foster self-interest rather than justice!
Even you put your economic interests
Ahead of Israel's imperiled existence!
And how this feeds Dayyan's will for conquest-
How he has played on everyone's avarice!
The only way in which this world unites
Is in the lax agreement of its vice!
Proving, with opportunity and power,
One can fulfill the most evil desire

While a world stands by - like workmen for hire!
Through every winding has he not stole,
Through the weak ports of every human soul?

The way forward, the only one Dayyan knows,
Is to seize him by force and go for his throat!

E. Hawkins: He will not let up, he has real momentum;
He won't allow time to make assessments,
He will not allow anyone to take pause
To judge what events today are true or false!

Ben David: She's right! A bomb has gone off: a war exists,
The time is past, when we might prevent it!
And now the world will pay in death for it -
Where now will anyone attain their profit?

Sec. Hawkins: I am prepared to answer Dayyan's aggression,
We've our attack scenarios plotted in,
Though they involve massive populations!

Ben David: We are prepared, too, to do what we must,
Even if it means pounding him into dust!

Dayyan turns to face his camera again, the microphone is activated.

Dayyan Hasan: Time is up! Will you stand down your armies?
Will you allow my people to push out the Israelis?
Exiles, prisoners or casualties,
Choose what they'll be, for it's your doing!

Sec. Hawkins: And what will we do? How will we respond?
What will result from your acts? Shall I go on!
You are marked and the program is installed,
You must stand down or your acts may end us all!

Dayyan Hasan: You know, I really don't think so.

| Arif Hasan: | Dayyan, NO! |

Br. Elias:	You used and came through God's own church gate,
Yelling	To open this door to Hell's living hate!
	I will not be staid! I will speak before it's too late!

Sec. Hawkins: You have no place here, Brother! Arrest him!

Br. Elias: War rooms have no place for faith, that's the problem!

Dayyan Hasan: Are you so uncontrolled? I must face a lunatic?

| Arif Hasan: | Keep rushing into death, Dayyan, you'll find it! |
| | Perhaps you should take time and be quiet! |

Ariel Ben David and a security team seize Br. Elias.

| Rabbi Gamliel: | Ariel! Perhaps we should take time to listen, |
| | If only to calm our warlike passion! |

Following Ariel's example, the officers loosen their grip on Br. Elias, but keep hold of him.

Br. Elias:	Gentlemen! We've time to test many paths to death!
	Should we not try the one path to life instead?
	Here you stand, ready to carve each other's hearts,
	Ready to tear peoples and continents apart,
	And leave this half of the Earth, this vast arc,
	In a state of death and a perpetual dark.
	I can no longer sit. I can no longer be staid.
	Halt while you may to see the light of day
	And allow me moments, for one tale to relate!

The room stops in a stunned silence.

Dear brethren, brethren yourselves, it's not long since
When Jesus stood atop this Mount of Olives.
Not long since he entered Jerusalem's gates,

Surrounded by adherents, singing his praise:
He knew then he might master all he surveyed,
But chose sacrifice instead. May I explain?
Jerusalem was then lightly garrisoned
Pilate's troops numbered not above a thousand,
His headquarters was away in Caeserea,[207]
Where the port now stands against the sea!
The number of Christ's followers were many;
In part they were Zealots, poised for anything,
They wanted a warrior; they wanted a King!
Like the sons of Matthias,[208] like Maccabeus!
If a tenth of the populace then in the city
Would have attached to Christ in an uprising,
Christ could have rallied two hundred thousand
And have easily overwhelmed the Romans!

Instead, he harbored in a borrowed garden,
Gazing on a crimson river, the Kidron,
Flooded with the sacrificed blood of lambs,
Knowing he would soon so bleed to save man!
Christ stood there in thrall of intense prayer
For as a man, he could do whate'er he dared:
He chose freely to follow God's holy word,
Than to be Jerusalem's next conqueror!
He overcame human pride, mortal envy
Of the palaces and the crowns of kings,
Surrendering instead to God's teachings!

He had faith that God lives in all living things,
That his light is channeled through all beings.
Thus, what need had God to conquer anything?
Who needs conquer who lives in everything?
Jesus viewed God as the light in all living men
In the Jewish zealot and in the centurion;
Christ viewed God's light in the least of us,
Compounded with various material dust,
And he'd not kill God in man for kingdoms!

---

207 Caeserea: The ancient port city located between Tel-Aviv and Haifa on the Mediterranean coast.
208 Like sons of Matthias: Refers to the Maccabees, who rebelled against Seleucid rule.

Christ knew conquering man comes at the cost:
Some of God's own light and self might be lost,
Even in the conqueror who wins the assault;
Therefore, he did what he did for everyone,
For the Roman, the Jew and the Samaritan!
For Christ did then as God himself does:
He sacrificed himself for the least of us!
Christ saw past man's material semblance;
He viewed God through spectrums and in opposites
He saw God in every living breast,
He revered one God and forgave the rest:
With understanding of human weakness,
To the point of forgiving his opposites!
Thus, he allowed himself to be surrounded;
He allowed himself to be bound and hounded,
For his love of God was never confounded:
So he confirmed his faith in God through action.

Christ was arrested here, in a borrowed garden,
Lone on Gethsemane, where he was abandoned,
Abandoned by his own, his very brethren,
His followers by adverse winds scattered forth
Yet Christ followed One Word of our One Lord,
And did so as he cast down - Peter's sword!

Ben David: So for Israel to do what you desire,
We must follow Christ with what he required,
Follow him to die through crucifixion or fire![209]

Br. Elias: You forget that horrible night's other lesson:
We should never leave just brethren abandoned,
But we must stand fast together, beside them.
If we each sacrifice for our common defense,
Then the unjust never chance to flourish!
You are not the conqueror, but the prey,
That the world unjustly abandons this day!

---

209 Crucifixion or fire: Christians were martyred for their faith during the first three centuries of the existence of Christianity. The martyrs were typically stoned, crucified or burned alive.

Arif Hasan: You over-praise this single prophet's name!
You heap on a prophet far too much fame!

Br. Elias: Christ cared not for the sound or print of his name,
Or for saturnalia of ineffectual fame
He would be crucified again the same.
If mankind would once learn how to trace
The signature which Christ's acts relate!

You would all war over material names,
Rather than follow the light of true faith!
Rather than deprive so many of life,
Take council of our own, our same inner vice:
And determine on the proper sacrifice!
We needn't carve the weakness from someone else,
We have only to sacrifice weakness from ourselves.
We needn't look for who sounds or looks different,
And classify and range them according to opposites.
We all share in the same human weakness,
Whether Jews, Christians, Hindus or Muslims…
And we have all to learn the proper sacrifices!
Sacrifice the blindness that views differences,
And join in the One Word that should unite us!
In all human advance and all time historical,
We have yet to overcome… the last obstacle!

Dayyan Hasan: I have no time for this! Do you surrender?

Ben David: In a word. Never!

Dayyan Hasan: You pull a fatal lever!

A sonic boom follows a growing high-pitched screaming noise and shakes the intel chamber. Several persons fall to ground as ceiling lamps and video monitors crash to the floor and shatter amidst the screams of those insufficiently sheltered. The intense sound lingers like thunder.

E. Hawkins: What unexampled evil with this is loosed
               Upon unwary innocence from an ambush!

Dr. Bethe: We can trace heat emissions: it came from Dayyan!
               And has struck down on the city of Hebron!
               There is after burn and there is radiation.

Rabbi Gamliel: Where Ismael and Isaac stood hand in hand,
               In Hebron?

Arif Hasan: Struck where both buried Abraham![210]

Rabbi Gamliel: Where Jacob buried all of his twelve sons,
               How many to bury? So many, dear God!

Br. Elias: He bursts matter's most fundamental bond!
               So strained is this relation of brethren,
               That to murder, he's shattered even the atom!

Dayyan Hasan: I will break Israel down to its foundations
               To discern if there is any good in them!
               When will you leave the Palestinians' home?

Ben David: What Palestinians? You've turned them to bone!

Arif Hasan: Brother! Your missile fell on Old Hebron
               And left no remains of a population!

Dayyan Hasan: You know the damned Jews were attacking them.
               I attacked so, to come to their defense!

Arif Hasan: You bombed the resting place of Ibrahim
               And reduced the teeming city to ruins!
               Rather than sacrifice hecatombs to fire -
               Why can't you sacrifice your wrongful desire?

---

210 Abraham's burial place: The Cave of the Patriarchs in the ancient city of Hebron, where Isaac and Ishmael buried Abraham together.

Dayyan Hasan: It's I who serve Islam and Allah best!
It's I who will exercise no more patience
With Jews or brothers who are traitorous!
It is Zion's fault the Palestinians suffer.
I demand Israel's immediate surrender!
I demand the surrender of all U.S. forces
Housed within Middle Eastern garrisons!
You have no more time. I want an answer!
Only by surrender will peace be delivered!
I will perforce see this misled world evolve
Under a single master, beneath one God!

Ben David: We must all go on to the elevator!
We must go! To deeper depths of this crater!

Rabbi Gamliel: If we go further below in our descent
We go where man first broke God's covenant.
Where Adam broke faith, at the birth of Eden!
Of all covenants broken, that one was first,
And see! Man lives with the same ancient curse!
All mankind may soon curse that horrid hour,
When man first tasted this forbidden power!

Br. Elias: What can I say? How louder can I warn?
When Christ's frail boat upon the sea was swarmed,
Only God's given Word could calm the storm!

End Act One Scene Four

ACT ONE
SCENE FIVE

CATARACT

Place: The deepest subfloor of the joint Israeli and U.S. intel center, beneath the Dominus Flevit Church, Mount of Olives, Jerusalem

Present: John Hawkins, Elena Hawkins, the Hawkins sons, Ariel Ben David, Arif Hasan, U.S. Gen. Jim Reiss, Israeli Col. Ethan Rosen, Dr. Lars Bethe, Br. Elias, Maj. Patrick Killean, various soldiers and security personnel. Later appearing via monitors: Indian Prime Minister Chandra Sengupta and Pakistani President Faiz Laghari

Scene: *The same party of persons has descended to an impenetrable chamber deeper beneath the intel center. The chamber is an impersonal colorless vault; its walls are blank and overhead lighting casts a too-bright and lifeless ambience. The chamber features a similar general configuration of desks and monitors as the previous intelligence center. The personnel arrive breathlessly, as if in a state of physical shock. Military and security personnel forthrightly discharge their responsibilities; they know where to go and what to do. Yet they work in a state of nervous panic.*

Sec. Hawkins: Update!

Gen. Reiss: Calculating, we have changes,
From here to Himalayan mountain ranges:
Iraq's is being invaded by Iran;
There's conflict along the borders of Syria
As Syria brings missiles to bear on Israel;
India and Pakistan raze the frontier,
Warring through contested jungles of Kashmir!

Ben David: Opponents move like fire and water at war,
Pouring elastically, fighting through every pore!

Sec. Hawkins: Accelerating beyond means of arrest,
We've no means to leap this pace of events!
The time to peacefully stop Dayyan is past...

Ben David: Let's get back to that meteor, that menace,
The mad Dayyan, the destroyer of a planet!
His damned evil should have been killed in the shell,
Before he was unleashed like some fury of hell!
This conqueror, with the world's cowards combined
In a collusion of everyone's vice:
That's made war theater-wide! The priest's right!
How otherwise, if our virtues had allied!

He leaves us no choice, no other design,
Than extinguishing an eye for an eye!
If he is so swift to detonate Hebron,
He will waste no time launching another bomb!
If we waste time with being delusional,
One more launch will be the end of Israel!

Gen. Reiss: Come on! We need to get through to Cent Comm.
It's past time we give guidance to our bombs!
I am personally going to find this devil's lair
And with every means bury him there!

Ben David: There is one thing on which we can rely:
In his quest, Dayyan will show no mercy.

Maj. Killean: We've located Dayyan by his sound traffic
I'm sending Cent Com the coordinates.

Sec. Hawkins: We need approval to move; where's Washington?

Maj. Killean: We have tried! There's no communication.
I've tested the system; it comes to one result:
Washington's been struck by a magnetic pulse![211]

---

211 Electromagnetic pulse, EMP: Burst of radiation resulting from a high-energy explosion that may cause disruption and destruction of electric systems.

We have no communication via the skies,
They have attacked and downed our satellites!
Only in this region have we ears or eyes.

Sec. Hawkins: Then send through communication beacons
Of the fleet to Western Pacific stations,
Our request for nuclear retaliation!

E. Hawkins: My God, John, what will become of our sons?

Sec. Hawkins: Elena! Israel contains four million.

Maj. Killean: This takes time, this communication recourse.

Sec. Hawkins: A moment's time is time we can't afford!
Authority to launch I assume as mine -
Tell the subs: launch on Dayyan's coordinates!
We have no time, nor other means to stop him!
We need to make use of every edge
Which prevails in this struggle to the death!

Rabbi Gamliel: It soon will be here, at the impenetrable,
About to separate the inseparable!
God's womb, man's cradle in the world,
Where the light of Adam's soul was figured:
This monumental temple of the earth,
From which so many prayers have emerged,
Will soon be set fire by an unearthly scourge!

Sec. Hawkins: What can possibly end this growing storm;
What power can we devise, of what form?
At this precipice, at life's utmost verge,
It will not permitted us twice to err!
We've ventured beyond all the laws ever writ,
To the unknown frontier of a lawless abyss!

E. Hawkins: There's precedent of the Kellogg-Briand Pact.[212]

---

212 Kellogg-Briand Pact: Signed in 1928 by the great powers, prohibiting use of war as an instrument of national policy.

Ben David: The law that was supposed to hold Hitler back?
It served to shield him, while he prepared to attack!

Rabbi Gamliel: There's the "Law of Reciprocity" to stand on.

E. Hawkins: Which one? If we follow Nature's canon
Of predator and prey, and so act on,
We, and all we know, will as soon be gone!

Br. Elias: Reciprocity, as I was just stating,
Is the law Christ died for - by obeying.

Arif Hasan: This priest must suffer some correction!
It is a law diffused through civilization,
Allah never made that law exclusive,
But gave man, through ages, the like directive,
That with Muhammad achieved its perfection
When he gave to man the following direction:
"None of you truly believes, until he wishes
For his brother what he wishes for himself."[213]

This Law, or one akin, is found in Hinduism,
In Bhuddism, Confucianism and Taoism,
In Jainism, in Sikism and in Humanism:[214]
It's not confined to Issa or Judaism!
It's the single law all religions implore:

---

213 An-Nawawi's Forty Hadith 13 Islam

214 Pittacus, Greek philosopher (640? – 568 B.C.E.): "Do not do to your neighbor what you would take ill from him."

Brihaspati, Mahabharata Anusasana Parva, Hinudism: "One should never do that to another which one regards as injurious to one's own self. Other behavior is due to selfish desires."

Bahá'u'lláh, Bahai : "And if thine eyes be turned towards justice, choose thou for thy neighbor that which thou choosest for thyself."

Confucius, Chinese philosopher (551 – 479 B.C.E.) Analects XV.24, Confucianism: "Never impose on others what you would not choose for yourself."

Buddha 563 – 483 B.C.E., Buddhism: "Putting oneself in the place of another, one should not kill nor cause another to kill."

Suman Suttam, verse 151, Jainism: "Killing a living being is killing one's own self; showing compassion to a living being is showing compassion to oneself. He who desires his own good, should avoid causing any harm to a living being."

Var Sarang, Guru Granth Sahib, Sikhism: "Whom should I despise, since the One Lord made us all."

T'ai Shang Kan Ying P'ien, Taoism: "Regard your neighbor's gain as your own gain, and your neighbor's loss as your own loss."

Hillel, The Elder (110 B.C.E. – 10 C.E.), Judaism: "That which is hateful to you, do not do to your fellow. That is the whole Torah; the rest is the explanation."

Matthew 7:12, Christian: "In everything, do to others what you would want them to do to you."

	The law of every spiritual lord,
	And the common law all mankind ignores!

Br. Elias:	So Christ perceived God in all creation,
	In the Jew, the Roman, the Samaritan,
	So did he try to heal the deaf or blinded.

Arif Hasan:	One's color or name shouldn't make us one-sided!
	But the virtues of the soul which are inherent
	Should make us embrace those of just spirit,
	Despite differences, which are merely apparent!

Rabbi Gamliel:	It's the law man's rejected and left alone...
	But if life is to go on and the law enthroned,
	The rejected one must become the cornerstone![215]

Dr. Bethe:	As we have overcome nature's obstacles,
	And have discovered a power ungovernable,
	As we've penetrated the impenetrable!

Arif Hasan:	So we must congress the incongressable!
	We must overcome the insurmountable,
	Overcome the last, the fatal obstacle!
	We must assume one law that's relational!
	We must embrace and love our opposites,
	By common will, for a surviving justice,
	The one neglected law must combine us!
	If a Muslim can ignite these hostilities,
	So a Muslim can bring forth a peace!
	By embracing law of the ultimate realm
	Where opposites reconcile in a commonwealth!

As Arif begins furiously writing, the scene shifts to Maj. Killean.

Maj. Killean:	China's firing on India in Lahore,
	Here too, over Nepal, their jets are aswarm.

215 Cornerstone: Acts 4:1-12.

475

E. Hawkins: Why would China be firing on India!

Sec. Hawkins: By reciprocal ties with states of Arabia!
                The world separates in camps of enemies,
                Which were convened to keep the peace!

Maj. Killean: To China's east, her missiles now bear on
                And fire on disputed straits of Taiwan!
                Nuclear plumes rise in the Gobi basin:
                On borders China shares with the Russians…

E. Hawkins: As the former age changes and cracks,
                Foes issue forth from poles, all to attack!
                And we all converge in a cataract!

Maj. Killean: There's activity beneath Pacific Seas,
                Among U.S., Russian and Chinese navies:
                Battle groups sail in converging sorties!

                Who has a degree in geography
                Now has a great degree that's worth nothing!
                From the highest heights of achievable space
                To the deepest depths beneath ocean waves
                Unbridled war is beginning to be waged!

Col. Rosen: All these motions look very mechanistic,
                Occurring at once, almost synchronistic.

Dr. Bethe: Man's aggressions show a wondrous feature:
                He moves in sync, like a chronometer.

Sec. Hawkins: Have we communication with India?
                Get a line to Prime Minister Chandra!
                We need intervene in this, starting there!

Maj. Killean: There are several channels, most dead I fear,
                Here! I have a satellite that is capable,
                But the din of all Asia is remarkable!
                As though we live in a tower of Babel,
                All the voices cascade in a rabble!
                I have the frequency: I have India!

A screaming din occurs.

PM Sengupta: How could you fire the bomb on Mathura?
You've set afire the whole Vale of Yamuna!

Pres. Laghari: We have intelligence you have silos there!
Can you assure you'll not attack from that sphere?
We demand that all your aggression stop
Or we'll further attack - aided by Dayyan!

PM Sengupta: Siva himself would never have been so cruel,
Though he was born the Destroyer of Worlds!
When he destroys, he destroys weakness in things -
You commit murder indiscriminately!
More dead than we have gods! Where is mercy?

What difference if God has a million names,
If acts don't follow false syllables of praise!

Gen. Reiss: Damn it! We're past hoping for containment,
Someone's hit Germany, our U.S. stations,
Amidst our nuclear installations!

Sec. Hawkins: All the forces of man are in full career,
Propelled together by their shock and fear!
No one knows the extent of this new war,
Or knows where the bombs come from anymore,
So everyone lets loose of all their stores!
Like a ferocious panther goes for the throat,
To protect his own, he overleaps the moat!
Witness the dark tragedy that occurs
When all nations react like predators!

Dr. Bethe: It resembles a style of Cytokine Storm
When defensive reactions over perform!

Video screens show missiles ascending out of various silos. On scrolling maps, the globe changes shades of colors with bombings or the advance or retreat of forces.

E. Hawkins: Fire's ascending out of the world's lost tombs,
                  Rising with alarms through gaseous fumes:
                  Like lava pushing up in wrathful advance,
                  Through permeable channels of volcanic shafts!
                  Nothing any longer holds the fury back,
                  No more than we can calm the cataract!

Br. Elias: We have ourselves to blame! We ourselves hurled
                  In depthless gulfs of a war-encircled world!
                  We fall upon our prey like predators
                  As though instinctually, as by our natures!
                  Man always returns to primordial law
                  When in the fell passes of war enthralled.

E. Hawkins: It is true!   It has always been man's curse,
                  We only learn by means that are adverse!
                  But who will live to claim they're mightier,
                  When there may not be found a sole survivor?

Arif Hasan hands Sec. Hawkins a hurriedly written proposal based on "Reciprocity." The Secretary reads it.

Arif Hasan: Send this law as a proposal by e-mail
                  To all states and embassies within hail!

Br. Elias: It costs you just the price of transmission;
                  It cost another crucifixion.

Sec. Hawkins: *Handing over the message*   Send it!

Maj. Killean: Message is uploaded and transmitted!

Rabbi Gamliel: Too late, Arif! To stop what we all fear,
                  Too late, after we've shared six thousand years!

Arif Hasan: We always see with our material sight
                  Without noting God's underlying light.
                  We always divide people by appearance
                  Rather than unite through virtuous actions.

Rabbi Gamliel: We react in a manner predatory,
Rather than unite in the cause of mercy!

Br. Elias: We always are violent in how we react,
Rather than learn, that to live, we must adapt!

E. Hawkins: We react according to survive as the fittest,
Rather than learn strength lies in forgiveness!

Br. Elias: We always enslave our brethren through conquest,
Rather than to embrace in reconcilement!
We always leave prone brethren abandoned,
When for justice, we need to protect them!

Rabbi Gamliel: We always raze the world's various life,
Rather than learn it's pride we need sacrifice!

Arif Hasan: We always cite the hundred laws that divide,
Rather than God's highest law, which unites!

Br. Elias: We always break the covenant of God's word,
Rather than realize, it is we whom it serves!

Arif Hasan: Will we hear the ancient, universal call,
And abide mankind's highest common law?

Br. Elias: And enjoin in a new, constant relation,
Which survives time's material changes?

*A scrambled voice overpowers the room as a wavering image of
Prime Minister Sengupta reappears on monitor.*

PM Sengupta: Secretary! I've received your urgent plea
Regarding enactment of "Reciprocity" -
We'll abide! If so shall the Pakistanis,
Though now we are attacked by the Chinese!
In order to end this end of order,
We cease activities on our border!

Pres. Laghari: We will commit this proposal to study;
Unless approved, there will be hostility!

Maj. Killean: A message from China has been received:
"We are for peace, is not everybody?
But we're surrounded by hostile enemies,
And defend our and our allies' integrity!"

A sonic boom resounds deeply into the earth. The walls shake even at the vault's steep depth, and screams reverberate through the chamber.

Sen. Hawkins: Damn it! What was that? Do we have our Comm?

Maj. Killean: A bomb has just detonated Jerusalem!

Rabbi Gamliel: Feel what comes to matter's slightest basis,
When the atom's shredded by human hatreds!
What God, in his wisdom, would fain preserve
He immerses in floods of healing waters.
What man in ignorance would destroy entire,
He strangles in a wilderness of nuclear fire!
The prayers, glories, hopes Moriah held yet,
Are dead and strewn over a new Gulggolet![216]
The world's aflame, the air full of fume,
God! Look how your breath returns to you…
Must this be the sculpture mankind designs,
This scarred being that becomes the face of Time!

Arif Hasan: As we have corrupted matter at its most slight,
Weeping We must ascend spiritualism's highest height.
We must clasp and unite with our opponents:
Unite and combine in a brotherhood of justice!

On a central monitor, a satellite image shows a massive nuclear explosion.

Gen. Reiss: We've got him! Goodbye Dayyan! We've got him!
He can feel that we have reciprocated!

---

216 Gulggolet: Hebrew name for Golgotha, a hill outside Jerusalem used in the ancient era for executions.

I don't know if he has met his deserved death,
But Dayyan is buried in a grave of great depth,
Buried alive, beneath the burning planet!

Ben David: He still believes the whole world will surrender,
               So doing, he mistook Israel's measure!
               But the fight he started still rages on,
               Spreading east and west, like a contagion!

Sec. Hawkins: We are all prisoners now; the world's a prison,
               We're all locked in a lunatic's ambition,
               While above is a swarm with confrontation!
               The fracture of a single human being,
               Framed insignificantly as a mustard seed,
               Given the amplified powers of a god
               And loosed to destroy where he would trod:
               This evil, let slip from one fractured soul,
               Has lost control and made the world explode!

E. Hawkins: One human soul, like a bacillum, radicalized,
               And moves violently to raze half the Earth's life?
               'Twas for us the beast in Nature to subdue,
               But look you, we have only amplified her!

Br. Elias: 'Twas for us the beast in Nature to subdue,
               But it's the beast in us that subdues the world!

Rabbi Gamliel: Out goes the light from humanity's eye,
               That's been cradled there since the birth of time!

Arif Hasan: Our crime is the same, we are equally to blame
               For the common covenant we've all betrayed!
               Only love and reconciliation make things one;
               All other means end up destroying them!

Sec. Hawkins: How many bombs have fallen?

E. Hawkins: How much radiation?

481

Dr. Bethe: Earth having suffered so many eruptions,
                Her atmosphere, her air, will be corrupted!
                Above this sphere, ignition may acquire;
                Through the liable air will roll living fire:
                While oxygen feeds it, the flame will aspire,
                Devouring the vital air that life requires!

Sec. Hawkins: The only shields mankind has anymore
                Protect those who are making the war!

E. Hawkins: All the losers of the war have been vanquished,
                While the victors await a certain death?

Arif Hasan: We would not reconcile with our opposites
                To battle the common enemy of us all:
                The evil that operates this common fall!
                The first failings of mankind are always moral,
                And herewith it's proved, in the end are mortal!
                We should do no harm, nor allow harm be done,
                But must move, and act, according to what's just!
                We may well have followed a thousand laws,
                But we betrayed the one that would prevent our fall!

Another blast and shock reverberate through the shelter. The video monitors and lamps flash on and off, on and then off. A generator and reserve light mechanically kick on. The company of the intel center stands in vivid horror. They pale and sweat and cry and quake in the anguish of the blank, white aura of a moment's realization that at this time there occurs the end of their former age…and world.

Maj. Killean: We have lost Comm. There's no communication.

E. Hawkins: The air we have at this depth is very thin!
                In a doomed prison are my beautiful children!

Ben David: Our air is pulling from a storage element
                On battery power; a nuclear bomb's hit.

Col. Rosen: To see if civilization's rubble bounces!

Sec. Hawkins: We overcame all challenges of Nature's realms,
                To be overcome by weakness in ourselves!

Ben David: We are cut off and on back-up systems.
                We have three days to return to surface!

E. Hawkins: We have to do something! We have to get help!
                We can't just sit here quietly by ourselves!
                We have to work to stem that moving tide of war -
                We have to move! To stop the gathering storm!
                The fury building in that chain reaction
                Will gain momentum and acceleration -
                What then will hold the gathering fury back?
                Or will make calm the moving cataract?

Ben David: Calm down! The earth is still burning up there,
                It's poisonous death to breathe that atmosphere!

E. Hawkins: We have to move up! And return to the light!

Sec. Hawkins: It's all right, Elena! We have to bide some time…
                Trust time remains for mankind to act aright!

E. Hawkins: Oh God! Oh please God! Can you not help us?
                John! What is to become of our poor sons?

Rabbi Gamliel: How often have we such petitions sent?
                How oft have we returned spurned prophets!
                As usual, Man errs, and then asks too much.

Br. Elias: Look how man returned God's prophet of love!
                Gaze on man's treatment of God's burdened son!
                Romans mocked, abused and scourged him -
                They broke, bled and led him to crucifixion!
                How was it, do you think, for God to witness?
                That arc of the whip, its ripping through the flesh!

483

Do you think it stung God as deep as death?
The descent of the hammer, its crash on the nail!
Do you think it drove God's grieving soul to wail?
Thorns of a crown, driven in his bleeding brow -
Do you think God wept? Do you think he howled?
View the rising crucifix, bleeding with his son!
How did God behold His messenger of love?

E. Hawkins: How does God view this burning death of millions?
How does he take the wails of all his children,
Crushed in the fires of this churning instant!
Oh God! Can you not rescue us from this?

Br. Elias: Perhaps all this horror God himself observes
From a quiet throne and a still universe,
Just as he viewed the suffering that occurred
When His true son died for keeping his Father's word!
Perhaps God prefers that man's freedom be preserved!
If God were once to show his divine face,
One slave would be made of our whole human race!
As he viewed Christ die for his faith's resolve -
Perhaps now He waits see: if we'll obey His law!
Will we finally learn that we must adapt
Or be buried by the sins that hold us back?
It's still in our decision: whether we listen,
Or whether continue our timeless rebellion.

The End
But By The Chance Of War

ACKNOWLEDGEMENTS

Special thanks to:

Editors Fern Schumer Chapman and Susan Figiulo,
Book Designer Kevin McHugh,
Printer Michael Mueller
and
Executive Assistant Kelly Ryan.

For their roles in helping to make the final product.